Defendant Participation in the Criminal Process

Requirements for the defendant to actively participate in the English criminal process have been increasing in recent years such that the defendant can now be penalised for their non-cooperation. This book explores the changes to the defendant's role as a participant in the criminal process and the ramifications of penalising a defendant's non-cooperation, particularly its effect on the adversarial system.

The book develops a normative theory which proposes that the criminal process should operate as a mechanism for calling the state to account for its accusations and request for official condemnation and punishment of the accused. It goes on to examine the limitations placed on the privilege against self-incrimination, the curtailment of the right to silence, and the defendant's duty to disclose the details of his or her case prior to trial. The book shows that, by placing participatory requirements on defendants and penalising them for their non-cooperation, a system of obligatory participation has developed. This development is the consequence of pursuing efficient fact-finding with little regard for principles of fairness or the rights of the defendant.

Abenaa Owusu-Bempah is Lecturer in Law at City, University of London.

Defendant Participation in the Criminal Process

Abenaa Owusu-Bempah

Routledge
Taylor & Francis Group
LONDON AND NEW YORK

First published 2017
by Routledge

2 Park Square, Milton Park, Abingdon, Oxfordshire OX14 4RN
52 Vanderbilt Avenue, New York, NY 10017

Routledge is an imprint of the Taylor & Francis Group, an informa business

First issued in paperback 2018

British Library Cataloguing in Publication Data
A catalogue record for this book is available from the British Library

Library of Congress Cataloging in Publication Data
Names: Owusu-Bempah, Abenaa, author.
Title: Defendant participation in the criminal process/Abenaa Owusu-Bempah.
Description: New York, NY: Routledge, 2016. | Includes bibliographical references and index.
Identifiers: LCCN 2016020589 | ISBN 9781138019577 (hbk) | ISBN 9781315767857 (ebk)
Subjects: LCSH: Defense (Criminal procedure)—Great Britain. | Actions and defenses—Great Britain. | Criminal procedure—Great Britain.
Classification: LCC KD8358.O98 2016 | DDC 345.41/03—dc23
LC record available at https://lccn.loc.gov/2016020589

ISBN: 978-1-138-01957-7 (hbk)
ISBN: 978-0-367-07554-5 (pbk)

Typeset in Galliard
by Keystroke, Neville Lodge, Tettenhall, Wolverhampton

For my father

Contents

Preface

There has been no shortage of reform to criminal procedure and the law of evidence in England and Wales in recent years. While much has been written about individual areas of reform, little attention has been paid to the effect of reform on the role of the defendant in the criminal process. Over the past 25 years, the role of the defendant has been affected by, *inter alia*, legislative reform to the right to silence and pre-trial disclosure, the introduction of the Criminal Procedure Rules and an increasingly narrow interpretation and application of the privilege against self-incrimination. The defendant is no longer able to put the prosecution to proof without fear of being penalised; if the defendant fails to answer questions or provide information which may assist in his or her prosecution, he or she now faces the risk of adverse legal consequences, such as criminal sanction and inferences of guilt.

This book provides a critical exploration of defendant participation in the criminal process by considering the various requirements which have been placed on defendants to actively participate. The development of the defendant's new participatory role is exposed through an in-depth examination of the law in relation to the privilege against self-incrimination, the right to silence and pre-trial disclosure. As well as a doctrinal exploration of the law, consideration is given to the wider implications of requiring defendant participation, particularly in respect of the application of fair trial rights and the nature of criminal procedure. It is contended that England's traditionally 'adversarial' system has transformed into a system of 'obligatory participation'. The exploration of the law and its wider consequences is underpinned by a normative theory of the criminal process as a process of calling the state to account for its accusations against the accused. The book, therefore, draws together various strands of criminal procedure and the law of evidence from both a doctrinal and theoretical perspective, while presenting a novel means of characterising criminal procedure, based on the participatory role of the defendant.

The themes of the book were originally explored in a doctoral thesis which was completed in 2012. There have since been significant developments to the relevant areas of law and procedure, and every attempt has been made to keep up to date with new material. Writing was completed in early 2016 and the book attempts to state the law as at March 2016.

I would like to thank the staff at Routledge, and in particular Katie Carpenter, Olivia Manley, Zoe Everitt and Sarahjayne Smith, for their patience and assistance during the preparation of the book. I would also like to thank Sue Cope for copy-editing the manuscript. I have had the opportunity to explore some specific aspects of my work in published articles, and I am grateful to Sweet and Maxwell Limited and SAGE Publications Limited for granting permission to reprint material from the following articles: A Owusu-Bempah, 'Judging the Desirability of a Defendant's Evidence: An Unfortunate Approach to s.35(1)(b) of the Criminal Justice and Public Order Act 1994' [2011] *Crim LR* 690; A Owusu-Bempah, 'Defence Participation through Pre-Trial Disclosure: Issues and Implications' (2013) 17 *E & P* 183; A Owusu-Bempah, 'Silence in Suspicious Circumstances' [2014] *Crim LR* 126.

I would like to thank Ian Dennis and Jonathan Rogers for supervising the doctoral thesis which formed the basis of this project, and for providing helpful comments and advice during the preparation of the book. I am also grateful to Andrew Choo for providing comments on numerous draft chapters and for being an invaluable source of advice throughout the preparation of the book. I would also like to thank Tom Frost and Hannah Quirk for their helpful comments on draft chapters. I am indebted to many other scholars of criminal procedure, evidence, criminal law and philosophy who have provided inspiration for my arguments and the direction of my work. Finally, I would like to thank my family, friends and colleagues for all of their advice, support, encouragement and patience throughout the duration of this project.

Table of cases

Canada

European Court of Human Rights

United Kingdom

United States of America

Table of legislation

Primary legislation

Australia

Italy

United Kingdom

Statutory instruments

United States of America

Table of international instruments and treaties

List of abbreviations

Abbreviation	Full title
CJA	Criminal Justice Act 2003
CJPOA	Criminal Justice and Public Order Act 1994
CPIA	Criminal Procedure and Investigations Act 1996
Crim LR	*Criminal Law Review*
CrimPR	Criminal Procedure Rules 2015
E & P	*International Journal of Evidence and Proof*
ECHR	European Convention on Human Rights
MLR	*Modern Law Review*
PACE	Police and Criminal Evidence Act 1984
YJCEA	Youth Justice and Criminal Evidence Act 1999

1 Introduction: participatory requirements and rights

'In England, the defendant acts no kind of part: his hat stuck on a pole might without inconvenience be his substitute at the trial.'[1]

The above statement was made by a French observer of the English criminal trial in the early nineteenth century. It reflects a long-standing perception that, within England and Wales, those accused of criminal wrongdoing are free to sit back and wait for the state to prove their guilt. Accordingly, the defendant need not play an active role in pre-trial proceedings, nor is he obliged to speak on his own behalf at trial. However, times have changed. A hat stand is no longer an accurate descriptor of the defendant in court, nor is it a convincing symbol of his role during criminal investigations and pre-trial proceedings. Active and cooperative defendants can provide information which can assist the police and prosecution in building and presenting a case. Active and cooperative defendants can also prevent unnecessary delay by, for example, ensuring early identification of the issues in the case. Over the past two decades in particular, there has been an increase in demand from government and some criminal justice professionals for accused persons to actively participate throughout the criminal process. The increase in demand for participation has accompanied an increase in demand for convictions and efficiency in criminal proceedings.

The increase in demand for participation has resulted in the imposition of requirements on defendants to actively participate, backed by penalties for non-cooperation. These requirements derive from legislation and have been given effect by the courts. The purpose of this book is to critically examine the participatory role of the defendant during the pre-trial and trial stages of the criminal process, from charge to verdict,[2] and to assess the impact which requiring active

1 C Cottu, *On the Administration of Criminal Justice in England; and the Spirit of the English Government* (anon tr, London, Richard Stevens, 1822) 105.

2 The term 'charge' is used in the autonomous sense, as provided for by Article 6(1) of the European Convention on Human Rights (ECHR), which includes pending or anticipated criminal proceedings. See, for example, *Deweer v Belgium* (1980) 2 EHRR 439 [42], where the term 'charge' is said to be 'very wide in scope'.

participation has had on the nature of criminal procedure. The position taken is that it is wrong to require defendants to actively participate in proceedings against themselves. This argument is based on a broad approach to fair trial rights and a normative position, or theory, which holds that the criminal process should operate as a mechanism for calling the state to account for its accusations and request for official condemnation and punishment of the accused. When fair trial rights are interpreted broadly, as they ought to be, they allow defendants to take a passive role, while challenging the state and holding it to account for its accusations of criminal wrongdoing. Moreover, if defendants are to be treated as free and dignified citizens of a liberal democracy, as they ought to be, they must be at liberty to choose whether or not to actively participate in criminal proceedings. This normative theory of the criminal process not only provides a basis for the argument against requiring active participation, but also provides a framework, or yardstick, from which to approach and examine wider developments in criminal procedure and the law of evidence.

Before outlining the participatory requirements at issue, and further explaining the normative position, a distinction must be made between active and passive participation. The focus of this book is active participation. The defendant is an active participant when he is actively involved in the criminal process, as an individual, through means such as answering questions beyond statements of 'no comment',[3] providing material evidence and testifying in court. Active participation involves mental effort or voluntary physical movement on the part of the defendant, which results in the production of information. Passive participation, on the other hand, requires no direct action on the part of the defendant, beyond submission. Arrest, searches, detention in police custody, being subjected to police questioning without answering and being presented to and being present in court are all forms of passive participation in the criminal process. As Leng notes, they are events 'which happen to the suspect rather than requiring action by her'.[4]

The focus of this book is on active participation rather than passive participation because the increase in requirements to actively participate is relatively recent and far-reaching. It has, therefore, become necessary to consider the consequences of the defendant's new participatory role. Requirements of active participation have implications for the enforceability of fair trial rights, even when they are interpreted narrowly.[5] These rights can provide the defendant with a choice of

3 In practice, where an accused responds to police questioning by stating 'no comment', the response is treated in the same way as silence, and adverse inferences may be drawn against the accused under the Criminal Justice and Public Order Act 1994 (CJPOA 1994).

4 R Leng, 'The Right to Silence Reformed: A Re-appraisal of the Royal Commission's Influence' (2001) 6 *Journal of Civil Liberties* 107, 128.

5 See, for example, the scope of the privilege against self-incrimination, which has been interpreted narrowly and has also been set aside in pursuit of the public interest. See ch 5. See also *Brown v Stott* [2003] 1 AC 681 (PC); *O'Halloran and Francis v UK* (2008) 46 EHRR 21.

whether or not to cooperate in the criminal process. Depriving the defendant of that choice has significant implications for the nature of criminal procedure. England and Wales can no longer be characterised as 'adversarial' in any strict sense of the term, such as Mirjan Damaska's core meaning of it: 'a contest or a dispute [which] unfolds as an engagement of two adversaries before a relatively passive decision maker whose principal duty is to reach a verdict'.[6] While it is natural for systems to transform over time, it is of concern that there has been a departure from legal norms and rights which became workable as part of an adversarial system.[7]

1.1 Participatory requirements

In order to demonstrate the way in which an increase in demand for participation has transformed the role of the defendant and the nature of criminal procedure, three areas of the law of evidence and criminal procedure are examined in Chapters 5 through 7. These are: the privilege against self-incrimination; the right to silence; and pre-trial disclosure. As a result of an increasingly restrictive notion of the privilege against self-incrimination, and legislative reforms to the law concerning the right to silence and disclosure, defendants can be required to participate. It is appropriate to use the term 'required' because the defendant is subject to compulsion to participate. The compulsion stems from the penalties attached to non-cooperation.

In relation to the privilege against self-incrimination, defendants can face a direct compulsion to provide self-incriminating information, where non-compliance is a criminal offence, provided for by statute.[8] It is not a criminal offence or contempt of court to remain silent or refuse to disclose details of one's case before trial. Nonetheless, defendants are subject to indirect compulsion to participate; a failure to answer police questions, give evidence in court or comply with disclosure obligations can result in an adverse inference being drawn against the defendant.[9] The inference may be one of guilt and can contribute to a conviction. The defendant is, thus, subject to a penalty because a failure to participate can result in a detriment that would not otherwise be endured. That detriment is provided for by law and associates non-participation with guilt. To penalise the defendant is to treat him as though he had done something wrong.

6 M Damaska, *The Faces of Justice and State Authority: A Comparative Approach to the Legal Process* (New Haven, Yale University Press, 1986) 3.

7 While the shift away from adversarialism is a key theme of this book, this is not a historical study. However, aspects of the development of adversarialism and participatory rights are examined in ch 4.2. See also JM Beattie, *Crime and the Courts in England 1660–1800* (Oxford, Clarendon Press, 1986); JH Langbein, *The Origins of the Adversary Criminal Trial* (Oxford, Oxford University Press, 2003).

8 See, for example, Road Traffic Act 1988, s 172, discussed in ch 5.3.3.

9 As provided for by the CJPOA 1994, ss 34–37, and the Criminal Procedure and Investigations Act 1996, s 11.

By subjecting defendants to compulsion to actively participate, and then using the law to put them in a disadvantaged position if they do not comply, the message that is conveyed by the practices examined in this book is that it is wrong for defendants not to participate.

The privilege against self-incrimination, the right to silence and disclosure have been selected for analysis on the basis that these three areas of law provide the clearest and most striking examples of requirements to actively participate. In addition, these areas of law have long been the subject of controversy and debate. This book provides an important opportunity to not only consider the impact of reform on the defendant, but also the development and rationales of the privilege against self-incrimination, the right to silence and pre-trial disclosure.

There are, however, a number of other practices and rules through which defendants can be subject to compulsion to participate and penalised for non-compliance. The penalties include the loss of a sentence discount for those who do not plead guilty but are found guilty following a contested trial, as discussed in Chapter 3. In addition to a loss of sentence discount, a mandatory Criminal Courts Charge was introduced in 2015.[10] While the financial charge was imposed on all convicted adults, those who were found guilty following a contested trial faced a higher fixed-sum charge than those who pleaded guilty. The Criminal Courts Charge was met with heavy criticism from criminal justice professionals, in part due to the increased pressure on the innocent to plead guilty.[11] It has since been abolished.[12]

Ongoing concern over the pressure faced by defendants to plead guilty may, at times, overshadow the changing role of the defendant in contested cases. However, while the vast majority of criminal cases end in a guilty plea, the prospect of a trial shapes the pre-trial stages of the criminal process, and there continue to be a significant number of contested trials in England and Wales each year.[13] Most of the participatory requirements explored in this study are imposed on the defendant before the trial, while the penalty for non-cooperation is implemented during, or after, the trial stage of the criminal process.

The defendant can also be penalised through sanctions for failure to comply with case management directions under the Criminal Procedure Rules, as

10 The Criminal Courts Charge was introduced by Statutory Instrument in April 2015, just before Parliament was dissolved, allowing little or no opportunity for parliamentary debate. Prosecution of Offences Act 1985 (Criminal Courts Charge) Regulations 2015/796; Prosecution of Offences Act 1985, ss 21A–21F.

11 For a summary of the criticism and concerns, see House of Commons Justice Committee, *Criminal Courts Charge Second Report of Session 2015–16* HC586 (London, The Stationery Office, 2015).

12 Prosecution of Offences Act 1985 (Criminal Courts Charge) (Amendment) Regulations 2015/1970.

13 In 2014, there were 71,969 effective trials and 28,092 ineffective trials in the magistrates' courts of England and Wales. In the same year, 27,953 defendants were dealt with in the Crown Court following a plea of not-guilty. See Ministry of Justice, *Criminal Court Statistics: April–June 2015 (Main Tables)* (Ministry of Justice, September 2015) Tables M2 and C5.

examined in Chapters 3 and 7. In addition, where a reverse burden of proof is imposed on the defence at trial, it will often be necessary for the defendant to participate in order to discharge the burden. A failure to discharge the burden will result in the conviction of the defendant. Consideration is given to reverse burdens of proof as a participatory requirement in the final chapter. Many other situations in which non-participation can result in a detriment that would not otherwise be endured concern the passive participation of the accused, rather than his active participation. For example, a refusal to submit to a police stop and search could result in arrest, and a refusal to be subjected to police questioning could result in a longer period of detention. However, for the reasons outlined above, this study is concerned only with requirements to *actively* participate during the pre-trial and trial stages of the criminal process.

By omitting to consider coerced passive participation, it is by no means assumed that such coercion is unobjectionable.[14] For example, being subjected to a compulsory search, having bodily samples forcibly taken or being detained in police custody or on remand prior to trial can amount to intrusions of the right to privacy, the right to be free from inhuman and degrading treatment[15] and the right to liberty. These forms of passive participation must be regulated, and they require justification, such as being necessary in the interests of crime prevention or public safety.[16] Once the consequences of coerced active participation have been examined, and the case against requiring active participation has been established, a standard can be identified, and perhaps later applied, to assess whether the various forms of coerced passive participation are justifiable.

It should be noted that, along with the defendant as an individual, the defence as a party has faced an increase in expectations of participation.[17] The defence party consists of the defendant as well as his legal representatives. The defence party actively participates when it goes beyond simply putting the prosecution to proof by, for example, providing information about the defence case ahead of trial, raising a positive defence and adducing evidence in support of that defence at trial. As will be shown, defence representatives can face penalties for non-compliance with participatory requirements, and can be placed in the difficult position of having to choose between their conflicting duties to the defendant and to the court. However, the main focus is the participatory

14 Passive participation is coerced in so far as the accused has no choice but to participate and can be physically compelled to do so.

15 See, for example, *Jalloh v Germany* (2007) 44 EHRR 32, in which the forcible administration of emetics in order to obtain evidence of a drugs offence was contrary to Article 3 of the ECHR.

16 See, for example, Article 8(2) of the ECHR, which provides that the right to respect for private and family life can be interfered with by a public authority in accordance with the law and where necessary in a democratic society 'in the interests of national security, public safety or the economic wellbeing of the country, for the prevention of disorder or crime, for the protection of health or morals, or for the protection of the rights and freedoms of others'.

17 See, for example, pt 3 of the Criminal Procedure Rules 2015, discussed in chs 3 and 7.

requirements placed on the defendant as an individual, as the existence of the defence party should enable the defendant to take a passive role in the criminal process, without sacrificing the opportunity to test the prosecution's case.

1.2 Rights and participation

While the defendant's participation may prove useful to the pursuit of efficient fact-finding, it should be a choice and not a requirement. This position can be justified on the basis that the coerced participation of the accused undermines the right to put the prosecution to proof and to defend oneself. The defendant's right to see that the prosecution can prove the case against him is expressed through the presumption of innocence. As part of the right to a fair trial, the defendant must be presumed innocent. The presumption of innocence is an ancient and fundamental principle.[18] Its value lies in its role as a procedural protection against wrongful conviction, and also in the effect it gives to a claim to fair treatment by the state.[19]

The presumption of innocence requires the prosecution to bear the burden of proving the defendant's guilt at the criminal trial. In other words, it is a reflection of the prosecution's burden of proof. It ordinarily requires the prosecution to both prove that the defendant committed the offence for which he has been charged and to disprove any defence which is advanced by him or on his behalf.[20]

18 The presumption of innocence has been traced back to Roman times. It now has a place in every international human rights document, including Universal Declaration of Human Rights, International Covenant on Civil and Political Rights, European Convention on Human Rights and African Charter on Human and Peoples' Rights. On the history of the presumption, see A Stumer, *The Presumption of Innocence: Evidential and Human Rights Perspectives* (Oxford, Hart Publishing, 2010) 1–8. See also *Coffin v United States* 156 US 432 (1895).

19 On the presumption of innocence, see generally A Ashworth, 'Four Threats to the Presumption of Innocence' (2006) 10 *E & P* 241; V Tadros, 'Rethinking the Presumption of Innocence' (2007) 1 *Criminal Law and Philosophy* 193; A Stumer, *The Presumption of Innocence: Evidential and Human Rights Perspectives* (Oxford, Hart Publishing, 2010); HL Ho, 'The Presumption of Innocence as a Human Right' in P Roberts and J Hunter (eds), *Criminal Evidence and Human Rights: Reimagining Common Law Procedural Traditions* (Oxford, Hart Publishing, 2012); P Roberts, 'Loss of Innocence in Common Law Presumptions' (2014) 8 *Criminal Law and Philosophy* 317; H Stewart, 'The Right to be Presumed Innocent' (2014) 8 *Criminal Law and Philosophy* 407; V Tadros, 'The Ideal of the Presumption of Innocence' (2014) 8 *Criminal Law and Philosophy* 449.

20 There are, however, many instances in which the burden is reversed, and the defence is required to prove or disprove an issue at the trial. See ch 8.1. On reverse burdens of proof generally, see A Ashworth and M Blake, 'The Presumption of Innocence in English Criminal Law' [1996] *Crim LR* 306; P Roberts, 'The Presumption of Innocence Brought Home? *Kebilene* Deconstructed' (2002) 118 *Law Quarterly Review* 41; V Tadros and S Tierney, 'The Presumption of Innocence and the Human Rights Act' (2004) 67 *MLR* 402; I Dennis, 'Reverse Onuses and the Presumption of Innocence: In Search of Principle' [2005] *Crim LR* 901; D Hamer, 'The Presumption of Innocence and Reverse Burdens: A Balancing Act' (2007) 66 *Cambridge Law Journal* 142; A Stumer, *The Presumption of Innocence: Evidential*

This conception of the presumption of innocence was endorsed by Viscount Sankey LC in *Woolmington v DPP*, when the duty of the prosecution to prove the defendant's guilt was declared a 'golden thread' of the English criminal law.[21] However, placing the burden of proof on the prosecution at trial does not in itself reveal much about the role which the defendant should play throughout the criminal process. Nor does it reveal much about how and where the prosecution can ascertain the evidence on which it relies to prove guilt.

On a broader scale, the presumption of innocence operates throughout the criminal process, as a direction to officials to treat the accused as if he were innocent, until guilt is proved. This is not to say that state officials must believe that the accused is in fact innocent. However, the state has a duty to recognise the defendant's legal status of innocence at all stages prior to conviction and after acquittal.[22] These two approaches to the presumption have been explored by Ho as a common law rule on the one hand, and a human right on the other.[23] These, in part, correspond to what Ashworth has labelled the 'narrow' and 'wide' concepts of the presumption of innocence.[24] Precisely what a wide conception of the presumption should entail is contestable, and a comprehensive exploration of the meaning, nature and implications of the presumption of innocence is outside the scope of this work. However, a wide conception places more restrictions on what can be required of the defendant than the narrow conception, which simply reflects the prosecution's burden of proof at trial. Under a wide conception, the presumption can, and arguably should, act as a restraint on the various compulsory measures that may be taken against suspects in the period before trial.[25] These measures include requirements to cooperate with the police and prosecution by answering questions or providing evidence. To demand that the accused account for the allegations made against them, or provide information which may assist in their prosecution, is not to treat them as innocent.

and Human Rights Perspectives (Oxford, Hart Publishing, 2010); F Picinali, 'Innocence and Burdens of Proof in English Criminal Law' (2014) 13 *Law, Probability & Risk* 243.

21 *Woolmington v DPP* [1935] AC 462 (HL) 481.

22 European human rights law supports a wide approach to the presumption of innocence in so far as Article 6 of the ECHR applies to both the pre-trial and trial stages of the criminal process. For example, the presumption of innocence should be taken into consideration when determining whether to grant bail or remand the defendant in custody pending trial. See *Caballero v UK* (2000) 30 EHRR 643. The European Court of Human Rights has also recognised what Trechsel identifies as a 'reputation-related' aspect of the presumption; it should protect the accused from any official insinuation that he is guilty, and can be infringed by public figures as well as by judges and courts. See S Trechsel, *Human Rights in Criminal Proceedings* (Oxford, Oxford University Press, 2005) 164; *Allenet de Ribemont v France* (1995) 20 EHRR 557.

23 HL Ho, 'The Presumption of Innocence as a Human Right' in P Roberts and J Hunter (eds), *Criminal Evidence and Human Rights: Reimagining Common Law Procedural Traditions* (Oxford, Hart Publishing, 2012).

24 A Ashworth, 'Four Threats to the Presumption of Innocence' (2006) 10 *E & P* 241.

25 ibid 243.

The defendant's right to have the case against him proved beyond a reasonable doubt, whether viewed from a narrow trial-centred approach or from a wider human rights perspective, underpins the case against requiring active defendant participation and penalising non-cooperation. When the emphasis is on the defendant's participation, the presumption of innocence becomes much less pronounced, as the focus shifts from the prosecution to the defence. In many circumstances, to require the defendant to actively participate is to ease the prosecution's burden of proof and is also contrary to treating him as if he were innocent. This occurs where, for example, the defendant's failure to participate can be used by the prosecution as evidence of guilt, notwithstanding that the correlation between non-participation and guilt may be extremely tenuous.[26] This book advocates a wide interpretation of the presumption of innocence which is both a reflection of the prosecution's burden of proof at the trial and a direction to officials to treat the defendant as if he were innocent, until guilt is proved. To treat the defendant as innocent should mean that he is under no obligation to actively assist in the discharge of the state's obligation to prove guilt, either expressly or in consequence of a procedural requirement.

Requiring defendant participation and penalising non-cooperation also raises issues of compatibility with other fair trial rights. Article 6 of the European Convention on Human Rights (ECHR), which guarantees the right to a fair trial, sets out the minimum conditions of fairness. It has been influential in many cases in which the imposition of penalties for non-cooperation has been challenged. In addition to the presumption of innocence,[27] Article 6 provides for the privilege against self-incrimination and the right to silence.[28] These rights are discussed in detail in Chapters 5 and 6, so it is sufficient to mention here that they provide the defendant with specific rights not to actively participate in the criminal process. Consequently, requiring defendant participation, and penalising non-compliance, undermines the rights which guarantee defendants a fair trial, and, by extension, undermines the legitimacy of the criminal process as a whole. As contended in the following chapter, it is adherence to principles of fairness and respect for rights which legitimises the process and the outcome of criminal cases.

It will become clear throughout the following chapters that the rationale, definition and scope of the various rights under consideration are debatable. The broad interpretation of fair trial rights which is promoted in this book is sometimes contrary to the narrow way in which the rights have been interpreted and applied by the courts. As mentioned above, a broad interpretation of fair trial rights is linked to a normative theory of the criminal process as a mechanism for calling the state to account. The basis for this theory is explained in the following section. It is further developed and applied throughout the book.

26 See the discussion on inferences from silence and non-disclosure in chs 6 and 7.
27 ECHR, Article 6(2).
28 *Murray v UK* (1996) 22 EHRR 29.

1.3 A theory of the criminal process

Once the state has exercised the power to accuse and charge an individual for a criminal offence, it is for the state to prove those accusations. As previously argued, the criminal process should be conceived of as a process of calling the state to account for the accusations which it has brought against the individual, before that individual can be subjected to official condemnation or punishment.[29] The state can account for the accusations by proving the guilt of the accused, using its police and prosecuting agencies. Guilt can be proved by way of the accused's plea of guilty,[30] or by way of a verdict of guilty following a contested trial, at which due respect is paid to the rights of the defendant. The state is accountable to the defendant, who must have an opportunity to understand and challenge the basis for the accusations against him. The state is also accountable to the wider community, as the individuals within the community are subject to state power and have an interest in the state acting within its powers.

This theory of the criminal process takes an absolutist position as to the defendant's role. The defendant should be under no requirement to actively participate by answering questions or providing information during the pre-trial and trial stages, not least because to do so may assist the state in accounting for its accusations. It is, therefore, appropriate to take an absolutist 'no-assistance' approach. The state should justify and account for the accusations of wrongdoing which it has brought against the defendant, without the defendant's co-opted assistance.[31]

The theory, and its absolutist approach, is grounded in political liberal theory and in the values of dignity, autonomy and freedom. The importance of these values, in relation to the contemporary liberal state, can be traced back to the emphasis placed on individualism during the age of enlightenment, and to social contract theory. The meaning of dignity is often context specific, but at its core is a requirement that the intrinsic worth of every human being be recognised and

29 The theory of calling the state to account is inspired by Hock Lai Ho's argument that a central purpose of the adversarial criminal trial is to hold the executive arm of government to account in its quest to enforce the criminal law. The language of calling, or holding, the state to account has been adopted and applied to pre-trial procedures as well as the trial. However, it is not assumed that Ho would subscribe to the substance or grounding of the theory set out in this book, or the absolutist position which is taken. See HL Ho, 'Liberalism and the Criminal Trial' [2010] *Singapore Journal of Legal Studies* 87; HL Ho, 'The Presumption of Innocence as a Human Right' in P Roberts and J Hunter (eds), *Criminal Evidence and Human Rights: Reimagining Common Law Procedural Traditions* (Oxford, Hart Publishing, 2012).

30 A guilty plea does not necessarily mean that the defendant is in fact guilty. However, where the defendant has made a free and informed decision to plead guilty, he has forfeited the right to test the case against him at a trial. Conversely, if a guilty plea was coerced through, for example, the threat of a harsher sentence following conviction, the state cannot truly be said to have accounted for the accusations. On sentence reductions for guilty pleas, see ch 3.2.2.

31 Assistance, in this context, refers only to assistance obtained through the active participation of the accused.

respected.[32] As part of our intrinsic worth, we have the authority to demand respect for our autonomy. To be treated with dignity thus includes being treated as an autonomous individual; as self-governing and able to make choices for oneself.[33] Autonomy is freedom, and freedom, or liberty, is an inherent good. Kant, for example, conceived of freedom as an *a priori* principle on which the civil state is based; it is not afforded by the state.[34] Kant had a notable influence on Rawls. In the *original position,* as conceived by Rawls, citizens are free and equal rational persons, before the basic structures of society are determined.[35] As inherently autonomous beings, we should be at liberty to conduct our affairs, and make our choices, free from external interference. The conception of liberty advanced here is negative; we should be left to do as we would like to do, rather than our actions being controlled by an external source.[36]

However, our liberty is restricted by the laws of the state in the interests of other values, particularly the interests of freedom itself. As Isaiah Berlin wrote, 'the liberty of some must depend on the restraint of others'.[37] In particular, the criminal law can prohibit us from conducting ourselves in a way that interferes with the liberty of other people. Certain behaviour may thus be criminalised in order to maximise liberty for everyone, and to protect individuals from encroachment on their freedom from other individuals.[38] The normative theory of calling the state to account accepts this role of the criminal law; it does not advocate absolute freedom.[39] There is, however, an inherent good in free behaviours, and freedom must not be interfered with lightly or without very good reason.

The basis for allowing the law to restrict our freedom is the social contract, from which the state is brought into being. Social contract theorists differ in their conceptions of the social contract. In accordance with the theories of Locke and

32 C McCrudden, 'Human Dignity and Judicial Interpretation of Human Rights' (2008) 19 *European Journal of International Law* 655, 679. On the meaning and legal application of dignity, see also LR Barroso, 'Here, There, and Everywhere: Human Dignity in Contemporary Law and in the Transnational Discourse' (2012) 35 *Boston College International and Comparative Law Review* 331.

33 C McCrudden, 'Human Dignity and Judicial Interpretation of Human Rights' (2008) 19 *European Journal of International Law* 655, 659–660. Kant in particular has become closely affiliated with the idea of dignity as autonomy. See I Kant, *Groundwork of the Metaphysics of Morals* (New York, Cambridge University Press, 1996).

34 I Kant, *Political Writings* (HS Reiss ed, HB Nisbet tr, Cambridge, Cambridge University Press, 1991) 74.

35 J Rawls, *A Theory of Justice,* rev edn (Massachusetts, The Belknap Press of Harvard University Press, 1999).

36 On positive and negative liberty, see I Berlin, 'Two Concepts of Liberty' in I Berlin, *Four Essays on Liberty* (Oxford, Oxford University Press, 1969).

37 ibid 124.

38 C Beccaria, *On Crimes and Punishments and Other Writings* (R Bellamy ed, R Davies tr, Cambridge, Cambridge University Press, 1995) 10.

39 In developing a theory of the criminal process, no attempt is made to adopt or create an overarching theory of substantive criminal law. The basis for allowing particular criminal laws to interfere with individual liberty falls outside of the scope of this work.

Rawls, the individual agrees to obey the laws of the state and, in so doing, sacrifices a portion of their freedom in order to preserve the greatest possible liberty overall. The individual should only need to sacrifice the smallest possible portion of liberty necessary to enjoy what remains in security and calm.[40] Precisely what the smallest portion amounts to is open to debate. For the reasons expressed in the following paragraphs, it should not extend to the freedom to choose whether or not to actively participate in the criminal process. The criminal process is the process by which liability for a criminal offence is determined. It is the state's means of enforcing the criminal law through denunciation and punishment of those who are found to have breached it. It is submitted here that, to best realise, within the criminal process, that we are free and dignified human beings, we must be at liberty to choose whether or not to actively participate.

Freedom of choice is important in the criminal process because there is a structural imbalance between the state and those accused of breaching the criminal law, in terms of both power and resources. This imbalance is present throughout the process. The state has immense powers of investigation, prosecution, trial and sentencing. In a liberal society, the state's far-reaching powers should be exercised according to certain standards that show respect for the dignity and autonomy of each individual.[41] In terms of resources, the accused and the state are in divergent positions. Ordinarily, the accused, and the defence as a party, lack the independent investigatory and coercive powers of the prosecution party, and do not have access to the same type of information or technology, such as access to forensic services or the criminal records of witnesses. Of course, a disparity in resources will not always favour the state. Some defendants, such as major corporations or those involved in large scale organised crime, may have ample resources which could be used to fabricate a defence or cast doubt on the prosecution's case.[42] However, where a disparity favours the accused, it results from the initial decision as to the distribution of state resources to the prosecution authorities. As well as deciding how to distribute its resources, the state also chooses who to pursue for alleged criminal behaviour, and how to dispose of individuals once convicted.

Following conviction, the state has the power and resources to interfere substantially with one's liberty. It may exercise this power to remove liberty

40 C Beccaria, *On Crimes and Punishments and Other Writings* (R Bellamy ed, R Davies tr, Cambridge, Cambridge University Press, 1995) 9–11.

41 A Ashworth, 'Four Threats to the Presumption of Innocence' (2006) 10 *E & P* 241, 249. See also HL Ho, 'Liberalism and the Criminal Trial' [2010] *Singapore Journal of Legal Studies* 87.

42 This forms an element of what Langbein refers to as the 'wealth effect' of the adversarial system. Adversary procedure bestows an advantage upon people who can afford to hire skilled counsel. Because most persons accused of serious crime are not wealthy, the wealth effect is considered to be a profound structural flaw in adversary criminal procedure. See JH Langbein, *The Origins of the Adversary Criminal Trial* (Oxford, Oxford University Press, 2003) 2. While the availability of state funded legal representation in many modern systems undermines this criticism of the adversarial system, the defendant's wealth can affect certain aspects of the case, such as the ability to conduct investigations or commission expert witnesses.

completely. Even in the absence of official punishment, the public condemnatory statement of blameworthiness can have damaging consequences through, for example, an inability to gain employment. As noted by Barkow, 'the state poses no greater threat to individual liberty than when it proceeds in a criminal action'.[43] Since liberty is an inherent good, the onus must be on the state to justify its accusations wherever it seeks to curtail the liberty of its citizens.[44] As part of the social contract, individuals should be protected not only from the freedom-restricting conduct of other individuals, but also from the arbitrary use of state power, including punishment for breach of the criminal law where this is not justified.[45] There is, thus, a need to create fairness within a system of imbalance. This requires that guilt is proved by the state, that the accused is treated fairly and that the accused is protected from the potential for arbitrary and oppressive use of state power, as well as from the oppressive use of power itself.

To achieve fairness within a system of imbalance, the procedures used to determine allegations of criminal conduct must be consistent with the freedom of the persons whose conduct is in issue.[46] As is explained in Chapter 4, the protections afforded to defendants by fair trial rights developed historically as a means of ensuring fairness within a structurally imbalanced system. Many fair trial rights give effect to the freedom of the accused in the criminal process. They afford the defendant the freedom to choose whether or not to actively participate. Freedom of choice is exhibited, for example, in the freedom to plead guilty or not, in the right to silence, in the privilege against self-incrimination and other participatory and non-participatory rights.[47]

The freedom to choose whether or not to actively participate also gives effect to a further aspect of human dignity; recognition that the state exists for the sake of the individual human being, and not vice versa.[48] In the context of the criminal process, this should mean that the process exists in order for the state to establish the guilt of the accused, and justify its findings, rather than the accused being

43 RE Barkow, 'Separation of Powers and the Criminal Law' (2006) 58 *Stanford Law Review* 989, 995.

44 HL Ho, 'Liberalism and the Criminal Trial' [2010] *Singapore Journal of Legal Studies* 87, 89. See also RL Lippke, 'Justifying the Proof Structure of Criminal Trials' (2013) 17 *E & P* 323.

45 See J Jackson and S Summers, *The Internationalisation of Criminal Evidence: Beyond the Common Law and Civil Law Traditions* (Cambridge, Cambridge University Press, 2012) 203. For a further assessment of the influence of social contract theory on the development of modern principles of criminal justice, see J Jackson and S Summers, *The Internationalisation of Criminal Evidence: Beyond the Common Law and Civil Law Traditions* (Cambridge, Cambridge University Press, 2012) ch 1.

46 H Stewart, 'The Right to be Presumed Innocent' (2014) 8 *Criminal Law and Philosophy* 407, 408.

47 HL Ho, 'Liberalism and the Criminal Trial' [2010] *Singapore Journal of Legal Studies* 87, 99.

48 C McCrudden, 'Human Dignity and Judicial Interpretation of Human Rights' (2008) 19 *European Journal of International Law* 655, 679.

required to establish his innocence or actively contribute to his own conviction. In accordance with Kantian principles, each individual must be treated as dignified and autonomous; as an end in themselves and not simply as a means to an end.[49] Thus, one should not be treated as an object from which the state can extract information for use in criminal proceedings, as is often a purpose of requiring the defendant to actively participate.

The basic premise of the theory of the criminal process as a process of calling the state to account can be summarised as follows: Because we, as individuals, agree to abide by the criminal laws of the state which prohibit certain behaviours, and, in so doing, give up some of our freedom, the state should account for any allegation that we have breached those laws, before subjecting us to condemnation and punishment. The respect for our freedom, which is owed to us as individual citizens of society, and the maximum value which should be accorded to individual autonomy, mean that we should be at liberty to choose whether we actively respond to those allegations. The criminal process is itself a coercive process in which individuals may be required to passively participate by, for example, being searched, arrested or subjected to questioning. However, the principles of dignity, autonomy and freedom dictate that accused persons should, at least, be able to choose whether to actively participate in the criminal process, and how to conduct their defence.[50] To be required by the state to actively participate is to unjustifiably destroy our freedom at a time when it warrants maximum protection.

The theory has been developed within the cultural context of English criminal procedure, and primarily as a means of assessing a specific issue, namely the increase in requirements for the defendant to actively participate in the criminal process. A more ambitious project could seek to apply it to requirements of passive participation, and to assess the appropriate limits of state pressure on defendants to participate, short of penalising a failure to do so.[51] It could also be possible to take the theoretical grounding further, and apply it outside of the realm of criminal procedure, to consider, for example, whether and how it can provide a basis for determining the legitimacy of the substantive criminal law. However, within this book, the theory is limited to providing a tool for analysing developments in particular areas of criminal procedure and the law of evidence, and to act as a normative yardstick against which such developments can be measured.

Before moving on, it is worth noting the position of the complainant and the public in relation to the normative theory. Complainants of crime, witnesses and

49 See I Kant, *Groundwork of the Metaphysics of Morals* (New York, Cambridge University Press, 1996).

50 J Jackson and S Summers, *The Internationalisation of Criminal Evidence: Beyond the Common Law and Civil Law Traditions* (Cambridge, Cambridge University Press, 2012) 103.

51 This could include, for example, an analysis of the law in relation to obtaining confessions and consideration of the extent to which the police can, or should, pressure accused persons into answering questions.

the wider community will inevitably play an important role in the criminal process by reporting crimes and providing information. However, once the state, through the police and prosecuting agencies, initiates a criminal investigation or brings criminal charges against an individual, it becomes a matter between the state and the accused, not the complainant and the accused or the complainant and the state.[52] Because crimes are conceived of as public wrongs, and because the state has the power to prosecute and punish those who commit criminal offences, it is appropriate to frame a theory of the criminal process around the state's obligations in relation to establishing the guilt of the accused. Nonetheless, protecting the interests of complainants and other witnesses, and providing them with necessary support and information, has become a priority for criminal justice agencies.[53] The increasing emphasis on the interests of complainants and witnesses raises interesting questions about whether they should play a more central role in the criminal process, and whether they should have procedural rights.[54] The issue of the interests of complainants is revisited briefly in the following chapter, where it is argued that such interests do not provide a basis for requiring defendant participation. The issue, however, remains a matter which, for the most part, falls outside of the scope of this book.[55]

The public play an important role within the English criminal process and within the process of calling the state to account. The public nature of the criminal trial helps to ensure that the state can account for the accusations made against

52 Individuals have a right to bring private prosecutions. However, the Crown Prosecution Service retains the power to take over such prosecutions and either continue them or stop them. See Prosecution of Offences Act 1985, s 6.

53 See, for example, Crown Prosecution Service, *The Prosecutors' Pledge* <www.cps.gov.uk/publications/prosecution/prosecutor_pledge.html> accessed 1 April 2016; Ministry of Justice, *Code of Practice for Victims of Crime* (London, The Stationery Office, 2015). The 2015 Code of Practice implements relevant provisions of the EU Directive 2012/29/EU establishing minimum standards on the rights, support and protection of victims of crime. See also D Lawrence, P Neyroud and K Starmer, *Recommendations on a Victims' Law: Report for the Labour Party by the Victims' Taskforce* (The Labour Party, February 2015); Criminal Justice Joint Inspection, *Meeting the Needs of Victims in the Criminal Justice System* (CJJI, 2015).

54 See, for example, the Victims' Right to Review Scheme, launched in 2013, which grants complainants the right to request a review of any decision taken by the Crown Prosecution Service to not charge a suspect or to stop a prosecution. See Crown Prosecution Service, *Victims' Right to Review Scheme* <www.cps.gov.uk/victims_witnesses/victims_right_to_review/> accessed 1 April 2016. This scheme gives effect to the principles laid out in *R v Killick* [2011] EWCA Crim 1608, [2012] 1 Cr App R 10. See also K Starmer, 'Finality in Criminal Justice: When Should the CPS Reopen a Case?' [2012] *Crim LR* 526.

55 See I Edwards, 'An Ambiguous Participant: The Crime Victim and Criminal Justice Decision Making' (2004) 44 *British Journal of Criminology* 967; J Doak, *Victims' Rights, Human Rights and Criminal Justice* (Oxford, Hart Publishing, 2008); M Hall, 'The Relationship Between Victim and Prosecutors: Defending Victims Rights?' [2010] *Crim LR* 31; A Ashworth and M Redmayne, *The Criminal Process*, 4th edn (Oxford, Oxford University Press, 2010) 51–55; K Starmer, 'Human Rights and Victims: The Untold Story of the Human Rights Act' [2014] *European Human Rights Law Review* 215; K Starmer, 'Human Rights, Victims and the Prosecution of Crime in the 21st Century' [2014] *Crim LR* 777.

the defendant, and that it does so in a legitimate manner.[56] As noted above, the state is accountable not only to the defendant, but also to the wider community. Moreover, it is often members of the public, in the form of a jury or lay magistrate, that determine whether or not the state has accounted for the accusations made against the defendant. However, again, because the state takes responsibility for the prosecution of criminal wrongs, and because the wider public possess little control over the decision to prosecute or the way in which a case is dealt with, the theory does not directly address the role of the public as participants in the criminal process.[57]

1.4 Structure of the book

Having introduced the subject matter of this book, and outlined the arguments against requiring active defendant participation, the following chapters will proceed to evaluate the role of the defendant as a participant in the criminal process and the implications of participatory requirements. Chapter 2 sets out the aims and values of the criminal process. It considers which aims must necessarily be emphasised in order to justify requiring defendant participation, and why the values of the criminal process should prevent the imposition of participatory requirements. Chapter 3 examines the way in which the participatory role of the defendant can shape the nature of criminal procedure, and how criminal procedure can be characterised according to the defendant's role. Chapter 4 further develops the normative theory of calling the state to account by contrasting it with an alternative communicative theory of the criminal trial. Chapter 4 also examines the historical development of defence rights which can facilitate a lack of participation, and assesses the defendant's current position as a participant in the English criminal process, particularly at trial.

Chapters 5 through 7 present three specific examples of the way in which defendants can be required to actively participate and penalised for not doing so. Chapter 5 critically evaluates how the modern understanding of the privilege against self-incrimination has been limited through requirements of defendant participation. Reliance on the privilege can now, in some circumstances, lead

56 See the discussion on public trials in ch 4.1.

57 Other commentators assign a greater participatory role to the public. For example, Hoyano has developed a conception of a fair trial which accommodates a quadrangulation between defendant, the alleged victim, other witnesses and the public interest, all of whom are participants and can lay claim to the right to a fair trial. L Hoyano, 'What is Balanced in the Scales of Justice? In Search of the Essence of the Right to a Fair Trial' [2014] *Crim LR* 4, 25. See also R Vogler, *A World View of Criminal Justice* (Aldershot, Ashgate Publishing, 2005). Moreover, alternative methods of criminal justice, such as restorative justice, entail much greater involvement of the victim and the community. However, in order to be successful, restorative justice requires admission of guilt on the part of the accused as well as the accused's willingness to be actively involved in the process. On the role of state, community and victim in restorative justice, see A Ashworth, 'Responsibilities, Rights and Restorative Justice' (2002) 42 *British Journal of Criminology* 578.

to the direct penalty of criminal prosecution for non-cooperation. In Chapter 6, the law in relation to the right to silence is considered. The main point of interest is the Criminal Justice and Public Order Act 1994 and the case law surrounding it, which controversially allow the fact-finder to draw inferences of guilt from a defendant's silence. Chapter 7 examines the pre-trial disclosure obligations placed on the defendant by the Criminal Procedure and Investigations Act 1996, and the provisions for drawing adverse inferences where the defendant fails to comply with the obligations. Chapter 7 also considers the procedural implications of the case management provisions in the Criminal Procedure Rules, which augment the statutory disclosure provisions. The final chapter presents a means of characterising English criminal procedure in the light of the current participatory role of the defendant, and considers the future of the defendant as a participant in the criminal process.

2 The aims and values of the criminal process

The 'aims' of the criminal process are the desired outcomes of criminal cases; that which we seek to achieve by charging and trying an individual for a criminal offence.[1] The purpose of requiring defendant participation is usually to further one or more of these aims. Conversely, if we are to reject the practice of penalising defendant non-participation, certain criminal process values should be prioritised. These 'values' can influence the way in which the aims of the criminal process are sought to be achieved. One means of identifying the aims and values of the criminal process is through reference to the overriding objective of the Criminal Procedure Rules (CrimPR).[2] The Rules formalised the aims of criminal litigation in England and Wales for the first time when they were introduced in 2005. They do not apply to the entire criminal process. However, they have set the tone for developments in procedure and play an important role in establishing the duties of the parties and the court by, for example, prescribing deadlines and laying down the powers of the courts to deal with a variety of situations. They have also carved out a more active and cooperative role for the defence, increasing the ability to require participation and effecting a 'sea change'[3] in the way cases should be conducted.

Rule 1.1(2) sets out the overriding objective of the CrimPR as dealing with criminal cases 'justly'. This is followed by a list of seven criteria for meeting this objective:

(a) acquitting the innocent and convicting the guilty;
(b) dealing with the prosecution and the defence fairly;
(c) recognising the rights of a defendant, particularly those under Article 6 of the European Convention on Human Rights;

1 The term 'aims' is used here only in relation to the desired outcome of individual criminal cases, and not in relation to the wider aims of the criminal law or sentencing practices.

2 Throughout this book, reference to the Criminal Procedure Rules, or CrimPR, is reference to the Criminal Procedure Rules 2015, unless otherwise stated.

3 *R (on the application of DPP) v Chorley Magistrates' Court* [2006] EWHC 1795 (Admin) [24] (Thomas LJ).

(d) respecting the interests of witnesses, victims and jurors and keeping them informed of the progress of the case;
(e) dealing with the case efficiently and expeditiously;
(f) ensuring that appropriate information is available to the court when bail and sentence are considered; and
(g) dealing with the case in ways that take into account—

i. the gravity of the offence alleged,
ii. the complexity of what is in issue,
iii. the severity of the consequences for the defendant and others affected, and
iv. the needs of other cases.

Rules 1.1(2)(e) and (f) are concerned with efficiency and management. While efficiency and managerialist concerns have become a major preoccupation within criminal procedure, and influence the participatory role of the defence, they better reflect how the aims of the system are pursued and are considered in Chapter 3, as part of an assessment of the character of criminal procedure. Rule 1.1(2)(g) is an important provision for the parties and the court. It sets out specific elements of a case which should be taken into account, but, again, it is not an aim of the criminal process and, therefore, is not addressed here. Rules 1.1(2)(a) through (d), on the other hand, represent the primary aims and values of the criminal process. This chapter presents accurate fact-finding and conflict resolution as the aims, or desired end results, of a process which should itself be an exercise in calling the state to account. The constraints which requirements of fairness and respect for rights place on the pursuance of these aims legitimise the process and help to ensure that the state has accounted for its accusations.

2.1 Aims

2.1.1 Accurate fact-finding

Acquitting the innocent and convicting the guilty, as stated in rule 1.1(2)(a), is an obvious aim of the criminal process. This aim can be more succinctly expressed as 'accurate fact-finding'. In other words, accurately determining the facts surrounding the commission of a particular offence with a view to ascertaining whether the defendant is guilty of the offence charged.[4] Accurate fact-finding, as an aim of the criminal process, is predominantly concerned with what Williams has termed 'primary facts'.[5] Primary facts depend chiefly on whether a witness is to be believed about those facts which she did or perceived, such as what she saw. As a consequence of the primary facts, it may also become necessary to

4 This aim was referred to by Bentham as 'rectitude of decision'. J Bentham, *Rationale of Judicial Evidence, Specially Applied to English Practice* (London, Hunt & Clarke, 1827).
5 G Williams, 'Law and Fact' [1976] *Crim LR* 472.

establish the inferential facts (which concern the factual inferences to be drawn from the primary facts); the evaluative facts (which concern the legal assessment of facts as reasonable, negligent, *et cetera*); and the denotative facts (which are concerned with the application of words used in legal rules, for instance, whether something amounts to 'grievous bodily harm').[6] For example, in a case of murder, having concluded that the defendant caused another's death, the issue becomes whether he can be held responsible given his state of mind at the time; including whether he 'intended' to cause 'grievous bodily harm'. The assessment will then centre on the facts surrounding the primary facts.

By establishing all of these facts, one would hope to unveil the objective truth, namely whether a particular defendant did or did not commit the offence for which he has been charged. However, as Williams' analysis suggests, the truth, as determined through the criminal process, is rarely this objective. At trial, rules of evidence, including exclusionary rules, must be taken into account. The fact-finder may not be privy to all of the available or relevant information, leading to legal determinations that do not necessarily reflect the objective truth. Ashworth notes that reference to 'truth' and 'facts' carries an aura of objectivity and incontrovertibility that is often exaggerated.[7] Two other terms which he believes warrant consideration are 'selectivity' and 'interpretation'. In all cases that come to court, each party's version of the facts is a construction dependent on selection and may be open to different interpretations. One must, therefore, recognise that cases are constructed in a particular way. Although we work on the basis that the system is equipped to achieve accurate verdicts, this is not always the case.

Relatively recent reforms to the law of evidence and criminal procedure within England and Wales have emphasised the fact-finding aim, usually by focusing on increasing convictions of the guilty, and sometimes at the expense of concern for acquitting the innocent. Richardson contends that:

> [S]ince 1993, and at an accelerating pace, the perspective that has informed all reforms to the rules of criminal evidence and procedure has been that the great majority of those accused of crime are guilty of what is alleged or something similar to what is alleged, that too many of them are getting away with it, and that the rules need to be changed with a view to securing a higher conviction rate.[8]

This perspective has led to the imposition of penalties on defendants who fail to actively participate, where participation is thought to assist in establishing guilt. The right to silence, for example, was curtailed by the Criminal Justice and Public Order Act 1994 to prevent guilty suspects from hiding behind their silence,

6 ibid.

7 A Ashworth, 'Crime, Community and Creeping Consequentialism' [1996] *Crim LR* 220, 227.

8 J Richardson, 'A "Just" Outcome: Losing Sight of the Purpose of Criminal Procedure' (2011) *Journal of Commonwealth Criminal Law* 105, 106.

despite concern that this would put innocent suspects at risk of wrongful conviction.[9]

If accurate fact-finding (with an emphasis on obtaining convictions) were the only consideration of the criminal process, it would be difficult to argue against requiring defendant participation, since the defendant will often have at least some knowledge of the relevant facts. However, the pursuit of accurate fact-finding can, and should, be constrained by evidentiary rules and procedural norms which prohibit the state from requiring the defendant to participate. Many of these constitute, or further, the criminal process values, discussed below. As Ho contends, the criminal trial is 'much more than a search for truth';[10] it provides an opportunity to hold the state to account for the accusations that it makes and its request for official condemnation and punishment of individual citizens.

2.1.2 Conflict resolution

A further aim of the criminal process is conflict resolution. This aim is not expressly set out in the CrimPR. It can, however, be linked to accurate fact-finding, in that one way that a conflict can be resolved is through a determination of the true facts. Even so, conflict resolution is also an aim in itself. When the conflict arising from the alleged commission of a criminal offence is resolved, finality and closure can be achieved. Finality and closure, and thus conflict resolution, are desired outcomes of the criminal process. Conflict resolution can become an integral feature of any system of criminal justice, regardless of whether it is expressly designed as such.[11] As Markovits maintains, the moment the law is involved, 'the element of conflict, which gives rise to the need for law in the first place, is so omnipresent that it no longer can serve as a device for distinguishing some legal processes that resolve conflicts from others that supposedly do not'.[12]

A conflict can be resolved without necessarily discovering the objective truth. In many jurisdictions, including England and Wales, a resolution can be reached during the pre-trial stage by entry of a guilty plea, removing the need for a trial. An innocent defendant may be tempted to plead guilty where, for example, the case against him appears strong and he feels he would benefit from a sentence

9 See ch 6. Other examples of reforms aimed at accurate fact-finding include the introduction of exceptions to the double jeopardy rule, allowing those previously acquitted of certain offences to be retried where there is new and compelling evidence. See Criminal Justice Act 2003 (CJA 2003), pt 10. See also I Dennis, 'Quashing Acquittals: Applying the "New and Compelling Evidence" Exception to Double Jeopardy' [2014] *Crim LR* 247.

10 HL Ho, 'Liberalism and the Criminal Trial' [2010] *Singapore Journal of Legal Studies* 87, 105.

11 See, for example, Damaska's 'policy implementing' mode of government. M Damaska, *The Faces of Justice and State Authority: A Comparative Approach to the Legal Process* (New Haven, Yale University Press, 1986) 80–88.

12 I Markovits, 'Playing the Opposites Game: On Mirjan Damaska's The Faces of Justice and State Authority' (1989) 41 *Stanford Law Review* 1313, 1337.

reduction gained by pleading guilty at an early stage.[13] Guilty pleas can, therefore, be accepted from innocent defendants as determinative of the legal outcome in the case, effectively supplanting the role of the court in accurately determining the facts. Moreover, due to the limitations of establishing the objective truth, trial verdicts are not always accurate, resulting in both wrongful convictions and wrongful acquittals.[14] Jackson argues that in the absence of a definitive manner for establishing the truth and in the face of the uncertainty that attaches to making judgments about past events, the strength of the criminal trial has been that it establishes a basis for resolving disputes about evidence and justifying the outcome to the community.[15] The need for final decisions to be reached in conditions of uncertainty about disputed claims can impose a number of constraints on procedures for legal truth-finding, such as standards of proof setting out when facts will be considered proved.[16] Safeguards, such as public hearings, together with rules of evidence and fairness requirements, have also helped to establish a basis for resolving disputes, by providing a legitimate means for disputing the accusations made against the defendant. Where closure and finality are the main concerns, factors such as fairness and respect for rights can be given priority, to ensure that an individual is not convicted unless the state has accounted for the accusations against them.

The way in which the aim of conflict resolution is pursued will depend on the importance attached to other procedural concerns. Requiring defendants to participate may speed up the process of finality by uncovering information which will lead to a conclusion. However, it is entirely possible that a conflict can be resolved without the active participation of the defendant, either through the active participation of his legal representatives or by simply putting the prosecution to proof. The trend in reforms intended to secure the participation of the defendant place greater emphasis on the aim of accurate fact-finding than conflict resolution by any other means.

2.2 Values

The way in which the aims of accurate fact-finding and conflict resolution are pursued is fundamental to the legitimate operation of the criminal process. The need for fairness (rule 1.1(2)(b)) and respect for rights (rule 1.1(2)(c)) should act

13 See CJA 2003, s 144; Sentencing Guidelines Council, *Reduction in Sentence for a Guilty Plea: Revised Guideline* (Sentencing Guidelines Secretariat, 2007).

14 In the 1990s, for example, a string of high profile miscarriages of justice came to light, including *R v McIlkenny* (1991) 93 Cr App R 287 (CA) (the Birmingham Six), and *R v Paris* (1993) 97 Cr App R 99 (CA) (the Cardiff Three). More recent high profile cases include *R v Cannings* [2004] EWCA Crim 1, [2004] 1 WLR 2607.

15 J Jackson, 'Managing Uncertainty and Finality: The Function of the Criminal Trial in Legal Inquiry' in A Duff, L Farmer, S Marshall and V Tadros (eds), *The Trial on Trial 1: Truth and Due Process* (Oxford, Hart Publishing, 2004) 142.

16 ibid 127.

as a constraint on how the process aims are achieved. These are the core values of the criminal process. They ensure due process and can prevent, or at least limit, participatory requirements being imposed on the defendant. Respecting the interests of witnesses and complainants (rule 1.1(2)(d)) can also be regarded as a criminal process value. While it is submitted here that fairness and respect for rights are not process aims in themselves, this is not an uncontroversial view, as other commentators do recognise respecting rights as an aim of the criminal process.[17]

2.2.1 Fairness and respect for the rights of the defendant

The criminal process should not be accepted as legitimate unless the aims are pursued fairly and in accordance with the rights of the defendant. There is an overlap between these values, as fair procedures ordinarily require that the rights of the defendant are respected. Yet, fairness and respect for rights are presented as two separate aspects of the overriding objective in the CrimPR, and fairness can be conceived of as a broader conception than a collection of specific rights.

Principles of fairness have been said to lie at the heart of the criminal process.[18] In *R v Horncastle*,[19] Lord Phillips identified two principal objectives of a fair trial. These are that a defendant who is innocent should be acquitted; and a defendant who is guilty should be convicted.[20] Achieving fairness may, therefore, be tantamount to accurate fact-finding. However, this would link fairness only to outcome. Ensuring fairness goes beyond ensuring the discovery of the truth at trial; it also requires that the defendant be treated fairly and that his rights are upheld throughout the criminal process.[21] Lord Phillips went on to recognise that English law has different kinds of rules designed to ensure a fair trial. These rules relate to the procedure itself (including the defendant's rights under Article 6, European Convention on Human Rights (ECHR)) and to the evidence that can be placed before the tribunal (admissibility rules).[22] Yet, a violation of a fairness requirement will not necessarily result in a successful appeal against conviction. The appellate courts have been willing to uphold convictions where the safety, or accuracy, of

17 For example, Ashworth and Redmayne consider respect for rights to be a concomitant aim of the trial process. A Ashworth and M Redmayne, *The Criminal Process,* 4th edn (Oxford, Oxford University Press, 2010) 48. Similarly, Hoyano contends that fairness must not be relegated to the status of a side constraint on the accuracy of the verdict. L Hoyano, 'What is Balanced in the Scales of Justice? In Search of the Essence of the Right to a Fair Trial' [2014] *Crim LR* 4, 26.

18 A Ashworth and M Redmayne, *The Criminal Process,* 4th edn (Oxford, Oxford University Press, 2010) 25.

19 [2009] UKSC 14, [2010] 2 AC 373.

20 ibid [18].

21 See, HL Ho, *A Philosophy of Evidence Law* (Oxford, Oxford University Press, 2008). Ho argues that the law of evidence should be viewed from the perspective of a fact-finder seeking to do justice in the search for truth.

22 *R v Horncastle* [2009] UKSC 14, [2010] 2 AC 373 [19]–[20].

the verdict is not in doubt, despite an acknowledged violation of a fair trial right.[23] In practice, the fairness of criminal proceedings is considered to be directly linked to the accuracy of the outcome. Hoyano contends that the British courts have allowed a doctrine of 'harmless error' to contaminate a fundamental right.[24] This is an unfortunate position, as the criminal process cannot truly be accepted as having been 'fair' if the verdict was produced by a process which was unfair.

'Fairness' has been described as 'at best an indefinite and imprecise concept'.[25] The phrase 'dealing with the prosecution and defence fairly', as set out in rule 1.1(2)(b), seems to imply equality between the prosecution and defence parties. This is in line with the jurisprudence of the European Court of Human Rights on the principle of equality of arms. In accordance with this principle, the prosecution and defence should be on a procedurally equal footing. This includes the requirement that the prosecution disclose to the defence all material evidence in their possession for or against the accused. A failure to do so can give rise to a defect in the trial proceedings.[26] Fairness at the trial may thus depend upon fair disclosure before the trial.[27] At trial, equality of arms suggests equality in presenting and challenging evidence, as provided for by Article 6(3) of the ECHR. Although the concept of 'fairness' is ambiguous, it should arguably encompass all of the factors set out above; fairness in criminal proceedings requires the pursuit of accurate fact-finding in accordance with the rights of the defendant, including the right to equality of arms.

Identifying the defendant's rights which should be respected is more straightforward than determining the exact nature of fairness. Rule 1.1(2)(c) refers specifically to recognition of 'the rights of a defendant and the defence, particularly those under Article 6 of the European Convention on Human Rights'. The ECHR has become an integral aspect of criminal procedure and was given domestic force under the Human Rights Act 1998. Article 6 reads:

> 1. In the determination of his civil rights and obligations or of any criminal charge against him, everyone is entitled to a fair and public hearing within a reasonable time by an independent and impartial tribunal established by law. . . .

23 For example, in *Cadder v HM Advocate* [2010] UKSC 43, [2010] 1 WLR 2601, the Supreme Court held that the admission of evidence obtained under procedures denying access to a solicitor before or during police interrogation was a violation of Article 6. Yet, it would only be appropriate to quash the resulting conviction if there was insufficient evidence to sustain it without the police interview, or taking all the circumstances of the trial into account, there was a real possibility that the jury would have arrived at a different verdict had they not had that evidence before them.

24 L Hoyano, 'What is Balanced in the Scales of Justice? In Search of the Essence of the Right to a Fair Trial' [2014] *Crim LR* 4, 9.

25 N Taylor and D Ormerod, 'Mind the Gaps: Safety, Fairness and Moral Legitimacy' [2004] *Crim LR* 266, 268.

26 *Edwards v UK* (1992) 15 EHRR 417 [36]; *Rowe and Davis v UK* (2000) 30 EHRR 1 [60].

27 J Jackson, 'The Effects of Human Rights on Criminal Evidentiary Processes: Towards Convergence, Divergence or Realignment?' (2005) 68 *MLR* 737, 756.

2. Everyone charged with a criminal offence shall be presumed innocent until proved guilty according to law.
3. Everyone charged with a criminal offence has the following minimum rights:

   a) to be informed promptly, in a language which he understands and in detail, of the nature and cause of the accusation against him;
   b) to have adequate time and the facilities for the preparation of his defence;
   c) to defend himself in person or through legal assistance of his own choosing or, if he has not sufficient means to pay for legal assistance, to be given it free when the interests of justice so require;
   d) to examine or have examined witnesses against him and to obtain the attendance and examination of witnesses on his behalf under the same conditions as witnesses against him;
   e) to have the free assistance of an interpreter if he cannot understand or speak the language used in court.

Article 6 has become Europe's defining standard for determining fairness in criminal proceedings.[28] Several additional rights have been read into it, including the principle of equality of arms,[29] the right to effective participation,[30] the privilege against self-incrimination,[31] and the right to silence.[32] The rights which make up a fair trial are not limited to those expressed and inferred in the Convention; Member States are free to afford citizens a broader range of rights.

It is recognition of the defendant's rights which can allow criminal proceedings to be structured so as to require the prosecution to prove the state's accusations and limit the participatory obligations put on the defendant. However, Article 6 is not an absolute guarantee of respect for rights. Article 6 is not qualified in the way which a number of other Convention rights are. Unlike Articles 8 through 11, it cannot be interfered with in circumstances which are prescribed by law and necessary in a democratic society in the interests of specified public interests. For this reason, Ashworth and Redmayne refer to it as a 'strong right'.[33] They suggest that any argument for curtailing a strong right must at least be more

28 For a critical analysis of the European Court of Human Rights' case law on Article 6, see R Goss, *Criminal Fair Trial Rights: Article 6 of the European Convention on Human Rights* (Oxford, Hart Publishing, 2014).

29 *Edwards v UK* (1992) 15 EHRR 417.

30 *Stanford v UK* App no 16757/90 (ECHR, 23 February 1994).

31 *Funke v France* (1993) 16 EHRR 297.

32 *Murray v UK* (1996) 22 EHRR 29.

33 A Ashworth and M Redmayne, *The Criminal Process*, 4th edn (Oxford, Oxford University Press, 2010) 38. See also A Ashworth, 'The Exclusion of Evidence Obtained by Violating a Fundamental Right: Pragmatism Before Principle in the Strasbourg Jurisprudence' in P Roberts and J Hunter (eds), *Criminal Evidence and Human Rights: Reimagining Common Law Procedural Traditions* (Oxford, Hart Publishing, 2012).

powerful than the 'necessary in a democratic society' argument, and that it is not accurate to state that human rights can be 'balanced' against public interest considerations.[34] In principle, this is a sound argument. In practice, however, the rights conferred by Article 6 have been qualified and restricted by both the European Court and the domestic courts on a 'public interest' and 'proportionality' basis,[35] particularly in cases regarding reverse burdens of proof and the privilege against self-incrimination.[36] In *Brown v Stott,* for example, the Privy Council found that there was 'a clear public interest in enforcement of road traffic legislation' and that limiting the privilege against self-incrimination was not a disproportionate response to this.[37] The European Court has held that such restrictions must not destroy the 'very essence' of the right.[38] Yet, there has been a lack of clarity as to what constitutes the 'essence' of fair trial rights.[39]

When a defendant has rights he has a protection against the power of the state, irrespective of the role he plays in the criminal process. This makes it possible for him to demand that the case against him be proven. When rights are set aside, regardless of whether this is a proportionate response to a legitimate aim, the state can use its powers to coerce individuals into cooperating and, in so doing, undermine their freedom of choice. Ashworth and Redmayne rightly note that, too frequently, no account is taken of the increase in state power that accompanies curtailments of individual rights, whereas one of the fundamental purposes of human rights is to protect individuals against arbitrary exercises of power by state officials.[40] Moreover, it is important to appreciate that the public not only has an interest in the prosecution of criminals, but also in the delivery of individual rights. As Laws LJ put it, 'the delivery of rights by the State is itself an aspect of the public interest, which it is the State's duty to secure . . . The fundamental idea is to perceive rights as inherent in the public interest, and not the public interest's enemy.'[41]

34 A Ashworth and M Redmayne, *The Criminal Process,* 4th edn (Oxford, Oxford University Press, 2010) 38. On balancing rights, see also D Meyerson, 'Why Courts Should Not Balance Rights Against the Public Interest' (2007) 31 *Melbourne University Law Review* 873.

35 For a discussion on the genesis, form and content of balancing within Article 6, see L Hoyano, 'What is Balanced in the Scales of Justice? In Search of the Essence of the Right to a Fair Trial' [2014] *Crim LR* 4.

36 See ch 5.3.3.

37 *Brown v Stott* [2003] 1 AC 681 (PC) 705 (Lord Bingham). The Strasbourg Court had previously rejected the idea of balancing the privilege against self-incrimination against public interest concerns. See, for example, *Heaney and McGuinness v Ireland* (2001) 33 EHRR 12. However, the Court has since adopted a proportionality approach. See *O'Halloran and Francis v UK* (2008) 46 EHRR 21, discussed in ch 5.

38 *Heaney and McGuinness v Ireland* (2001) 33 EHRR 12.

39 See L Hoyano, 'What is Balanced in the Scales of Justice? In Search of the Essence of the Right to a Fair Trial' [2014] *Crim LR* 4.

40 A Ashworth and M Redmayne, *The Criminal Process,* 4th edn (Oxford, Oxford University Press, 2010) 45.

41 Lord Justice Laws, 'Do Human Rights Make Bad Citizens?' (Northumbria University Inaugural Lecture, November 2012) para 5.

The matter of balancing defence rights against the public interest (namely the interest in securing convictions) has become a familiar one, with a number of developments to the law of evidence suggesting that the good of accurate (namely guilty) verdicts is of primary concern. For example, the Criminal Justice Act 2003 (CJA 2003) substantially altered many important aspects of criminal evidence and procedure, including provisions for greater admissibility of hearsay and bad character evidence, in the name of rebalancing the system in favour of victims, witnesses and communities.[42] Ashworth and Redmayne view the metaphor of 'balance' as a rhetorical device of which one must be extremely wary. Many of those who adopt the terminology fail to stipulate exactly what is being balanced, what factors and interests are to be included, what weight is being assigned to particular values and interests and so on.[43] They maintain that, if there is to be balancing, there must be 'an empirically grounded, reasoned, and principled course of argument, not simply the pronouncement of a conclusion'.[44] In the absence of a considered argument, the balancing exercise may prove counter-productive, as many rights are of instrumental value to the outcome of the case. An example is the right to examine witnesses, provided for by Article 6(3)(d).[45] Cross-examination is a tool by which weaknesses in the opposing party's case may be exposed. This right has, to some extent, been curtailed in the interests of complainants and witnesses through greater admission of hearsay evidence,[46] witness anonymity orders[47] and the use of special measures for witnesses at trial.[48]

Ensuring fairness and respecting the rights of the defendant legitimises the criminal process and the outcome of individual cases. In any liberal and democratic society, it is essential that the state acts legitimately. Since the state has such vast resources for dealing with criminal matters, it is particularly important that the criminal justice system operates in a legitimate manner, and that there is a certain degree of consensus as to how it operates and what it aims to achieve. Like 'fairness', the term 'legitimacy' is ambiguous. There are differing understandings and uses of the term in the context of the criminal process.[49] Dennis, for example, puts forward a theory of legitimacy, arguing that the production of legitimate verdicts is the key aim of the law of evidence.[50] According to Dennis, a legitimate verdict should have three qualities: it should be factually accurate; it

42 Home Office, *Justice for All* (Cm 5563, 2002).

43 A Ashworth and M Redmayne, *The Criminal Process*, 4th edn (Oxford, Oxford University Press, 2010) 42.

44 ibid 45.

45 For a discussion of developments in relation to Article 6(3)(d), see I Dennis, 'The Right to Confront Witnesses: Meanings, Myths and Human Rights' [2010] *Crim LR* 225.

46 CJA 2003, pt 11, ch 2.

47 Coroners and Justice Act 2009, pt 3, ch 2.

48 Youth Justice and Criminal Evidence Act 1999, ss 16–33.

49 Some commentators prefer to avoid 'legitimacy theory' altogether. See, for example, L Hoyano, 'What is Balanced in the Scales of Justice? In Search of the Essence of the Right to a Fair Trial' [2014] *Crim LR* 4, 25.

50 I Dennis, *The Law of Evidence*, 5th edn (London, Sweet & Maxwell, 2013) 51–56.

should be morally authoritative; and it should be founded on respect for the rule of law. Although truth-finding becomes the primary means by which a legitimate verdict is secured, it is the legitimacy of that verdict which is the ultimate goal.[51] Ho believes that the legitimacy of a particular verdict depends on how the trial was conducted, on the quality of the interaction between state and accused in the process by which the outcome is reached.[52] According to Ho, the legitimacy of the verdict means its worthiness to be recognised, its moral weight, normative acceptability, rightful authority or some such notion.[53] When the accused is treated unfairly, the state's right to expect him, and the citizenry in general, to accept the resulting conviction is somehow undermined.[54] And, therefore, not legitimate.

It is submitted that the criminal process is legitimised through the pursuit of accurate fact-finding, respect for individual rights and fair procedures. This applies to pre-trial procedures as well as the trial. Thus, the criminal process is legitimate if its aims are pursued fairly and in accordance with the rights of the accused. As will become clear, requiring defendants to actively participate in the criminal process necessitates defence rights being set aside. A system which endeavours to respect defence rights cannot easily be reconciled with one that also penalises defendants for exercising those rights.

2.2.2 Respecting the interests of witnesses and victims

The final relevant aspect of the overriding objective of the CrimPR is set out in rule 1.1(2)(d) as 'respecting the interests of witnesses, victims and jurors and keeping them informed of the progress of the case'. Rule 1.1(2)(d) raises interesting questions about the appropriate role which complainants and other witnesses play in the criminal process which fall outside the scope of this book.[55] Suffice to note here that recent years have seen an increase in concern for the interests of complainants and other witnesses in the criminal process,[56] such that

51 ibid 56.

52 HL Ho, 'Liberalism and the Criminal Trial' [2010] *Singapore Journal of Legal Studies* 87, 90.

53 ibid 102.

54 ibid.

55 See, for example, I Edwards, 'An Ambiguous Participant: The Crime Victim and Criminal Justice Decision Making' (2004) 44 *British Journal of Criminology* 967; J Doak, *Victims' Rights, Human Rights and Criminal Justice* (Oxford, Hart Publishing, 2008); M Hall, 'The Relationship Between Victim and Prosecutors: Defending Victims Rights?' [2010] *Crim LR* 31.

56 See, for example, The Advocate's Gateway, which provides guidance for advocates on vulnerable witnesses <www.theadvocatesgateway.org/> accessed 1 April 2016; Crown Prosecution Service, *The Prosecutors' Pledge* <www.cps.gov.uk/publications/prosecution/prosecutor_pledge.html> accessed 1 April 2016; Crown Prosecution Service, *Victims' Right to Review Scheme* <www.cps.gov.uk/victims_witnesses/victims_right_to_review/> accessed 1 April 2016; Ministry of Justice, *Code of Practice for Victims of Crime* (London, The Stationery Office, 2015); Criminal Justice Joint Inspection, *Meeting the Needs of Victims in*

this can be conceived of as a value of the criminal process. While complainants and witnesses should be supported, informed and treated with respect and dignity, reforms in England and Wales have not gone so far as to grant them a set of procedural rights along the same lines as the defendant.[57] Nonetheless, the effect of recent case law and legislation makes it difficult to dismiss the notion of procedural rights for witnesses altogether, particularly in the light of the European Court's pronouncement that 'principles of fair trial . . . require that in appropriate cases the interests of the defence are balanced against those of witnesses or victims called upon to testify'.[58] The Court has also found that criminal procedure should be organised so that the Convention rights of complainants and witnesses (such as privacy, life and liberty) are not unjustifiably imperilled.[59]

Popular discourse about criminal justice has become dominated by perceptions of criminal versus victim. The defendant's gain is the victim's loss. Within this, a political logic has been established wherein being 'for' victims means being tough on defendants.[60] This implies that affording greater protection to an alleged victim or a witness necessarily means removing rights from the defence.[61] For example, section 100 of the CJA 2003 restricted the admissibility of evidence of a witness's previous bad character, whilst section 101 extended the realm of admissible bad character evidence against the defendant, despite concern that this could lead to an increase in wrongful convictions.[62] The balancing metaphor between complainant and defendant interests tends to suggest that complainants, and the wider public, have an interest in increased conviction rates, no matter how that increase is produced.[63] Yet, complainants have no legitimate interest in seeing defendants wrongly convicted, the likelihood of which may increase by limiting defence rights. While respecting the interests of complainants and other witnesses can rightly be conceived of as a value of the criminal process, this should not be considered analogous to increasing conviction rates. Thus, it should not be used

the Criminal Justice System (CJJI, 2015). For an account of the development of victim's rights over the past two decades, see K Starmer, 'Human Rights, Victims and the Prosecution of Crime in the 21st Century' [2014] *Crim LR* 777.

57 Some jurisdictions do accord victims a greater role. For example, in Italy, the victim can participate at trial through counsel. See, WT Pizzi and M Montagna, 'The Battle to Establish an Adversarial Trial System in Italy' (2004) 25 *Michigan Journal of International Law* 429, 433.

58 *Doorson v Netherlands* (1996) 22 EHRR 330 [70].

59 ibid. See also *R (on the application of B) v DPP* [2009] EWHC 106 (Admin), [2009] 1 WLR 2072; *HM Advocate v Murtagh* [2009] UKPC 36, [2011] 1 AC 731. See also K Starmer, 'Human Rights and Victims: The Untold Story of the Human Rights Act' [2014] *European Human Rights Law Review* 215.

60 I Edwards, 'An Ambiguous Participant: The Crime Victim and Criminal Justice Decision Making' (2004) 44 *British Journal of Criminology* 967, 969–970.

61 L Hoyano, 'What is Balanced in the Scales of Justice? In Search of the Essence of the Right to a Fair Trial' [2014] *Crim LR* 4, 6.

62 A Ashworth and M Redmayne, *The Criminal Process,* 4th edn (Oxford, Oxford University Press, 2010) 44.

63 ibid.

in support of limiting defence rights by requiring defendant participation and penalising non-cooperation.

2.3 Conclusion

A process that sets out to uncover the truth and resolve conflicts in a legitimate manner is consistent with a normative theory of the criminal process under which the state should account for its accusations against the accused and its request for his blame and punishment. In practice, however, the emphasis has shifted away from the values of fairness and respect for defence rights, leading to requirements of defendant participation and penalties for non-compliance with these requirements. By penalising defendants, the system is not changing its aims, since the defendant's participation is ordinarily intended to further them. However, it is giving less regard to the important values which legitimise the process and which can act as constraints on achieving the aims. The manner in which this has occurred, as well as its implications, is demonstrated in the remaining chapters.

3 Characterising criminal procedure

The role which the defendant plays in the criminal process is an important indicator of the nature of criminal procedure. It is also revealing of the importance which is attached to the process aims and values identified in the previous chapter. This chapter considers the way in which criminal procedure is commonly characterised and the way in which it can be characterised, according to the participatory role of the defendant.

3.1 Models of criminal procedure

It has been common for scholars of comparative criminal procedure to identify distinct models of procedure, and to use these models as a tool for characterising particular justice systems. These models are usually defined by a description of their central features.[1] They may be based on either the historical developments of certain legal systems or they may be fictitious entities, difficult to find in reality, but under certain conditions useful for analysing systems and making them intelligible.[2] Setting out distinct procedural models provides a means of identifying common and differing features when making comparisons between legal systems. Knowing where a system lies on the procedural spectrum may also clarify the primacy attached to particular aims and values within that system. However, most individual jurisdictions cannot easily be placed within a specific pre-defined model of criminal procedure. As such, the value of identifying particular models in relation to existing systems is not always clear. It has, therefore, become increasingly common for writers to emphasise the oversimplifications which come with categorising systems into certain procedural types.[3] These

1 See, for example, Packer's Crime Control and Due Process models and Damaska's Hierarchical and Coordinate models. H Packer, *The Limits of the Criminal Sanction* (Stanford, Stanford University Press, 1968); M Damaska, 'Structures of Authority and Comparative Criminal Procedure' (1975) 84 *Yale Law Journal* 480; M Damaska, *The Faces of Justice and State Authority: A Comparative Approach to the Legal Process* (New Haven, Yale University Press, 1986).

2 M Damaska, *The Faces of Justice and State Authority: A Comparative Approach to the Legal Process* (New Haven, Yale University Press, 1986) 5.

3 See, for example, R Vogler, *A World View of Criminal Justice* (Aldershot, Ashgate Publishing, 2005); S Summers, *Fair Trials: The European Criminal Procedural Tradition and the European*

oversimplifications are illustrated by the adversarial and inquisitorial models of criminal procedure.

The adversarial-inquisitorial divide is the most common way of distinguishing between different Western legal systems. It is often used to represent the division between Anglo-American common law procedures on the one hand, and continental European civil law procedures on the other. This distinction is derived from the historical developments and contrasting features of the two legal traditions.[4] The adversarial trial developed in England from the late seventeenth century[5] and modern English procedure continues to be described as 'adversarial'. Yet, there has been a clear shift away from adversarialism. It has been suggested that this shift is towards an inquisitorial model of procedure.[6] Thus, at the same time as demonstrating the oversimplicity of procedural models, the distinction between adversarialism and inquisitorialism is a convenient starting point for identifying and assessing the current nature of English criminal procedure, in the light of the defendant's participatory role.

The adversarial and inquisitorial models are distinguished by both the form of the process and their underlying rationale. While the adversarial trial is the centrepiece of the adversarial model, the focus of the inquisitorial model is the pre-trial investigation. The adversarial trial takes the form of a contest between two equal sides (prosecution and defence) who are in control of the case; they define the issues, gather evidence, call witnesses at trial and examine and cross-examine them. An impartial judge ordinarily settles issues of law and lay

Court of Human Rights (Oxford, Hart Publishing, 2007); J Jackson and S Summers, *The Internationalisation of Criminal Evidence: Beyond the Common Law and Civil Law Traditions* (Cambridge, Cambridge University Press, 2012).

4 See generally S Landsman, *The Adversary System: A Description and Defense* (Washington DC, American Institute for Public Policy Research, 1984); M Damaska, *The Faces of Justice and State Authority: A Comparative Approach to the Legal Process* (New Haven, Yale University Press, 1986); E Sward, 'Values, Ideology, and the Evolution of the Adversary System' (1989) 64 *Indiana Law Journal* 301; JF Nijboer, 'Common Law Tradition in Evidence Scholarship Observed from a Continental Perspective' (1993) 41 *American Journal of Comparative Law* 299; C Harding, P Fennell, N Jorg and B Swart (eds), *Criminal Justice in Europe: A Comparative Study* (Oxford, Clarendon Press, 1995); JH Langbein, *The Origins of the Adversary Criminal Trial* (Oxford, Oxford University Press, 2003); P van Koppen and S Penrod (eds), *Adversarial Versus Inquisitorial Justice: Psychological Perspectives on Criminal Justice Systems* (New York, Kluwer Academic/Plenum Publishers, 2003); J McEwan, 'Ritual, Fairness and Truth: The Adversarial and Inquisitorial Models of Criminal Justice' in A Duff, L Farmer, S Marshall and V Tadros (eds), *The Trial on Trial 1: Truth and Due Process* (Oxford, Hart Publishing, 2004); J Hodgson, 'Conceptions of the Trial in Inquisitorial and Adversarial Procedure' in A Duff, L Farmer, S Marshall and V Tadros (eds), *The Trial on Trial 2: Judgment and Calling to Account* (Oxford, Hart Publishing, 2006).

5 Aspects of this development are discussed in ch 4.2.

6 See, for example, J Hodgson, 'The Future of Adversarial Criminal Justice in 21st Century Britain' (2010) 35 *North Carolina Journal of International Law and Commercial Regulation* 319; J Richardson, 'A "Just" Outcome: Losing Sight of the Purpose of Criminal Procedure' (2011) *Journal of Commonwealth Criminal Law* 105.

people are often used to determine the facts. The inquisitorial trial, on the other hand, serves as more of a confirmation of what has already been judicially established during the pre-trial investigation.[7] A member of the judiciary typically investigates the case before a trial judge determines the facts, based primarily on a dossier of written evidence gathered during the investigation. Since the inquisitorial judge is familiar with the case prior to the trial, through the dossier of evidence, and is trusted to accord proper weight to the evidence, there is little need for complicated rules of admissibility. Conversely, in the adversarial model, there is a preference for procedural rules and laws of evidence, including rules relating to the admissibility of evidence.

The legitimacy of the inquisitorial model requires a great deal of faith in the integrity of the state and its capacity to pursue the objective truth unprompted by partisan pressures or individual self-interest. Public interest, not self-interest, is key.[8] This is in contrast to the adversarial model which is centred on the proposition that the state's power needs to be curtailed in order to protect its citizens. Consequently, the adversarial model is often thought to be concerned with proof rather than truth, with the adversarial trial providing an opportunity for defence counsel to put the prosecution to proof.[9] Damaska, for example, states that the procedural aim of the adversarial model (being structured as a dispute between two theoretically equal sides) is to settle the conflict stemming from the allegation of commission of a crime. 'The prosecutor's role is to obtain a conviction; the defendant's role is to block this effort.'[10] Although the competitive nature and individuality of adversarialism has the potential to provide an effective forum to ascertain the truth, the adversarial model is not structured in such a way that accurate fact-finding is the obvious or sole aim of the criminal process.

It is not possible to identify a purely adversarial or inquisitorial model within existing legal systems. Elements of adversarialism and inquisitorialism can be found in all modern Western legal systems, with some jurisdictions leaning more closely to one model than the other, and some jurisdictions not easily identifiable as correlating more closely to either. For this reason, it is more appropriate to refer to existing systems as being mixed systems than it is to label them as either adversarial or inquisitorial. The Netherlands, for example, might be thought to

7 J Hodgson, 'Conceptions of the Trial in Inquisitorial and Adversarial Procedure' in A Duff, L Farmer, S Marshall and V Tadros (eds), *The Trial on Trial 2: Judgment and Calling to Account* (Oxford, Hart Publishing, 2006) 225.

8 N Jorg, S Field and C Brants, 'Are Inquisitorial and Adversarial Systems Converging?' in C Harding, P Fennell, N Jorg and B Swart (eds), *Criminal Justice in Europe: A Comparative Study* (Oxford, Clarendon Press, 1995) 47.

9 JH Langbein, *The Origins of the Adversary Criminal Trial* (Oxford, Oxford University Press, 2003) 6.

10 M Damaska, 'Evidentiary Boundaries to Conviction and Two Models of Criminal Procedure: A Comparative Study' (1973) 121 *University of Pennsylvania Law Review* 506, 563.

correspond closely to the inquisitorial model.[11] The Dutch judiciary are responsible for investigation and adjudication; decision-making is the responsibility of professional judges; and most cases are decided on the basis of a written dossier without hearing witnesses at trial.[12] However, the police have significant investigative powers;[13] the Dutch courts adhere to some evidentiary rules, such as a rule requiring corroborative evidence in certain circumstances; and, unlike a typical 'inquisitorial' system, Dutch prosecutors have a broad discretion in deciding whether to pursue a case.[14] While there is no jury in Dutch trials, many continental European jurisdictions do use lay people in serious criminal cases, ranging from the Belgian jury to the mixed panel of judicial and lay decision makers in Germany.[15]

The United States, on the other hand, has a common law system which is often described as being adversarial. Yet, American judges have it within their discretion to take on an active role, for example, by calling and questioning witnesses, suggesting defences, commenting on the evidence and issuing warrants. Goldstein claims that, due to its proactive nature, American criminal procedure has developed strong inquisitorial elements which are rarely noted because, 'Americans tend to equate inquisitorial systems with coercive interrogation, unbridled search, and unduly efficient crime control.'[16] Likewise, English criminal procedure, in its current form, cannot accurately be described as adversarial. There remain strong adversarial characteristics within the English criminal process. These include a clear distinction between the prosecution and the judiciary, party control of the case[17] and the use of lay fact-finders. However, the increasing weight put on accurate fact-finding, at times above the values of fairness and respect for the defendant's rights, has influenced it to adopt what appear to be inquisitorial aspects. The inquisitorial influence can be seen, for example, in the

11 See P van Koppen and S Penrod (eds), *Adversarial Versus Inquisitorial Justice: Psychological Perspectives on Criminal Justice Systems* (New York, Kluwer Academic/Plenum Publishers, 2003).

12 ibid.

13 E Cape, J Hodgson, T Prakken and T Spronken (eds), *Suspects in Europe: Procedural Rights at the Investigative Stage of the Criminal Process* (Antwerp, Intersentia, 2007) 24.

14 See P van Koppen and S Penrod (eds), *Adversarial Versus Inquisitorial Justice: Psychological Perspectives on Criminal Justice Systems* (New York, Kluwer Academic/Plenum Publishers, 2003).

15 JF Nijboer, 'Common Law Tradition in Evidence Scholarship Observed from a Continental Perspective' (1993) 41 *American Journal of Comparative Law* 299; J Jackson and N Kovalev, 'Lay Adjudication and Human Rights in Europe' (2006) 13 *Columbia Journal of European Law* 83.

16 A Goldstein, 'Reflections on Two Models: Inquisitorial Themes in American Procedure' (1974) 26 *Stanford Law Review* 1009, 1018. See also WT Pizz, 'The American Adversary System' (1998) 100 *University of West Virginia Law Review* 847; D Sklansky, 'Anti-Inquisitorialism' (2009) 122 *Harvard Law Review* 1634.

17 However, the recent emphasis on efficiency and managerialist concerns has diluted this aspect of adversarialism. See J McEwan, 'From Adversarialism to Managerialism: Criminal Justice in Transition' (2011) 31 *Legal Studies* 519.

role of prosecutors, who take the decision to commence criminal proceedings; in the increased reliance on written evidence at trial;[18] and the restrictions to the defendant's right to confrontation.[19] In addition, the English 'adversarial' trial has been substantially qualified by greater judicial management over the criminal process and greater reliance on the defendant as a source of evidence.

The mixed nature of individual Anglo-American and European systems could lead one to believe that these systems are adopting so many of each other's characteristics, and responding to common demands in such a way, that they are converging.[20] While common law systems have been increasingly taking on direct truth-finding characteristics, countries which assume civil law procedure appear to be increasingly influenced by the necessity for fairness in truth-finding at the trial stage.[21] Converging trends that have been identified in civil law countries include increasing party control, the diminishing authority of professional judges, a shift in emphasis from the pre-trial to trial phase of adjudication, greater importance being attached to oral evidence and the right to confrontation and less reliance on the accused as a source of testimonial evidence.[22]

However, attempts to import foreign practices can lead to their being translated in different ways. This can result in fragmentation and divergence rather than convergence. As Jackson notes, it leads to a paradox in which evidentiary processes are said to be converging, yet may also be diverging through attempts at convergence.[23] In Italy, for example, the 1988 Code of Criminal Procedure was enacted with the intention of adopting an adversarial system to the extent that power over the control of the criminal trial was to be shifted from the trial judges to the prosecutors and defence lawyers.[24] The attempts to implant adversarial elements into a traditionally 'inquisitorial' system were initially met with resistance from the courts and have resulted in a unique hybrid system.[25] Each criminal justice system depends on its own historically evolved institutions, and the justice system is not self-contained; it is affected by external elements,

18 See, for example, the hearsay provisions in the Criminal Justice Act 2003 (CJA 2003).

19 See I Dennis, 'The Right to Confront Witnesses: Meanings, Myths and Human Rights' [2010] *Crim LR* 225.

20 See BS Markesinis (ed), *The Gradual Convergence: Foreign Ideas, Foreign Influences, and English Law on the Eve of the 21st Century* (Oxford, Clarendon Press, 1994).

21 N Jorg, S Field and C Brants, 'Are Inquisitorial and Adversarial Systems Converging?' in C Harding, P Fennell, N Jorg and B Swart (eds), *Criminal Justice in Europe: A Comparative Study* (Oxford, Clarendon Press, 1995) 53.

22 J Jackson and S Summers, *The Internationalisation of Criminal Evidence: Beyond the Common Law and Civil Law Traditions* (Cambridge, Cambridge University Press, 2012) 6.

23 J Jackson, 'The Effects of Human Rights on Criminal Evidentiary Processes: Towards Convergence, Divergence or Realignment?' (2005) 68 *MLR* 737, 739.

24 See WT Pizzi and M Montagna, 'The Battle to Establish an Adversarial Trial System in Italy' (2004) 25 *Michigan Journal of International Law* 429; M Panzavolta, 'Reforms and Counter Reforms in the Italian Struggle for an Accusatorial Criminal Law System' (2005) 30 *North Carolina Journal of International Law and Commercial Regulation* 577.

25 ibid.

such as politics, culture, media and technology. As Damaska notes, even textually identical rules acquire a different meaning and produce different consequences in the changed institutional setting. He writes: 'The music of the law changes, so to speak, when the musical instruments and the players are no longer the same.'[26] Convergence into a single system, or procedural model, as a result of individual jurisdictions adopting foreign procedures and ideologies may, therefore, be unfeasible.

While characterising legal systems as adversarial and inquisitorial fails to recognise the diverse nature of individual jurisdictions, it is not always inadequate to point out that some aspects of existing systems can be described or analysed in terms of being either inquisitorial or adversarial, or as belonging to some other pre-defined procedural model.[27] English criminal procedure has retained a number of traditionally adversarial characteristics, yet it has shifted away from adversarialism due, in part, to an increased focus on accurate fact-finding. At the same time, it does not fit into the inquisitorial mould. Nor is the shift away from adversarialism likely to be a sign of convergence with continental European systems, each of which has a distinct culture and characteristics.

What is clear, however, is that the shift away from adversarialism in England and Wales has affected, and has been affected by, changes to the role of the defendant. Rather than further analysing pre-defined procedural models, and reflecting on the convergence debate, the remainder of this chapter presents an alternative means of characterising criminal procedure which draws from the distinction between adversarialism and inquisitorialism. Consideration is given to two divergent approaches to criminal procedure, based on the participatory role of the defendant. The first approach is one of obligatory participation, whereby the defendant is required, whether through direct or indirect compulsion, to actively participate in the criminal process. The second approach is one of voluntary participation, whereby the defendant is accorded the freedom to choose whether or not to be an active participant in the criminal process. It is within a system of voluntary participation that the state can be called to account for the accusations which it makes and its request for official condemnation and punishment of the defendant.

The purpose of presenting this means of characterising criminal procedure is not to propose new models of procedure which require a particular form or structure, or which should be used to compare and contrast different legal systems. Rather, the purpose is to highlight the significant impact which the participatory role of the defendant can have on the nature of criminal procedure. This will be done in the light of the increase in requirements to participate within English

26 M Damaska, 'The Uncertain Fates of Evidentiary Transplants: Anglo-American and Continental Experiments' (1997) 45 *American Journal of Comparative Law* 839, 840. See also P Legrand, 'European Legal Systems Are Not Converging' (1996) 45 *International and Comparative Law Quarterly* 52.

27 JF Nijboer, 'Common Law Tradition in Evidence Scholarship Observed from a Continental Perspective' (1993) 41 *American Journal of Comparative Law* 299, 308.

criminal procedure and the existence of penalties for failing to comply with the requirements.

3.2 Obligatory participation

The defendant is obliged to actively participate where a failure to do so can be penalised. The obligation may take the form of direct compulsion, whereby non-compliance is an offence or contempt. Alternatively, there may be indirect compulsion, whereby a failure to comply can result in a detriment which is provided for by law, but falls short of an official sanction, such as adverse inferences of guilt. Taken to the extreme, a system of obligatory participation would resort to methods of torture in order to obtain the participation of the defendant. Such methods were employed throughout European legal systems until the eighteenth and early nineteenth century.[28] Torture is no longer considered acceptable,[29] and evidence obtained in this way should not be used against a defendant as proof of guilt.[30] However, according to the European Court of Human Rights, the use of real evidence obtained through inhuman and degrading treatment, falling short of torture, will not necessarily result in unfairness to a defendant and, so, is not subject to an automatic rule of exclusion.[31]

Where the defendant is obliged to actively participate, whatever the method, the purpose is likely to secure him as a source of evidence. Consequently, a system in which the defendant is required, or obliged, to actively participate will be more concerned with pursuing the aim of accurate fact-finding than respecting the rights of the defendant. The focus on fact-finding suggests that systems which are often characterised as 'inquisitorial' could adopt this approach to criminal procedure. The primary aim of inquisitorial procedure is to unearth a version of the truth which will be as objective as possible. Even in the face of a guilty plea, it remains the responsibility of the inquisitorial court to satisfy itself that the offence has been fully investigated and that the case against the defendant has been established.[32] This does not mean that the inquisitorial model is unconcerned with other aims or values, but that it is designed to encourage optimum truth-finding. The conflict is resolved once the facts have been accurately determined.

28 See JH Langbein, *Torture and the Law of Proof: Europe and England in the Ancien Régime* (Chicago, University of Chicago Press, 1977).

29 See, for example, United Nations Convention against Torture and Other Cruel, Inhuman or Degrading Treatment or Punishment; European Convention on Human Rights (ECHR), Article 3.

30 *A v Secretary of State for the Home Department* [2005] UKHL 71, [2006] 2 AC 221; *Jalloh v Germany* (2007) 44 EHRR 32; *Gafgen v Germany* (2011) 52 EHRR 1.

31 See *Gafgen v Germany* (2011) 52 EHRR 1.

32 J Hodgson, 'Conceptions of the Trial in Inquisitorial and Adversarial Procedure' in A Duff, L Farmer, S Marshall and V Tadros (eds), *The Trial on Trial 2: Judgment and Calling to Account* (Oxford, Hart Publishing, 2006) 224.

Within a system which incorporates inquisitorial structures or ideologies, it might be considered less objectionable to require defendants to actively participate. Once the defendant's role as an active participant is deeply engrained within the process, the expectation of participation, and the psychological pressure which accompanies it, may render formal compulsion unnecessary. In France, for example, the defendant is expected to contribute to the truth-finding process. Unlike English trials, where the defendant does not testify until the close of the prosecution case, the French defendant is addressed by the court at the outset. He is asked to comment on the accusations before any witnesses have been heard. The defendant has the right to remain silent, but, psychologically, this becomes almost impossible to maintain.[33] However, as discussed below, there is a tension within French criminal procedure between maintaining what are essentially inquisitorial ideologies and ensuring respect for the rights of the defence.[34]

If participatory obligations can be linked to the pursuit of truth-finding, then the rise in penalty-backed participatory requirements within English criminal procedure can, in part, be attributed to an enhanced focus on accurate fact-finding. There is now much more emphasis on defendant participation, evidenced by, *inter alia,* the penalty-backed pre-trial disclosure requirements and the expectation that the defendant will respond to questioning at the police station and in court, or else face the possibility of adverse inferences. The assumption behind these expectations is that an innocent person would be keen to assert their innocence, and, so, non-participation is an indicator of guilt and may be treated as such.

However, obligatory participation stems not only from a desire to secure the defendant as a source of evidence in pursuit of accurate fact-finding, but also from a desire for a more efficient criminal justice system. Efficiency in this context refers to time and cost of the criminal process; reaching outcomes by achieving process aims as time and cost effectively as possible. Many relatively recent reforms within England and Wales have been aimed at creating an efficient criminal justice process. In 1993, the Royal Commission on Criminal Justice arrived at their important proposals through practical considerations intended to make the system better capable of serving the interests of both justice and efficiency.[35] Efficiency remains high on the criminal justice agenda. In 2012, the government published a White Paper, *Swift and Sure Justice,* setting out a programme of reforms to tackle delay and waste across the criminal justice services.[36] In 2015, a

33 See J Hodgson, *French Criminal Justice* (Oxford, Hart Publishing, 2005); J Jackson and S Summers, *The Internationalisation of Criminal Evidence: Beyond the Common Law and Civil Law Traditions* (Cambridge, Cambridge University Press, 2012) 245.

34 See J Hodgson, *French Criminal Justice* (Oxford, Hart Publishing, 2005); A Dorange and S Field, 'Reforming Defence Rights in French Police Custody: A Coming Together in Europe?' (2012) 16 *E & P* 153.

35 Royal Commission on Criminal Justice, *Report* (Cm 2263, 1993) 3.

36 Ministry of Justice, *Swift and Sure Justice: The Government's Plans for Reform of the Criminal Justice System* (Cm 8388, 2012).

Review of Efficiency in Criminal Proceedings was published by the Judiciary of England and Wales. The aim of the review was to 'demonstrate ways in which, consistent with the interests of justice, it might be possible to streamline the disposal of criminal cases thereby reducing the cost of criminal proceedings for all public bodies'.[37]

A drive to secure accurate fact-finding as efficiently as possible has resulted in requirements of both defendant and defence party participation, backed by penalties for non-cooperation. In order to highlight the significance of efficiency in a system of obligatory participation, two such examples of penalising non-cooperation are presented here. These are derived from current practice within English criminal procedure. The first results from the case management duties imposed by the Criminal Procedure Rules (CrimPR). The second is by way of sentence discounts for guilty pleas. Later chapters provide a more detailed analysis of further examples of penalising defendant non-cooperation which have arisen not only in pursuit of accurate fact-finding, but also, and sometimes primarily, as a result of efficiency concerns.

3.2.1 Case management

As part of the drive towards efficiency in criminal procedure, there have been increasing demands for robust judicial case management as a means of controlling the cost and length of proceedings.[38] Granting judges an active role is something usually associated with inquisitorialism. However, managerial judges are not required to initiate or direct the gathering of evidence, or lines of legal arguments.[39] It has, thus, been suggested that English criminal procedure has shifted towards a managerial system of criminal justice, rather than inquisitorialism.[40] In consequence of the CrimPR, judges are now required to intervene proactively in the management of criminal cases, before and during trial, to encourage agreement

37 Sir Brian Leveson, *Review of Efficiency in Criminal Proceedings* (London, Judiciary of England and Wales, 2015) 1. The review recommended, *inter alia,* robust judicial case management and greater use of video technology. The government responded to the review by welcoming and, in principle, accepting all of the recommendations. See Ministry of Justice, 'Government Response to Review of Efficiency in Criminal Proceedings' (11 March 2015) available at <www.gov.uk/government/uploads/system/uploads/attachment_data/file/411854/response-to-leveson-review.pdf> accessed 1 April 2016.

38 See, for example, Lord Justice Auld, *Review of the Criminal Courts of England and Wales* (London, The Stationery Office, 2001); Ministry of Justice, *Swift and Sure Justice: The Government's Plans for Reform of the Criminal Justice System* (Cm 8388, 2012); Sir Brian Leveson, *Review of Efficiency in Criminal Proceedings* (London, Judiciary of England and Wales, 2015).

39 P Darbyshire, 'Judicial Case Management in Ten Crown Courts' [2014] *Crim LR* 30, 32. See also M Langer, 'The Rise of Managerial Judging in International Criminal Law' (2005) 53 *American Journal of Comparative Law* 835.

40 See J McEwan, 'From Adversarialism to Managerialism: Criminal Justice in Transition' (2011) 31 *Legal Studies* 519.

where possible and to ensure that trials begin promptly, are as narrowly focused as possible and do not last longer than necessary.[41] Some judges have perceived the CrimPR as irrelevant because judicial case management had already been established in their courts for decades, using statutory and common law powers.[42] This indicates that judges were themselves primary movers in the shift towards efficiency and managerialism, even before the CrimPR formalised their case management role.[43] Judges have, subsequently, tended to take their case management duties seriously.[44]

It was noted in the previous chapter that the overriding objective of the CrimPR requires 'dealing with cases efficiently and expeditiously'.[45] Part 3 of the CrimPR deals specifically with case management. Rule 3.2 places a duty on the court to further the overriding objective by actively managing the case, while rule 3.3 requires the parties to actively assist the court in fulfilling this duty. Active assistance under rule 3.3 requires early engagement of the parties and communication with each other. Rule 3.2 assigns the court an activist role far removed from the passive adversarial role that English judges have become associated with. This is furthered by rule 3.5 which grants power to the court to give *any* direction or take *any* step to actively manage the case unless that direction or step would be inconsistent with legislation.[46] Such steps can include requiring advocates to attend court.[47] In addition, rule 3.11 allows the court to place participatory requirements on the parties in its role as case manager. These requirements include identifying whether the parties intend to raise any points of law that could affect the conduct of the trial or appeal, and identifying information about witnesses and the order of their evidence. The significant powers accorded to judges under the CrimPR have been described as 'unimaginable under adversary principles'.[48]

Levels of compliance with case management orders and requirements vary across courts.[49] For defence lawyers, their client's best interests and the demands of legal professional privilege may lead to a failure to comply with case management

41 ibid 527. For a practical analysis of the Criminal Procedure Rules (CrimPR), see RL Denyer, *Case Management in Criminal Trials*, 2nd edn (Oxford, Hart Publishing, 2012).

42 See P Darbyshire, 'Judicial Case Management in Ten Crown Courts' [2014] *Crim LR* 30.

43 See *R v Chaaban* [2003] EWCA Crim 1012, [2003] Crim LR 658.

44 See P Darbyshire, 'Judicial Case Management in Ten Crown Courts' [2014] *Crim LR* 30. See also the comments made by the President of the Queen's Bench Division in *R (on the application of Drinkwater) v Solihull Magistrates' Court* [2012] EWHC 765 (Admin), (2012) 176 JP 401.

45 CrimPR, r 1.1(2)(e).

46 Emphasis added.

47 See *Re West* [2014] EWCA Crim 1480, [2015] 1 WLR 109.

48 M McConville and L Marsh, 'Adversarialism Goes West: Case Management in Criminal Courts' (2015) 19 *E & P* 172, 173.

49 See P Darbyshire, 'Judicial Case Management in Ten Crown Courts' [2014] *Crim LR* 30; F Garland and J McEwan, 'Embracing the Overriding Objective: Difficulties and Dilemmas in the New Criminal Climate' (2012) 16 *E & P* 233.

orders.[50] As originally drafted, the CrimPR said little about sanctions for non-compliance with case management directions. However, rule 3.5(6) now allows the court to: fix, postpone, bring forward, extend, cancel or adjourn a hearing; exercise its powers to make a costs order; and impose such other sanctions as may be appropriate. Sanctioning non-compliance with pre-trial orders, or failure to serve appropriate notices within time, provides an example of the increasing emphasis on defence participation as well as the state's willingness to impose penalties where this is not forthcoming.

It has, however, been claimed that non-compliance with the CrimPR rarely leads to any meaningful sanction in practice.[51] In a study of ten Crown Courts, Darbyshire found that most judges preferred to chastise the non-compliant party in court, rather than impose costs penalties.[52] Garland and McEwan also found that less formal sanctions are more important in practice, and judicial displeasure is particularly feared.[53] This approach was endorsed by Sir Brian Leveson P in the Review of Efficiency in Criminal Proceedings, in which it is recommended that courts maintain a record of failures to comply with the CrimPR and insist on a 'compliance court appearance' once a pattern of failure is identified.[54] Subsequent amendments to the Criminal Practice Directions have implemented this recommendation.[55] Paragraph 3A.26 of the Criminal Practice Directions 2015 provides that 'courts should maintain a record whenever a party to the proceedings has failed to comply with a direction made by the court. The parties may have to attend a hearing to explain any lack of compliance.'

Wasted costs orders are often not an appropriate penalty for non-compliance with case management requirements. If the order is resisted, it can be vastly more expensive to make the order than the value of the order itself.[56] A further problem with costs orders is that they can result in punishing the wrong person. It may be difficult to determine who is at fault. To order costs against the defence representatives would be inappropriate where the fault lies with the defendant, who may have been unwilling to provide instructions. However, some judges have

50 F Garland and J McEwan, 'Embracing the Overriding Objective: Difficulties and Dilemmas in the New Criminal Climate' (2012) 16 *E & P* 233, 245–248.

51 RL Denyer, 'Non-Compliance with Case Management Orders and Directions' [2008] *Crim LR* 784.

52 P Darbyshire, 'Judicial Case Management in Ten Crown Courts' [2014] *Crim LR* 30, 40–43.

53 F Garland and J McEwan, 'Embracing the Overriding Objective: Difficulties and Dilemmas in the New Criminal Climate' (2012) 16 *E & P* 233, 238.

54 Sir Brian Leveson, *Review of Efficiency in Criminal Proceedings* (London, Judiciary of England and Wales, 2015) 55.

55 See Criminal Practice Directions 2015 [2015] EWCA Crim 1567 paras 3A.26–3A.28.

56 On the problems with wasted costs orders, see Lord Justice Gross and Lord Justice Treacy, *Further Review of Disclosure in Criminal Proceedings: Sanctions for Disclosure Failure* (London, Judiciary of England and Wales, 2012) 4. See also the comments of Sir Brian Leveson P in *DPP v Radziwilowicz* [2014] EWHC 2283 (Admin), (2014) 178 JP 432 [13]–[14].

been willing to impose significant sanctions for non-compliance, including wasted costs orders. In the case of *SVS Solicitors*,[57] a wasted costs order was upheld against a solicitors firm who had opposed a prosecution application to adduce hearsay evidence without setting out their grounds for doing so, in contravention of the CrimPR.[58] This led to the unnecessary expense of a prosecution witness being flown in from Australia. The court held that, if their client would not allow them to comply with the CrimPR, the solicitors should have withdrawn from the case. They owed a duty to the court and were not entitled to break the rules in order to act on their client's instructions. This case has raised important questions about where the balance lies between the duties of defence lawyers to their clients and their duties to the courts. It seems that defence lawyers are now expected to act in the interests of the administration of justice rather than the interests of their clients.[59] This is inconsistent with their historically adversarial role in which, subject to the ethical position of the defence lawyer, the defence serve to zealously represent the interests of the defendant.[60] The current approach reflects a move from an atmosphere of adversarial competitiveness to one of cooperation.[61]

Defence non-compliance has also been penalised through the exclusion of relevant evidence. In *Musone*,[62] the trial judge had been entitled to exclude evidence of an alleged confession where the defendant attempted to ambush his co-defendant. There had been a breach of rule 35,[63] as the defence had not given notice of intention to introduce the evidence. However, rule 35 contained no express provision dealing with a sanction for non-compliance, and the Court of Appeal acknowledged that the circumstances in which a breach of the CrimPR would entitle a court to exclude evidence of substantive probative value would be rare.[64] Nonetheless, the Court was of the view that the power to make rules requiring a co-defendant to serve notice of evidence of another defendant's bad character, under section 111 of the Criminal Justice Act 2003 (CJA 2003),

57 [2012] EWCA Crim 319, [2012] 3 Costs LR 502.

58 Under the CrimPR 2015, the relevant provision is r 20.3(2)(d). At the time of the case it was r 34.3(2)(d).

59 See also *Re Joseph Hill & Company Solicitors* [2013] EWCA Crim 775, [2014] 1 WLR 786, in which the Court of Appeal felt that, even if the defendant would not be specific about his alibi witnesses, defence counsel should have disclosed the identity of all potential alibi witnesses ahead of the trial, as required by s 6A of the Criminal Procedure and Investigations Act 1996.

60 On the impact of case management on traditional understandings of the adversarial advocate, see M McConville and L Marsh, 'Adversarialism Goes West: Case Management in Criminal Courts' (2015) 19 *E & P* 172.

61 F Garland and J McEwan, 'Embracing the Overriding Objective: Difficulties and Dilemmas in the New Criminal Climate' (2012) 16 *E & P* 233, 234.

62 [2007] EWCA Crim 1237, [2007] 1 WLR 2467.

63 The CrimPR have since been rearranged. The bad character provisions are contained in pt 21 of the CrimPR 2015.

64 *R v Musone* [2007] EWCA Crim 1237, [2007] 1 WLR 2467 [60].

confers power on a court to exclude such evidence in circumstances where there has been a breach of a prescribed requirement (in this case giving notice as required by the CrimPR). It was also felt that, in order to further the overriding objective of the CrimPR, the courts must have power to prevent a deliberate manipulation of the rules by refusing to admit evidence which it is sought to adduce in deliberate breach of those rules.[65]

The decision in *Musone* was largely framed in terms of ensuring fairness to the co-defendant and prosecution, but it does demonstrate a willingness to sanction defence non-cooperation where efficiency and managerialism are at stake. The desire for efficiency can also impact the admissibility of other types of evidence. For example, expert evidence can be excluded where the party has not complied with requirements under part 19 of the CrimPR. Likewise, hearsay evidence can be excluded where notice to introduce the evidence was served late, contrary to the requirements of part 20 of the CrimPR.[66] Hearsay evidence can also be excluded under section 126 of the CJA 2003, on grounds which include undue waste of time, weighed against the value of the evidence.

Breaches of the CrimPR or case management orders can also result in a refusal of a requested adjournment which could, in practice, render items of evidence unavailable.[67] Moreover, in the Review of Disclosure in Criminal Proceedings, undertaken for the Judiciary of England and Wales in 2011, it was anticipated that, subject to the interests of justice, late disclosure of material by any party may be capable of resulting in the exclusion of such material from trial.[68] However, the Further Review of Disclosure in Criminal Proceedings found no demand for a general exclusionary rule when there has been a disclosure failure. It was considered that a general discretionary power to exclude otherwise admissible evidence, which is relevant to an issue in the case, would be contrary to the principles of a fair trial and carry the risk of miscarriages of justice.[69] Yet, it was accepted that the common law may develop 'nuanced and necessary' exceptions, as in the case of *Musone*.[70]

65 ibid.

66 CJA 2003, s 132(5).

67 F Garland and J McEwan, 'Embracing the Overriding Objective: Difficulties and Dilemmas in the New Criminal Climate' (2012) 16 *E & P* 233, 249.

68 Lord Justice Gross, *Review of Disclosure in Criminal Proceedings* (London, Judiciary of England and Wales, 2011) 9.

69 Lord Justice Gross and Lord Justice Treacy, *Further Review of Disclosure in Criminal Proceedings: Sanctions for Disclosure Failure* (London, Judiciary of England and Wales, 2012) 3. See *R (on the application of Tinnion) v Reading Crown Court* [2009] EWHC 2930 (Admin), (2010) 174 JP 36, in which the trial judge had been wrong to refuse to admit previously undisclosed alibi evidence. See also *R v Ullah* [2011] EWCA Crim 3275; *R v T* [2012] EWCA Crim 2358, [2013] Crim LR 596.

70 Lord Justice Gross and Lord Justice Treacy, *Further Review of Disclosure in Criminal Proceedings: Sanctions for Disclosure Failure* (London, Judiciary of England and Wales, 2012) 6.

3.2.2 Sentence discounts

Aside from the creation of case management duties, efficiency concerns have led to other practices which disadvantage those who fail to participate, including 'sentence discounts' for guilty pleas. Section 144 of the CJA 2003 gives legislative authority for a reduction in sentence for guilty pleas. This reduction, or discount, can range from one third to one tenth, and can influence the decision between a custodial and non-custodial sentence.[71] As such, it places enormous pressure on the accused to actively participate in the criminal process by entering a guilty plea. A guilty plea requires active participation because, when asked how he pleads, the accused must respond by stating that he pleads guilty. A plea of not-guilty, on the other hand, does not require the active participation of the accused; if the accused refuses to enter a plea, a plea of not-guilty will be entered on his behalf. In this respect, the accused can demand that the state account for its accusations without actively participating in the process. By pleading guilty in return for a sentence discount, the accused forfeits his right to a trial and to put the prosecution to proof.

The Sentencing Council felt that sentence discounts for guilty pleas are appropriate because:

> A guilty plea avoids the need for a trial (thus enabling other cases to be disposed of more expeditiously), shortens the gap between charge and sentence, saves considerable cost, and, in the case of an early plea, saves victims and witnesses from the concern about having to give evidence. The reduction principle derives from the need for the effective administration of justice and not as an aspect of mitigation.[72]

Sentence discounts are framed as an incentive to plead guilty in order to save the system time and money. Yet, the effect is to significantly disadvantage those who do not cooperate; an inevitable consequence of the discount for pleading guilty is that a plea of not-guilty has its price for defendants.[73] In this regard, the harsher sentence imposed following a plea of not-guilty constitutes a penalty for non-compliance.[74] The convicted defendant automatically becomes subject to a detriment that would not be endured if he were to participate by entering a guilty plea.

The 'incentive' to cooperate is also contentious because it affects principles which the criminal justice system ought to protect. The presumption of innocence

71 Sentencing Guidelines Council, *Reduction in Sentence for a Guilty Plea: Revised Guideline* (Sentencing Guidelines Secretariat, 2007) para 2.3.

72 ibid para 2.2.

73 A Ashworth, *Sentencing and Criminal Justice*, 6th edn (Cambridge, Cambridge University Press, 2015) 187.

74 Darbyshire, for example, states that '[t]he discount undeniably punishes those who exercise their right to trial then are found guilty'. P Darbyshire, 'The Mischief of Plea Bargaining and Sentencing Rewards' [2000] *Crim LR* 895, 901.

means that it is the defendant's right to have the case against him proved beyond a reasonable doubt. It is not then proper that a person who exercises this right should be treated more severely, and, as argued by Ashworth, it is a weak response to maintain that pleading not-guilty is not an aggravating factor.[75] Likewise, Bridges submits that the guidelines on sentence discounts have led to, if not an abandonment of the principle of the presumption of innocence, then, at least, to its further subordination to other political and administrative priorities.[76] Sentence discounts also have a discriminatory effect which raises issues of compliance with Article 14 of the European Convention on Human Rights (ECHR).[77] Since black defendants tend to plead not-guilty more often than white defendants, and tend to receive longer sentences, partly due to having forfeited their discount,[78] sentence discounts operate as a form of indirect racial discrimination. The general principle of a sentence discount has a disproportionate impact on members of minority ethnic groups simply because they more frequently exercise their right to be presumed innocent.[79] In this instance, minority ethnic defendants are at greater risk of being penalised for their failure to cooperate in the criminal process than white defendants.

As argued by Bridges, the formalisation and systematisation of the sentence discount has, at the very least, introduced a more explicit and, arguably, stronger constraint on the voluntary nature of the guilty plea.[80] Likewise, Blake and Ashworth have stated that the English system 'militates against the "free choice" of the defendant'.[81] This sits uneasily with a concept of the criminal process based on calling the state to account; the pursuit of efficiency has taken precedence over the defendant's ability to exercise his autonomy and test the case against him. In order to ensure that guilty pleas are voluntary and properly made, any reduction in sentence for a guilty plea should be kept modest, and should be applied as a mitigating factor on a case by case basis, rather than as a blanket incentive to save the state time and money and to avoid a penalty for non-cooperation.[82]

By interfering with the freedom to choose whether or not to actively participate in the criminal process, case management and sentencing practices are indicative

75 A Ashworth, *Sentencing and Criminal Justice*, 6th edn (Cambridge, Cambridge University Press, 2015) 187.

76 L Bridges, 'The Ethics of Representation on Guilty Pleas' (2006) 9 *Legal Ethics* 80, 85.

77 A Ashworth, *Sentencing and Criminal Justice*, 6th edn (Cambridge, Cambridge University Press, 2015) 188.

78 R Hood, *Race and Sentencing* (Oxford, Oxford University Press, 1992) 125.

79 A Ashworth, *Sentencing and Criminal Justice*, 6th edn (Cambridge, Cambridge University Press, 2015) 188.

80 L Bridges, 'The Ethics of Representation on Guilty Pleas' (2006) 9 *Legal Ethics* 80, 85.

81 M Blake and A Ashworth, 'Ethics and the Criminal Defence Lawyer' (2004) 7 *Legal Ethics* 167, 182.

82 See generally RL Lippke, *The Ethics of Plea Bargaining* (Oxford, Oxford University Press, 2011).

of a system of obligatory participation. This approach to criminal procedure has little concern for the criminal process values directed towards legitimising case outcomes. Instead, it is focused on obtaining defendant participation in order to reach verdicts, namely convictions, as quickly and cost effectively as possible. A system which can be characterised by the obligatory nature of defendant participation is difficult to reconcile with a process based on calling the state to account, as the purpose of requiring participation is to speed up the process and secure the defendant as an evidential resource. In so doing, the defendant may be subjected to a requirement to account for the accusations being made against him, shifting the focus from the state to the defendant, and limiting the opportunity to put the prosecution to proof.

3.3 Voluntary participation

Whereas a system which requires the active participation of the defendant is likely to put the pursuit of efficient fact-finding ahead of fairness and respect for defence rights, a system which values the latter is more likely to afford the defendant the freedom to choose whether or not to actively participate in the criminal process. Such a system would remain concerned with obtaining accurate outcomes. It may also exert some degree of pressure on the defendant to actively participate, even if only by highlighting the risks inherent in leaving the accusations unchallenged. However, it would not attach legal consequences to non-participation and it would endeavour to pay due respect to the post-enlightenment ideals of the autonomous rights-bearing individual, who should be treated with dignity and respect in the determination of a criminal charge.

Systems which adopt strong 'adversarial' ideologies may be in a position to take this approach to criminal procedure. The adversarial model is highly individualistic and, in theory at least, allows the parties to control their case, including the defendant's control over his participatory role. It was during the development of the adversarial system within England and Wales that many participatory and non-participatory rights became workable. Accordingly, once adversarial procedure had become established, the defendant could utilise his position as an autonomous rights-bearing individual during the criminal process. This development, and the link between the rise of adversarialism and participation, is explored in the following chapter. What is most relevant for current purposes is the adversarial notion of the trial as a forum for testing the prosecution's case. This forms an element of the theory of the criminal process in which the state must account for the accusations it makes against the defendant. Within this, the defendant should not be required to actively assist or participate. It is not possible to reconcile a system of voluntary participation, whether that be an 'adversarial' system or otherwise, with one that is willing to penalise defendant non-cooperation.

Many of the rights which show respect for the defendant's autonomy and, as such, accord the freedom to choose whether or not to participate, exist within

Article 6 of the ECHR. These include the right to silence and the privilege against self-incrimination.[83] These rights, when interpreted broadly, provide the defendant with a means of insisting that the state account for the accusations made against him. Thus, in principle, the ECHR may promote a voluntary approach to the defendant's role as a participant in the criminal process; the defendant should not be compelled, or subjected to undue pressure, to actively participate. The ECHR also provides the equally important right to participate. Article 6(3) sets out the right to confrontation and the role of the parties in presenting their own evidence. Thus, at the same time as not requiring the defendant to actively participate, Member States should ensure that the defendant has the opportunity to do so. The procedural changes which have occurred within individual European jurisdictions over recent years, and which have led to suggestions of convergence, may, at least in part, be attributed to this effect of the ECHR.

Jackson and Summers, for example, argue that the European Court has been developing a new procedural model best characterised as 'participatory' because it seeks to enable all those capable of giving relevant evidence to do so in as least a coercive manner as possible.[84] They identify four broad strands in the development of defence participation in the criminal processes of proof that require to be accommodated within national systems: non-compulsion; informed involvement; an opportunity to challenge evidence; and a reasoned judgment that can be challenged.[85] Jackson and Summers' arguments have been advanced in the light of the Court's recognition of a right to adversarial procedure. Reference to 'adversarial procedure' began to appear in European Court judgments in the late 1980s, often in relation to the equality of arms principle.[86] Given the debate surrounding the value of procedural models within comparative law scholarship, the use of the term 'adversarial' might have been expected to prove controversial, yet it has received little attention.[87] This may reflect the Court's use of the terminology; the right to adversarial procedure in this context refers only to the entitlement of the defendant to be present at trial, and that the prosecution and defence be given the opportunity to have knowledge and comment on the observations filed and the evidence adduced by the other party.[88]

Yet, the notion of adversarial procedure, and the emphasis on party participation, has had an impact on the procedural traditions of some Member States, particularly

83 *Murray v UK* (1996) 22 EHRR 29.

84 J Jackson and S Summers, *The Internationalisation of Criminal Evidence: Beyond the Common Law and Civil Law Traditions* (Cambridge, Cambridge University Press, 2012).

85 ibid 102–103.

86 See, for example, *Rowe and Davis v UK* (2000) 30 EHRR 1 [60], where the Court states: 'It is a fundamental aspect of the right to a fair trial that criminal proceedings, including elements of such proceeding which relate to procedure, should be adversarial and that there should be equality of arms between the prosecution and defence.'

87 S Summers, *Fair Trials: The European Criminal Procedural Tradition and the European Court of Human Rights* (Oxford, Hart Publishing, 2007) 113.

88 J Jackson and S Summers, *The Internationalisation of Criminal Evidence: Beyond the Common Law and Civil Law Traditions* (Cambridge, Cambridge University Press, 2012) 86–91.

those with inquisitorial roots, where the defence traditionally played a subsidiary role. Perhaps the biggest impact of Article 6 has been through Article 6(3) which includes the rights to 'adversarial' proceedings. The emphasis given to equal participation by the parties has also underlined the need to distinguish those responsible for prosecuting and those responsible for judging and, in doing so, has broken with old continental practices which tended to blur the distinction.[89] The impact of the ECHR has not been welcomed by all of the Member States. The translation of Convention rights into the French 'inquisitorial' context, for example, has been problematic, creating tensions within prevailing legal cultures.[90] This is evident from the high level of condemnation by the European Court for faults which seemed endemic to the French system, such as police brutality, disregard for defence rights and excessive periods of detention before trial.[91] France has even been found to have violated Article 3 in a case involving the torture of a suspect in police custody.[92] The purpose of such practices is to secure the active participation of the defendant and to elicit incriminatory evidence from him. During the period of police detention and interrogation, French supervising prosecutors have generally been tolerant of police pressure exerted on suspects to make them tell 'the truth'.[93]

It seemed to be contrary to the attitude within French criminal procedure to equip suspects and defendants with workable defence rights, such as the right to silence and access to lawyers, since it potentially undermines the search for the truth, and is thought to give them an unfair advantage.[94] Legislation enacted in 1993, 2000 and 2011 sought explicitly to bring French criminal procedure into line with the ECHR. However, Hodgson identifies two faces of French criminal justice which have emerged as a result. On the one hand, there is a claim to embrace the ECHR and to incorporate it through formal legal mechanisms. On the other hand, there is a parallel domestic discourse which seeks to downplay the impact of the ECHR on criminal procedure, reassuring those responsible for its implementation that police powers are not significantly curbed, and that any change in procedure is minimal.[95] Thus, although the ECHR has undoubtedly had some impact, in practice, its ability to create systems of voluntary participation, in which the defendant can neither be required to participate nor prevented from doing so, may not be as stark as it appears.

89 J Jackson, 'The Effects of Human Rights on Criminal Evidentiary Processes: Towards Convergence, Divergence or Realignment?' (2005) 68 *MLR* 737, 751.

90 J Hodgson, *French Criminal Justice* (Oxford, Hart Publishing, 2005) 33. See also A Dorange and S Field, 'Reforming Defence Rights in French Police Custody: A Coming Together in Europe?' (2012) 16 *E & P* 153.

91 J Hodgson, *French Criminal Justice* (Oxford, Hart Publishing, 2005) 35.

92 *Selmouni v France* (2000) 29 EHRR 403.

93 J Hodgson, *French Criminal Justice* (Oxford, Hart Publishing, 2005) 171.

94 See J Hodgson, 'Human Rights and French Criminal Justice: Opening the Door to Pre-Trial Defence Rights' in S Halliday and P Schmidt (eds), *Human Rights Brought Home: Socio-legal Perspectives on Human Rights in the National Context* (Oxford, Hart Publishing, 2004).

95 ibid 200.

Within England and Wales, there has been some reluctance to embrace the conception of fairness advanced by the Article 6 rights. The domestic courts have made it clear that Europe does not have the final say in the determination of fairness. In *Horncastle*,[96] the Supreme Court stated that there would be rare occasions where the Court had concerns as to whether a decision in Strasbourg sufficiently appreciated or accommodated particular aspects of the domestic process. In such circumstances, it was open to the Court to decline to follow the Strasbourg decision, giving reasons for adopting this course.[97] In this particular case, the Court found that the European Court's rule against admitting hearsay evidence which formed the 'sole or decisive' evidence against the defendant did not apply. Where such evidence is relied upon, the defendant's participatory right to confront and challenge the evidence is curtailed. The Court reasoned that England had sufficient safeguards to ensure fairness in cases where such evidence was relied upon. The Grand Chamber of the European Court has since conceded to this view, finding that the 'sole or decisive rule' should not be applied inflexibly.[98]

Section 2 of the Human Rights Act 1998 provides that the domestic courts must take into account decisions of the European Court in determining a question that has arisen in connection with a Convention right. Dennis has noted that, in the context of the law of evidence, there has been some tendency for the English courts to treat Strasbourg jurisprudence as a resource to be drawn upon when useful, in contrast to treating it in all cases as authoritative on the meaning and application of Convention rights.[99] Even so, there have been suggestions that British judges have been, and should not be, too quick to accept Strasbourg decisions as determinate. For example, Lord Irvine, architect of the 1998 Act, has called for a more critical approach to Strasbourg jurisprudence, arguing that it is the constitutional duty of judges to reject Strasbourg decisions they feel are flawed in favour of their own judgments.[100] Recent comments from a number of senior members of the judiciary and ex-judiciary appear to reflect this attitude.[101] There has also been significant government animosity towards the European Court, culminating in a proposal to abolish the Human Rights Act 1998 and enact a

96 [2009] UKSC 14, [2010] 2 AC 373.

97 ibid [11].

98 *Al-Khawaja v UK* (2012) 54 EHRR 23. See also *Horncastle v UK* (2015) 60 EHRR 31.

99 I Dennis, 'The Human Rights Act and the Law of Evidence Ten Years On' (2011) 33 *Sydney Law Review* 333, 337.

100 M Wolfe-Robinson and O Bowcott, 'Lord Irvine: Human Rights Law Developed on False Premise' *The Guardian* (London, 14 December 2011) <www.theguardian.com/law/2011/dec/14/lord-irvine-human-rights-law> accessed 1 April 2016.

101 See, for example, Lord Sumption, 'The Limits of the Law' (27th Sultan Azlan Shah Lecture, Kuala Lumpur, 20 November 2013); Lord Judge, 'Constitutional Change: Unfinished Business' (University College London, 4 December 2013); Lord Justice Laws, 'The Common Law Constitution' *The Hamlyn Lectures* (Cambridge University Press, July 2014); Lord Neuberger, 'The Role of Judges in Human Rights Jurisprudence: A Comparison of the Australian and UK Experience' (Conference at the Supreme Court of Victoria, Melbourne, 8 August 2014).

British Bill of Rights.[102] As a result of a reluctance to give effect to certain European doctrines and decisions, there has been a tendency to downplay the Article 6 rights which provide for voluntary participation.

While the ECHR does not dictate the form or structure of criminal procedure, or what individual jurisdictions aim to achieve, it should influence how the aims are pursued. The formulation of defence rights within Article 6, and the adversary ideologies they impose, suggests that restrictions apply. Since Article 6 provides the defence with both the right to participate and the right not to participate, it should limit, if not prevent, the state's ability to penalise a defendant for failing to actively participate in the criminal process. Yet, as is demonstrated in later chapters, in practice, internationally recognised defence rights have failed to protect defendants from penalties for non-compliance. The failure results from a judicial willingness to limit access to certain rights, often on a proportionality basis, as well as a tendency to interpret Article 6 rights narrowly. This has occurred at both the domestic and European level. On the one hand, the ECHR has undoubtedly had an impact on many European jurisdictions, in attempting to bring standards and practices closer together.[103] On the other hand, the significance of the deeply engrained traditions of different legal systems within Europe, as well as shifting priorities and concerns about national subsidiarity, will affect the ECHR's ability to create systems of voluntary participation.

3.4 Conclusion

Characterising English criminal procedure as, *inter alia*, adversarial, or a mix of adversarialism and inquisitorialism, or as a model of efficiency and managerialism, does not in itself adequately capture the participatory nature of the criminal process. The process has become one in which the defendant's freedom of choice has been curtailed by both direct compulsion and indirect compulsion to actively participate.[104] The role which the defendant plays can tell us much about the aims of the criminal process, about the manner in which those aims are pursued and about the extent to which fairness and respect for defence rights are valued. The analysis thus far suggests that the pursuit of efficient fact-finding has taken precedence over fairness and respect for defence rights, particularly those which provide for voluntary participation. The remaining chapters further examine the

102 See the Conservative Party Manifesto 2015.

103 A coming together of criminal procedure and defence rights across Europe has also been encouraged by the European Union. For example, the 2009 Roadmap for strengthening procedural rights of suspected or accused persons, has been given substance through a series of EU Directives on the right to translation and interpretation, the right to information, the right to legal assistance and the presumption of innocence.

104 The defendant faces direct compulsion to participate where, for example, a failure to provide incriminatory information can result in prosecution for non-compliance. See ch 5. The defendant faces indirect compulsion where, for example, a failure to actively participate can result in adverse inferences being drawn against the defendant. See chs 6 and 7.

defendant's participatory role in the criminal process and present specific examples of the way in which defendants can be penalised for failing to actively participate in the criminal process, in the light of the normative theory of calling the state to account. The question of the impact this has had on the nature of English criminal procedure, and how best to characterise it, is returned to in the final chapter.

4 Defendant participation

The key concern of this book is the increase in requirements for the defendant to actively participate in the criminal process and the implications this has for the nature of criminal procedure. The purpose of this chapter is to further establish the case against requiring defendant participation and to consider, in broad terms, the defendant's role as a participant in the criminal process, particularly at the trial. The chapter begins by further developing the theory of the criminal process as a process of calling the state to account, which was set out in Chapter 1. It does this by comparing it to an alternative theory based on calling the accused to account. A brief and critical examination of this alternative theory raises important issues with regards to defendant participation. The historical development, or decline, of the defendant's role as a participant during the emergence of the adversarial system is then examined. Developments during this time shaped many of the norms which now govern matters of fairness, and these norms should limit the extent to which a defendant can be expected to participate in the criminal process. Finally, the defendant's current position as a participant in the criminal process is considered, highlighting the trend towards an obligation to actively participate, irrespective of fundamental rights not to do so.

4.1 Calling to account

The normative theory of the criminal process put forward in this book is one in which the state should be held to account for its accusations and request for condemnation and punishment of the defendant. However, there is an alternative school of thought which holds that the participation of, and communication with, the defendant should be central to the criminal trial. In *The Trial on Trial* book series, Duff *et al.* develop a theory of the criminal trial aimed at calling the defendant to account for his criminal wrongdoing.[1] It builds on Duff's previous

1 A Duff, L Farmer, S Marshall and V Tadros (eds), *The Trial on Trial 1: Truth and Due Process* (Oxford, Hart Publishing, 2004); A Duff, L Farmer, S Marshall and V Tadros (eds), *The Trial on Trial 2: Judgment and Calling to Account* (Oxford, Hart Publishing, 2006); A Duff, L Farmer, S Marshall and V Tadros (eds), *The Trial on Trial 3: Towards a Normative Theory of the Criminal Trial* (Oxford, Hart Publishing, 2007).

work which envisages the criminal process as one in which the defendant is called to participate as a rational moral agent.[2] The core argument of the theory is that the criminal trial is a process through which defendants are called to answer a charge of criminal wrongdoing and, if they are proved to have committed the offence charged, to answer for their conduct. The defendant can answer for his conduct by offering a defence, if the commission of the offence is admitted or proved; or by accepting guilt.[3] If the defendant is found not only to have committed the offence, but also to have no defence, he is condemned through a guilty verdict which holds him to account for his wrongdoing.[4]

Duff *et al.* argue that calling defendants to account accords them the respect they are due as responsible agents and citizens. In a separate work, Duff writes: 'We are criminally responsible, in a liberal democracy, to our fellow citizens: we must answer to them, through the criminal courts, for our alleged criminal wrongs.'[5] We are thus held responsible, or called to account, by and in the criminal courts on behalf of, and in the name of, the polity as a whole.[6] Much emphasis is placed on the communicative nature of the trial; to call a person to account for wrongdoing through a communicative judgment involves an attempt to persuade him or her to accept the judgment that he or she did wrong, and make it his or her own.[7] Within this view of the trial, the court does not presuppose responsibility or liability for the commission of the criminal wrongdoing, but does presuppose responsibility to answer to the charge.[8]

Duff *et al.* reject the traditional instrumentalist, or standard, approach which sees the trial process as geared towards aims identified in Chapter 2, namely, ensuring the accuracy of the verdict subject to constraints such as fairness and respect for rights. They see this as not completely wrong, but suggest that it is too simplistic.[9] Calling to account, on the other hand, is:

> to give the defendant a central, and at least ideally an active, role in the trial – as the person to whom the criminal charge is addressed; who is summoned to answer that charge; and to answer for his conduct if proved to be criminal; and who is expected to accept responsibility for what he has done, and to accept the condemnation that a conviction expresses if his guilt is proved.[10]

2 See A Duff, *Trials and Punishments* (Cambridge, Cambridge University Press, 1986).
3 A Duff, L Farmer, S Marshall and V Tadros (eds), *The Trial on Trial 3: Towards a Normative Theory of the Criminal Trial* (Oxford, Hart Publishing, 2007) 108, fn 47.
4 ibid 3.
5 A Duff, 'Who is Responsible, for What, to Whom?' (2005) 2 *Ohio State Journal of Criminal Law* 441, 441.
6 A Duff, L Farmer, S Marshall and V Tadros (eds), *The Trial on Trial 3: Towards a Normative Theory of the Criminal Trial* (Oxford, Hart Publishing, 2007) 134.
7 ibid 140.
8 ibid.
9 ibid 64.
10 A Duff, L Farmer, S Marshall and V Tadros (eds), *The Trial on Trial 2: Judgment and Calling to Account* (Oxford, Hart Publishing, 2006) 3.

Although Duff *et al.* suggest that there is reciprocity in the practice of calling to account, as in the defendant can also call the prosecution and court to account,[11] they concentrate so much on calling the defendant to account that this seems to be the primary purpose of the trial.

A distinction should be made at this point between the substance and the form of the trial. The form of the existing criminal trial may, on the face of it, appear to lend support to Duff *et al.'s* normative conception. The prosecution presents a case against the defendant and, if the court is satisfied that there is a case to answer, the defence has the opportunity to present its own case, or further test the prosecution's evidence. However, in substance, the trial does not operate in the way proposed by Duff *et al.* It is not assumed that the defendant has anything to 'answer' for until a guilty verdict has been reached. There is a difference between finding that there is a case to answer for the defence, and the normative account put forward by Duff *et al.* which seems to imply that the defendant should answer for his alleged conduct during the trial, ahead of a verdict having been reached.

As a general principle, if a defendant pleads 'not-guilty', then, given the presumption of innocence, it is for the prosecution to prove his guilt. As Duff *et al.* see it, a criminal trial in which guilt is contested consists of three stages.[12] The first stage of proving guilt is to prove that the defendant committed the offence charged. Until that is proved, there is nothing for which the defendant has to answer. If the prosecution succeeds in proving guilt, the second stage is for the defendant to answer by offering a defence.[13] Finally, if the prosecution completes its whole task, both proving that the defendant did commit the offence charged, and disproving any defence for which evidence is adduced, it is then for the fact-finder to convict the defendant. This account is flawed both in terms of the substance of existing trials and from a normative standpoint. Deciding whether the defence has a case to answer at the close of the prosecution case is not tantamount to finding that it is proved that the defendant committed the offence charged.[14] It simply means that there is sufficient evidence on which a reasonable jury could convict, but not that they will or must do so.[15]

11 For example, they claim that 'calling to answer or account is properly a two-way process'. A Duff, L Farmer, S Marshall and V Tadros (eds), *The Trial on Trial 3: Towards a Normative Theory of the Criminal Trial* (Oxford, Hart Publishing, 2007) 96.

12 ibid 147–148.

13 ibid 147. The authors use the word 'prove' several times when discussing the first stages of the process, i.e. the prosecution having a requirement to 'prove' that the defendant committed the offence before the defence presents its case.

14 HL Ho, 'Book Review: Duff, Farmer, Marshall and Tadros, The Trial on Trial (vol. 3): Towards a Normative Theory of the Criminal Trial' (2008) 6 *International Commentary on Evidence* Article 3, 3. For a similar line of criticism of this aspect of Duff *et al.*'s theory, see also J Jackson and S Summers, *The Internationalisation of Criminal Evidence: Beyond the Common Law and Civil Law Traditions* (Cambridge, Cambridge University Press, 2012) 25–27.

15 The general approach to the issue of 'no case to answer' was laid down by Lord Lane CJ in *R v Galbraith* [1981] 1 WLR 1039 (CA).

The decision as to whether the prosecution has proved its case comes at the close of the trial, after all of the evidence has been heard, including that of the defence. In the landmark case of *Woolmington v DPP,* Viscount Sankey LC stated that, 'it is not till the end of the evidence that a verdict can properly be found and that at the end of the evidence it is not for the prisoner to establish his innocence, but for the prosecution to establish his guilt'.[16] Furthermore, if the defence choose not to 'answer' the prosecution case, a conviction, no matter how likely, does not automatically follow. A judge may direct a jury to acquit a defendant where there is no evidence that could justify a conviction, but there are no circumstances in which a judge is entitled to direct a jury to return a verdict of guilty.[17] The right to challenge the prosecution's case does not imply a requirement to account for oneself. The latter is difficult to justify in terms of the presumption of innocence and the burden of proof.

It is not completely clear what is envisaged by stating that the defendant is 'called to answer' a charge. The defendant's right to a jury verdict applies even if he makes no attempt to address the prosecution's case.[18] If an acquittal is not dependent on the defendant providing any answers to the prosecution's case, then how plausible is it to construe the trial as having the point of calling him to answer to the charge?[19] Duff *et al.*'s theory seems strained when it tries to accommodate the defendant's choice not to participate. They believe that there is a normative expectation that the defendant should take part.[20] In their view, the right to silence and the right to participate are not on an equal footing. The right to participate and be heard is a feature of the trial's positive aims which are fully achieved only if that right is exercised, whereas the right to silence flows from constraints which should be placed on the pursuit of that end: 'a trial in which the right [to silence] is exercised is a legitimate trial, but its positive purpose is frustrated'.[21] The theory is so focused on defendant participation that any right not to participate becomes difficult to accommodate. Within a criminal process based on calling the state to account, on the other hand, exercising the right to silence may constrain and delay the aims of accurate fact-finding and conflict resolution, but the purpose of the trial cannot be said to be frustrated, as the trial provides a forum to test the prosecution's case. This can be done by a silent defendant putting the prosecution to proof. When the trial is viewed as part of the process of calling the state to account for its accusations and request for punishment, there should be no such normative expectation on the defendant to participate.

16 *Woolmington v DPP* [1935] AC 462 (HL) 481.
17 *R v Wang* [2005] UKHL 9, [2005] 1 WLR 661 [18].
18 ibid.
19 HL Ho, 'Book Review: Duff, Farmer, Marshall and Tadros, The Trial on Trial (vol. 3): Towards a Normative Theory of the Criminal Trial' (2008) 6 *International Commentary on Evidence* Article 3, 3.
20 A Duff, L Farmer, S Marshall and V Tadros (eds), *The Trial on Trial 3: Towards a Normative Theory of the Criminal Trial* (Oxford, Hart Publishing, 2007) 101.
21 ibid 102.

Duff *et al.* acknowledge that, within their approach, there would ideally be a civic duty, and even a legal duty, to participate in one's own trial.[22] From this, Ho suggests, it also follows that the defendant would carry the legal burden of proving any defence he wishes to claim,[23] and that 'the heavy emphasis on calling the defendant to account is likely to lack appeal in liberal democracies'.[24] Prior to 1935, there was considerable authority to show that the defendant carried a legal burden of proving any common law defence he wished to raise.[25] However, in *Woolmington*, Viscount Sankey LC declared that, 'No matter what the charge or where the trial, the principle that the prosecution must prove the guilt of the prisoner is part of the common law of England and no attempt to whittle it down can be entertained.'[26] There may be means of enforcing a legal duty to participate, aside from the imposition of legal burdens of proof, for example, through an offence of contempt for failure to participate. Yet, any such legal duty would undermine the relationship between citizen and state in a liberal democracy, in which citizens should be treated as law abiding and individual autonomy should be respected. Duff *et al.* appear to perceive the defendant's role in the trial as one in which he is responsible for disproving the case against him. Under their theory, if the prosecution is taken to have proven the defendant's guilt before the defence presents its case, a failure to participate could inevitably lead to a conviction.

Viewing the trial as part of the process of calling the state to account is a more logical approach than calling the defendant to account, at least in terms of the values of fairness and respect for rights. These values must be adhered to if the defendant is to be treated as a free, dignified and autonomous member of society.[27] Moreover, the state has powerful resources for the detection, investigation and prosecution of crimes that may be wrongfully used against citizens. The trial provides a safeguard against abuses of state resources and protects the defendant from being wrongly stigmatised as a criminal. The trial should, therefore, be construed as a means of holding the state to account for its request for blame and punishment of the defendant, and not as a means of calling the defendant to account for why he is undeserving of the same. The defendant should not be required to participate in order to disprove guilt, just as he should not be required to actively assist the prosecution in proving guilt. As contended by Ho, the central point of the criminal trial is the provision by the state of their

22 ibid 120.

23 In this context, 'defence' is considered to mean substantive defences that go beyond a simple denial.

24 HL Ho, 'Book Review: Duff, Farmer, Marshall and Tadros, The Trial on Trial (vol. 3): Towards a Normative Theory of the Criminal Trial' (2008) 6 *International Commentary on Evidence* Article 3, 5.

25 A Stumer, *The Presumption of Innocence: Evidential and Human Rights Perspectives* (Oxford, Hart Publishing, 2010) 5–8.

26 *Woolmington v DPP* [1935] AC 462 (HL) 481. This is subject to the common law defence of insanity and any statutory exception. See the discussion on reverse burdens of proof in ch 8.1.

27 On the importance of respect for the defendant's dignity and autonomy, see ch 1.3.

justification for the conviction they seek from the court, and critical scrutiny by the court of the justification that is provided by the state.[28] This can be achieved even if the defendant declines to answer the charge or give an account of his conduct. Where the defendant chooses to plead guilty, without being coerced, the purpose of the trial is not frustrated, as he is effectively waiving his right to a trial and is forfeiting the opportunity to test the prosecution's case. In this situation, the criminal process has achieved conflict resolution and, assuming the defendant is in fact guilty, accurate fact-finding.

This is not to say that the defendant has no role to play during the trial. The defendant is a party to the proceedings and has a right to effective participation, but this is a choice and not a requirement. As Ho puts it:

> [A liberal trial] attempts to engage the accused in a dialogue because he or she is intrinsically worthy of dialogue, employing reasons to justify his or her conviction and sentence that appeal to our collective sense of justice. It is in recognition of the person's autonomy that we do not force him or her to participate at the trial and, at the same time, give that person the cherished right to do so.[29]

That criminal trials are public supports the assertion that they provide a means of calling the state to account. The public nature of the trial is a well-recognised requirement and a right.[30] One reason frequently offered in support of the rule is that public justice is accountable and that it promotes confidence in the courts. A public trial can assist in ensuring that the aims of the criminal process are pursued in a legitimate manner. The public nature allows the credibility and reliability of prosecution evidence to be tested, and helps to safeguard the defendant's rights, particularly those allowing confrontation.[31] Early common law writers, such as Bentham, were proponents of the claim that the trial must be public in order to limit the power of the state and discourage perjury. Bentham criticised the secrecy of European inquisitorial procedures as leaving the door wide open to 'mendacity, falsehood, and partiality'.[32]

28 HL Ho, 'Book Review: Duff, Farmer, Marshall and Tadros, The Trial on Trial (vol. 3): Towards a Normative Theory of the Criminal Trial' (2008) 6 *International Commentary on Evidence* Article 3, 4. See also HL Ho, 'Liberalism and the Criminal Trial' [2010] *Singapore Journal of Legal Studies* 87.

29 HL Ho, 'Liberalism and the Criminal Trial' [2010] *Singapore Journal of Legal Studies* 87, 105.

30 See generally J Jaconelli, *Open Justice: A Critique of the Public Trial* (Oxford, Oxford University Press, 2002).

31 Namely, the rights under the European Convention on Human Rights (ECHR), Article 6(3)(d).

32 J Bentham, *Rationale of Judicial Evidence, Specially Applied to English Practice* (London, Hunt & Clarke, 1827) Vol 2, Book III, 404.

The public nature of the criminal trial may also be accounted for on the basis that, since crimes are public wrongs, from which the criminal law seeks to protect citizens, the public have an interest in the trial of those accused of committing them. As both potential victims and defendants, the general public have a broad interest in the criminal process. Duff *et al.* rely on the idea of public interest, believing that the value of holding trials in public lies in the critical scrutiny that it allows. They argue that there is a clear connection to be found in the idea that breaches of criminal law constitute public wrongdoing for which members of the community are publicly called to account and through which members of the criminal justice system can themselves be held accountable. In this sense, public justice must be seen as a core element of the process of calling to account.[33] This concept of public justice can be viewed in terms of calling the state to account, since the public have an interest in ensuring that the state is acting within its powers, that innocent people are not convicted and that there is accountability in the enforcement of the criminal law. The state is accountable not only to the defendant, but also to the wider community, as the individual citizens within the community are subject to the laws and power of the state. The citizenry can examine and evaluate the grounds for the exercise by the state of its coercive powers only if those grounds are presented for public scrutiny.[34] Where a verdict is delivered by a jury or lay magistrate, it is members of the public who decide whether the accusations have been accounted for.

These justifications for public justice do not explain why it is framed as a defence right.[35] According to Duff *et al.*, the defendant's right to a public trial should be seen as a right to have his trial subject to critical scrutiny.[36] However, the defendant has no choice but to have his trial open to scrutiny. Indeed, this may be detrimental for the defendant, principally due to the stigma and social consequences that often follow an association with crime. Jaconelli questions the 'right' to a public trial, arguing that, whereas most rights claims are capable of being analysed in terms of the will and interest theories, neither can accommodate the right to a public trial.[37] The defendant can neither exercise a choice over the operation of the right nor necessarily benefit from it. Despite the difficulties encountered in labelling the public trial requirement as a 'right', openness is arguably in the best interest of

33 A Duff, L Farmer, S Marshall and V Tadros (eds), *The Trial on Trial 3: Towards a Normative Theory of the Criminal Trial* (Oxford, Hart Publishing, 2007) 261.

34 HL Ho, 'Liberalism and the Criminal Trial' [2010] *Singapore Journal of Legal Studies* 87, 101.

35 ECHR, Article 6(1) provides that 'everyone is entitled to a fair and public hearing' and that 'judgment shall be pronounced publicly'.

36 A Duff, L Farmer, S Marshall and V Tadros (eds), *The Trial on Trial 3: Towards a Normative Theory of the Criminal Trial* (Oxford, Hart Publishing, 2007) 270.

37 J Jaconelli, 'Rights Theories and Public Trial' (1997) 14 *Journal of Applied Philosophy* 169, 169. See also S Trechsel, *Human Rights in Criminal Proceedings* (Oxford, Oxford University Press, 2005) 126.

the defendant. Dennis notes that, when a liberal polity seeks to enforce the criminal law against a citizen, it is required to demonstrate to the defendant and to the public at large how and why conviction and punishment is justified.[38] The defendant has an interest in publicity as a means of potentially increasing the factual accuracy of adjudication.[39] By achieving factual accuracy, and by doing so fairly, the state can account for its accusations in a legitimate manner. Thus, while the public trial may not always appear to be in the defendant's personal interest, it is in his greater interest to ensure that the state can account for the accusations it makes against him.

In consequence of the arguments presented above, the defendant cannot truly be called to account for his criminal conduct until guilt has been established through a guilty verdict, at the end of the trial, or as a result of a guilty plea. It is, therefore, not until the sentencing stage that he can begin to account, or answer, for that conduct. Although Duff *et al.* did not consider the sentencing stage of the criminal process, it is at this stage that the communicative nature of the process is most prevalent; it is where mitigating and aggravating factors can be explored, and Victim Personal Statements can be presented. Since communication between the court and those involved in the offence is not as constrained by procedural and evidential rules as at the trial, the sentencing hearing is where the wrongness of the act, as well as its consequences, can be communicated to the defendant and the public.

Duff *et al.*'s theory was developed in the 'social and historical context that is particular to the modern adversarial trial',[40] but they state that it will be 'relevant to any polity that claims to be a liberal democracy'.[41] They believe that their model of communicative participation favours neither an adversarial nor an inquisitorial system.[42] However, the success of a trial or process aim will, at least to some extent, be contingent on the institutional setting. Given the emphasis on partisanship, the adversarial system does not seems as well placed to accommodate Duff *et al.'s* theory as does the truth seeking inquisitorial system that already places greater emphasis on the defendant's participation. It may be more successful in mixed jurisdictions which lean more closely towards inquisitorialism, such as France, where, according to Hodgson, the accused is required to take responsibility for his actions, to reflect on the consequences of what he has done and to participate in the process.[43] This is played out in practice by defendants being questioned directly by the judge in court; 'there is a sense in which they are held to account as erring citizens'.[44] Likewise, it would provide a more suitable theoretical

38 I Dennis, 'The Right to Confront Witnesses: Meanings, Myths and Human Rights' [2010] *Crim LR* 225, 262.

39 ibid 261.

40 A Duff, L Farmer, S Marshall and V Tadros (eds), *The Trial on Trial 3: Towards a Normative Theory of the Criminal Trial* (Oxford, Hart Publishing, 2007) 11.

41 ibid 57.

42 ibid 201.

43 J Hodgson, *French Criminal Justice* (Oxford, Hart Publishing, 2005) 21.

44 ibid.

underpinning for a system of obligatory participation than one of voluntary participation.

The theory of calling the state to account, on the other hand, provides an underpinning for a voluntary approach to the defendant's participatory role. It could be applied more readily within an adversarial-type system, though it is founded upon factors which should be upheld in any liberal democracy, regardless of its procedural form. The following section illustrates why the notion of calling the defendant to account, and requiring participation, fits uncomfortably within the adversarial model which views the trial as a forum for testing the prosecution's case rather than communicating with the defendant. Although English criminal procedure has become preoccupied with efficient fact-finding, and cannot accurately be described as adversarial, many of the values associated with the adversarial system remain relevant. The historical development of the adversarial system within England and Wales provided many of the legal norms which underpin the theory of calling the state to account, and which create an important link between the existence of workable rights and the defendant's capacity to choose whether or not to actively participate.

4.2 The development of the adversarial trial

The adversarial system began to develop in the late seventeenth century and took shape throughout the eighteenth and nineteenth centuries. However, many of its components had been developing for centuries, including the rise of the jury and the idea of party participation.[45] While examining the development of the modern criminal trial provides a key to understanding some of the values which underpin the criminal process, an account of the history of the English criminal process is unavoidably messy. Important developments occurred gradually and inconsistently throughout the whole realm of criminal law and procedure. As such, historical exploration can easily become oversimplified or overly complicated and drawn-out. What is significant for present purposes is the shift in the role of the defendant at the trial from active participant to potentially passive observer. The following examination is intended to focus on this narrow aspect of adversarial history and draw out those elements that are most relevant to it.

Immediately before the emergence of the adversarial trial, the defendant was an active participant and played a central role. The trial, during this period, is often referred to as the 'altercation trial'. However, Langbein describes it as the 'accused speaks' trial because the defendant was effectively forced to speak in order to defend himself.[46] The altercation trial emerged at the end of the Middle Ages, replacing older methods of proof, such as trial by wager and ordeal, and when the

45 See S Landsman, *The Adversary System: A Description and Defense* (Washington DC, American Institute for Public Policy Research, 1984) 8–10.

46 See JH Langbein, *The Origins of the Adversary Criminal Trial* (Oxford, Oxford University Press, 2003).

shifting population made it difficult to have a self-informing active jury. The purpose of the altercation trial was to give the defendant the opportunity to respond to accusing evidence, hence the image of the 'accused speaks' trial.[47] It was based on the active participation of the accuser and the accused, and was much less structured than the adversarial trial. Because of the private nature of the majority of prosecutions, the trial was comparable to civil cases, thus creating an expectation that the defendant would participate. Moreover, the criminal law was focused on protecting property,[48] and there were many similarities between the law of evidence applied in civil and criminal trials at the time.[49]

Securing the defendant as an informational resource was a central preoccupation of the altercation trial.[50] Contemporaries seemed to have believed that subjecting the defendant to the pressures and hardships of having to defend himself unprepared and unaided was truth promoting. The defendant had no access to the indictment and would usually enter court completely ignorant of the case against him. Facing the defendant with the evidence in court for the first time was thought to help the judge and jury ascertain the sincerity of his denials.[51] Accurate fact-finding was, thus, the key aim of the process. This formed a primary justification for the rule denying defence counsel in felony cases; the defendant was better suited than counsel to respond to questions of fact. However, the reality was seldom so straightforward. Beattie sums up the situation:

> Under this system of prosecution, which lasted well into the eighteenth century, the accused had few rights. He or she was to be committed to trial without knowing the exact nature of the charge as it would appear on the indictment, or without having access to the depositions of the prosecution witnesses. Virtually all accused felons were held in jail to await trial, and in conditions that made preparation difficult. It had been the magistrate's duty to bind over the prosecution witnesses in recognizances to appear in court to give their evidence. The accused could not compel the attendance of witnesses. At the trial itself, accused felons had to speak in their own defense and to respond to prosecution evidence as it was given, and as they heard it for the first time. If they did not or could not defend themselves, no one would do it for them.[52]

47 ibid 48.

48 See D Hay, 'Property, Authority and the Criminal Law' in D Hay, P Linebaugh, JG Rule, EP Thompson and C Winslow (eds), *Albion's Fatal Tree: Crime and Society in Eighteenth Century England* (New York, Pantheon Books, 1975).

49 A Stumer, *The Presumption of Innocence: Evidential and Human Rights Perspectives* (Oxford, Hart Publishing, 2010) 6.

50 JH Langbein, *The Origins of the Adversary Criminal Trial* (Oxford, Oxford University Press, 2003) 61.

51 ibid 63.

52 JM Beattie, 'Scales of Justice: Defense Counsel and the English Criminal Trial in the Eighteenth and Nineteenth Centuries' (1991) 9 *Law and History Review* 221, 223.

This system allowed no room for a workable privilege against self-incrimination or right to silence. In fact, the defendant effectively had no trial or pre-trial rights, making the 'accused speaks' trial the ultimate means of calling the defendant to account. There is an important link here between holding rights and having a choice to participate which is returned to later. When a defendant has rights he has a protection against the power of the state, irrespective of the role he plays at trial. It then becomes harder to hold him to account and easier for him to demand that the case against him be proved.

Not only did the defendant have to speak in order to mount a defence, but also a lack of participation could have serious consequences given the widespread use of capital punishment in felony cases. This was especially true at the end of the eighteenth century, when 'capital punishment overshadowed the whole of the criminal law'.[53] According to Langbein, contemporaries in the late eighteenth and early nineteenth century were willing to tolerate the truth defeating consequences of the emerging adversary procedure because in the realm of the criminal trial 'too much truth brought too much death'.[54] Although a powerful phrase, this may be overstating the situation, as roughly half of those condemned to death during the eighteenth century did not go to the gallows.[55] It was felt that the law over-threatened the use of capital punishment and jurors and judges would use techniques, such as down charging and clemency, to avoid it.[56] Nevertheless, the defendant's participation remained a crucial factor in his fate.

The assumption that denying defence counsel promoted truthful outcomes was undermined in the celebrated treason trials of the late 1600s.[57] These trials often involved perjured evidence which resulted in the execution of innocent persons. Public revulsion at this led to the Treason Trials Act 1696, a momentous step in the emergence of the adversarial system. The Act granted the defendant the right to a copy of the indictment, pre-trial assistance of counsel, full assistance of counsel at trial and the ability to compel the attendance of defence witnesses. It also allowed the defendant's witnesses to testify on oath.[58] Even though the central purpose of the criminal trial was to hear the defendant speak, he spoke unsworn until the Criminal Evidence Act of 1898.

53 L Radzinowicz, *A History of English Criminal Law and its Administration from 1750, Volume 4: Grappling for Control* (London, Stevens and Sons, 1968) v.

54 JH Langbein, *The Origins of the Adversary Criminal Trial* (Oxford, Oxford University Press, 2003) 334.

55 D Hay, 'Property, Authority and the Criminal Law' in D Hay, P Linebaugh, JG Rule, EP Thompson and C Winslow (eds), *Albion's Fatal Tree: Crime and Society in Eighteenth Century England* (New York, Pantheon Books, 1975) 43.

56 JH Langbein, *The Origins of the Adversary Criminal Trial* (Oxford, Oxford University Press, 2003) 336.

57 ibid 3.

58 An Act of 1702 extended this reform to cases of felony, although there had been some judicial discretion to subpoena defence witnesses prior to this. See JH Langbein, *The Origins of the Adversary Criminal Trial* (Oxford, Oxford University Press, 2003) 53.

The 1696 Act applied only in relation to defendants accused of high treason. In the 1730s, lawyers began to appear for defendants in ordinary felony trials, but it was not until the Prisoners' Counsel Act of 1836 that legislation provided for this. When defence lawyers first entered the felony trial they were permitted only to do what judges had previously done for the defendant: cross-examine witnesses and speak to issues of law. They could not speak to the jury or offer a defence against the facts put in evidence. It was essential that the judge and jury hear the defendant's account.[59] The rule against defence counsel did not apply to misdemeanour trials. There is no clear account of why this was, but the thinking at the time may have been that it was particularly important to avoid counsel interfering with the court's access to the defendant as an informational resource in cases of serious crime, where much was at stake.[60]

The presence of defence counsel in ordinary felony trials has largely been inferred from information within the *Old Bailey Sessions Papers* which were in existence from the 1670s into the nineteenth century with varying degrees of detail and consistency. The number of counsel employed cannot be known for sure, but there was a definite increase from the mid-eighteenth century, even though the majority of defendants remained unrepresented.[61] The reason for the increase in defence counsel activity is unknown. However, it is thought to be a result of a judicial perception that the balance in the courtroom had been shifting further to the detriment of the defendant.[62] Most prosecutions in the early eighteenth century were initiated by complainants, who could hire counsel to run their whole case without the restrictions faced by defence counsel. The apparent equality and appearance of balance that existed in the altercation trial courtroom, arising from the confrontation between the accuser and accused, was breaking down.[63] This was exacerbated by government efforts to increase the level of prosecution by offering monetary rewards for the successful prosecution of offenders who committed certain crimes. Those who took on this task were known as thieftakers. The reward system (which also operated privately) was fraught with incentives for false accusations and perjured witnesses, something of which judges were very aware.[64] The judicial concern about these factors, and the resulting unfairness to the defendant, may have contributed to the increase in defence counsel.

59 JM Beattie, 'Scales of Justice: Defense Counsel and the English Criminal Trial in the Eighteenth and Nineteenth Centuries' (1991) 9 *Law and History Review* 221, 231.

60 JH Langbein, *The Origins of the Adversary Criminal Trial* (Oxford, Oxford University Press, 2003) 39.

61 Beattie estimates that in 1740, 3.1 per cent of cases had prosecution counsel and 0.5 per cent had defence counsel but by 1800, 21.2 per cent had prosecution counsel and 27.9 per cent had defence counsel. JM Beattie, 'Scales of Justice: Defense Counsel and the English Criminal Trial in the Eighteenth and Nineteenth Centuries' (1991) 9 *Law and History Review* 221, 227.

62 ibid 224.

63 ibid.

64 JH Langbein, *The Origins of the Adversary Criminal Trial* (Oxford, Oxford University Press, 2003) 157.

By the 1780s, there was not only an increase in the number of lawyers involved in felony trials, but also an apparent change in their attitudes and behaviour, especially those acting for the defence.[65] Even though their role remained restricted, counsel became more aggressive and actively committed to the defendant's interest. They found ways to effectively speak to the jury through clever cross-examination and by disguising their remarks as comments to the judge on points of law.[66] They would cast doubt on the truth of prosecution evidence and the credibility of prosecution witnesses, leading to a more sceptical view of the prosecution than previously.[67] According to Langbein, 'Defense counsel would ultimately end the altercation trial, silence the accused, marginalize the judge, and break up the working relationship of judge and jury'.[68] The role of defence counsel that developed at this time can be observed in England's current system; they are expected to use their special knowledge of the law and criminal procedure to act in the best interests of their clients.[69] In so doing, it may be necessary, or at least beneficial, for the defendant to take a passive role. Langbein attributes the development of the adversarial system to the development of the role of defence counsel.[70] Thus, a system within which the defendant can play a passive role may be attributable to the role played by his advocate.

The emergence of the adversarial system also impacted defendant participation through the development and enforceability of defence rights. One example is the burden of proof. As with present practices, in the early adversarial trial, the court could dismiss a case if the prosecution did not present sufficient evidence against the defendant. Allowing defence counsel had the effect of separating the tasks of probing for whether the prosecution had presented its case, and offering defensive evidence.[71] Defence counsel insisted on asking the judge whether the prosecution had discharged its burden. Where they were successful, the defendant was completely silenced. Accordingly, 'the recognition of the prosecution's burden, combined with the use of defense counsel to test whether that burden had been met, materially reduced the amount of speaking that the accused had to do in order to defend effectively'.[72] However, the burden of proof was not fully

65 JM Beattie, 'Scales of Justice: Defense Counsel and the English Criminal Trial in the Eighteenth and Nineteenth Centuries' (1991) 9 *Law and History Review* 221, 229.

66 ibid 233.

67 ibid 235.

68 JH Langbein, *The Origins of the Adversary Criminal Trial* (Oxford, Oxford University Press, 2003) 177.

69 See Bar Standards Board, *Handbook,* 2nd edn (April 2015); www.barstandardsboard.org.uk/media/1731225/bsb_handbook_sept_2015.pdf (accessed 1 April 2016). However, in consequence of the increasing emphasis on case management, the lawyer's duty to act in the best interests of their client may, at times, be at odds with their duty to the court. See the discussion on case management in chs 3.2.1 and 7.4.

70 JH Langbein, *The Origins of the Adversary Criminal Trial* (Oxford, Oxford University Press, 2003) 177.

71 ibid 258.

72 ibid 261.

established until the decision in *Woolmington*, in the early twentieth century. The defendant's participation was also stifled by the formulation and acceptance of the beyond reasonable doubt standard of proof which was crystallised in the later eighteenth century. Setting a high standard of proof encouraged the jury to probe the prosecution case, rather than focusing on whether or how the defendant gave evidence.[73]

Unlike the burden and standard of proof, the underlying presumption of innocence is ancient and can be traced to Classical Roman law.[74] However, our modern understanding of the principle as a statement of the prosecution's burden, and as a direction to officials on how to treat the accused, arose towards the end of the seventeenth century. Beattie states that, within the old altercation trial, the assumption:

> was not that [the defendant] was innocent until the case against him was proved beyond a reasonable doubt, but that if he *were* innocent he ought to be able to demonstrate it for the jury by the quality and character of his reply to the prosecutor's evidence.[75]

It was only when the trial could be conceived as a contest between two parties, rather than between two individuals, that the defendant could remain silent and the trial could be organised around the presumption of innocence.[76] As a consequence of the presumption of innocence, even in a narrow trial-centred sense, it is the defendant's right to have the case against him proved beyond reasonable doubt.

By the end of the nineteenth century, the majority of European countries had accepted an understanding of criminal proceedings as based on two opposing parties and an independent judge. Summers notes that it was the rights of the defence as a party and not of the accused as an individual that were seen as important in the works of the nineteenth century writers.[77] Only through the assistance of counsel would those accused of criminal offences be able to engage with legal formalities and make proper use of the guarantees afforded to them in presenting their defence.[78] There is, thus, a distinction between the institutional rights of the defence and the personal rights of the defendant which he can insist on exercising himself. This distinction between the defendant as a person and the defence as a party remains an important aspect of criminal procedure. For example,

73 ibid 266.

74 See A Stumer, *The Presumption of Innocence: Evidential and Human Rights Perspectives* (Oxford, Hart Publishing, 2010). See also *Coffin v United States* 156 US 432 (1895).

75 JM Beattie, *Crime and the Courts in England 1660–1800* (Oxford, Clarendon Press, 1986) 341. Original emphasis.

76 ibid 349.

77 S Summers, *Fair Trials: The European Criminal Procedural Tradition and the European Court of Human Rights* (Oxford, Hart Publishing, 2007) 61.

78 ibid 71.

while the defendant is prohibited from cross-examining certain witnesses in person, his counsel remains able to exercise the right to confrontation on his behalf.[79] In many situations, as long as the defence is conceived of as a party that can exercise rights to participate, the defendant can successfully put the prosecution to proof while exercising his personal rights not to participate.

Important defence rights became workable within a system which effectively discouraged defendant participation, and it was these rights which, in turn, facilitated that lack of participation. The burden and standard of proof on the prosecution meant that the defendant did not have to prove his case, and that the presumption of innocence could be given much greater force, again, turning the attention of the court to the prosecution. Two other significant factors which emerged during the rise of adversarialism were the defendant's right to silence and privilege against self-incrimination. These rights became a workable part of the common law criminal procedure when defence counsel succeeded in restructuring the criminal trial in the way described above, and made it possible to defend a silent defendant.[80] Through an examination of the *Old Bailey Sessions Papers* from 1670, Langbein did not find one instance of a defendant remaining silent on the grounds of a right to do so until the late 1780s, when defence counsel had become a regular trial feature and had alleviated the defendant of his participatory burden.[81]

The privilege against self-incrimination has become an integral element of many legal systems. It exists as an implicit part of Article 6 of the European Convention on Human Rights (ECHR).[82] It is also expressly catered for in Article 14 of the International Covenant on Civil and Political Rights. The presumption of innocence is also acknowledged in these international documents. Its international status can be traced back to the Universal Declaration of Human Rights which was adopted by the United Nations General Assembly in 1948. Although these documents stem from the mid-twentieth century, they are a restatement of what was already recognised in a significant number of legal systems. Thus, what emerged in response to, and which now facilitates, the defendant's ability to choose whether to actively participate in the criminal process has a significant link to the development of the adversarial system as a means of protecting the defendant from the potentially oppressive power of the state, which had previously seen defendants face the allegations against them unprepared and unaided.

Following the development of the adversarial system, defendants did not need to be active participants at the criminal trial. Strengthening their rights and allowing counsel to run their case meant that they did not even have to speak.

79 Youth Justice and Criminal Evidence Act 1999 (YJCEA 1999), ss 34–40.

80 See JH Langbein, 'The Historic Origins of the Privilege Against Self-Incrimination at Common Law' (1994) 92 *Michigan Law Review* 1047.

81 JH Langbein, *The Origins of the Adversary Criminal Trial* (Oxford, Oxford University Press, 2003) 279–281.

82 *Murray v UK* (1996) 22 EHRR 29.

The onus was firmly on the prosecution. The trial had shifted from the 'accused speaks' trial, in which the defendant was truly called to account, to one which allowed the state's powers to be limited and the prosecution's case to be tested. Concern for fairness and respect for rights became necessary constraints on the achievement of accurate fact-finding and conflict resolution. Langbein asserts that with the development of the adversarial trial came a new theory of the purpose of the trial, which endures to this day, that it is primarily an opportunity for the defence to probe the prosecution case.[83] The concept of adversarialism has become so well entrenched in criminal procedure that the European Court recognised a right to adversarial proceedings in so far as 'both prosecution and defence must be given the opportunity to have knowledge of and comment on the observations filed and the evidence adduced by the other party'.[84]

A criminal process operating on the basis of adversarialism, and testing the prosecution's case, cannot easily be reconciled with the idea of requiring defendant participation and penalising disobliging defendants. An assessment of the history of adversarialism does not in itself uncover a normative theory of the criminal process. However, it does highlight the developments that led to the rights and procedures which underpin the theory of the criminal process in which the state is called to account for its accusations against the accused. In order to respect those rights which we have come to accept as fundamental,[85] and pay due respect to the freedom and dignity of the defendant in the criminal process, participation must be a choice and not a requirement.

4.3 The defendant's current role

Many of the rights that developed as part of the adversarial system continue to govern issues of fairness and legitimise the process. However, while the English criminal trial remains structured largely on an adversarial basis, it cannot be labelled as strictly adversarial. The increasing concern for efficiency in fact-finding has influenced criminal procedure, such that greater emphasis has been placed on the defendant's participation. Before turning to a detailed exploration of specific participatory requirements, and the accompanying penalties for non-cooperation, this section considers more broadly the defendant's current role as a participant in the criminal process, particularly at the trial stage.

83 JH Langbein, *The Origins of the Adversary Criminal Trial* (Oxford, Oxford University Press, 2003) 253.

84 *Laukkanen and Manninen v Finland* App no 50230/99 (ECHR, 3 February 2004) [34].

85 Rights are accepted as fundamental in so far as they have become well established in domestic law and internationally, through provisions such as Article 6 of the ECHR. They protect essential aspects of human dignity and secure crucial human interests. See HL Ho, 'The Presumption of Innocence as a Human Right' in P Roberts and J Hunter (eds), *Criminal Evidence and Human Rights: Reimagining Common Law Procedural Traditions* (Oxford, Hart Publishing, 2012) 261.

The defendant has a right to be present at his trial.[86] Yet, his absence is not, in principle, incompatible with the right to a fair trial. There are different procedures for dealing with the absence of a defendant at summary trials and trials on indictment. In trials on indictment, the defendant is normally required to be present to plead and remain present throughout the trial. The rationale behind this general rule might be to prevent the jury from drawing an impermissible inference from the defendant's absence.[87] It might also promote fairness by ensuring that the defendant hears the evidence against him and has an opportunity to participate, if he so chooses. The defendant may wish to respond to unforeseen arguments or evidence that emerge during the trial. The fact that the defendant is required, rather than given a choice, to be present might be thought to undercut this rationale. Alternatively, the presence requirement may stem from the historical continuation of the trial into sentencing and punishment. Historically, the trial was a very quick process, averaging half an hour by the mid-eighteenth century.[88] The defendant was virtually always the most efficient potential witness, and so his presence and participation would have contributed to the brevity of the trial. The defendant was sentenced immediately following conviction,[89] and his presence may have been necessary to ensure that punishment was carried out.

Like the public trial requirement, it is difficult to reconcile the defendant's duty to be present with the fact that it is a right and, therefore, presumably for his benefit. However, also like the public trial requirement, the defendant's presence is in his greater interest, by ensuring that he has the opportunity to hold the state to account and test the prosecution's case. Moreover, both the defendant and the public may be more willing to accept that the state has, or has not, accounted for its accusations if the defendant is present throughout the process, particularly in the Crown Court, where there is much at stake. Thus, the requirement to be present is a requirement to passively participate which may prove necessary if we are to accept condemnation and punishment of the defendant following a conviction. However, the requirement to be present does not infer a requirement to actively participate or to account for oneself.

If the defendant fails to appear in the Crown Court, the trial may proceed in his absence. In *Haywood*,[90] the Court of Appeal held that the right to be present can be waived if the defendant deliberately and voluntarily absents himself or if he behaves in such a way as to obstruct the proper course of the proceedings. In *Jones*,[91] the House of Lords confirmed that the courts have a discretion to commence a trial in the absence of the defendant. However, it is 'a discretion to be exercised with great caution and with close regard to the overall fairness of

86 See *Colozza v Italy* (1985) 7 EHRR 516.
87 H Riddle and S Jones, 'Trial in Absence in a Magistrates' Court' [2013] *Crim LR* 750, 755.
88 JH Langbein, *The Origins of the Adversary Criminal Trial* (Oxford, Oxford University Press, 2003) 19.
89 ibid 57.
90 [2001] EWCA Crim 168, [2001] QB 862.
91 [2002] UKHL 5, [2003] 1 AC 1.

the proceedings'.[92] The focus on fairness suggests the importance of the defendant's choice to participate; it does not imply that he must be present in order to take part in the proceedings.

Summary trials can, and often do, take place in the defendant's absence.[93] Section 12 of the Magistrates' Courts Act 1980 allows the defendant to plead guilty by post, and sections 11 and 13 set out the options open to the magistrates when a defendant, who has not pleaded guilty by post, fails to appear at the trial.[94] An important provision in summary trials is that if a defendant does not physically attend but his legal representative does, he is for most purposes deemed to be present.[95] In this situation, the defendant's presence may make little difference in the exercise of holding the state to account if the defence is able to participate as a party.[96] Although there is no general requirement for the defendant to be present at a summary trial, and a trial can proceed in his absence at the Crown Court, if a defendant has been granted bail and fails to surrender to custody he may be charged with absconding under the Bail Act 1976.

There are no *prima facie* legal obligations on the defendant to actively participate at the trial. A legal culture which discourages active participation developed over a long period of time, as a result of the emergence of the adversarial system. There are now many bars to effective communication between the defendant and the court, including the formality of the legal process which is dominated by legal professionals. As explained in the previous chapter, the judge now has extensive case management duties, and the prosecution and defence lawyers can also be tasked with specific duties to ensure the efficient running of the case. Consequently, it is the legal professionals who dictate the management and progress of the case. The trial itself remains a formal affair and this may cause the defendant to feel uncomfortable and intimidated. In the Crown Court, for example, counsel wear wigs and gowns and employ legal terminology that may be unfamiliar to the defendant. In *SC v UK*, the European Court of Human

92 ibid [6] (Lord Bingham).

93 Magistrates' Courts Act 1980, s 11(1)(b) provides that, subject to certain provisions, 'if the accused has attained the age of 18 years, the court *shall* proceed in his absence unless it appears to the court to be contrary to the interests of justice to do so'. Emphasis added. See also Criminal Procedure Rules (CrimPR), r 24.12(3), which states that, where the defendant is absent, the general rule is that the court will proceed as if the defendant were present, and had pleaded not guilty (unless a plea has already been taken).

94 For a discussion on whether trial of a defendant in his absence in the magistrates' courts should be routine or should occur only in an exceptional case, see H Riddle and S Jones, 'Trial in Absence in a Magistrates' Court' [2013] *Crim LR* 750.

95 Magistrates' Courts Act 1980, s 122(2).

96 In *R v Kepple* [2007] EWCA Crim 1339, (2007) 104(26) LSG 32, the court held that defence counsel for an absent defendant can ask questions of prosecution witnesses in as much detail as they wish based on their instructions, but without indicating what the defendant's evidence might have been and in the knowledge that he cannot call evidence to contradict the answers given. They may do this in the hope of either showing that the defendant's account is accepted by the witnesses or to cast doubt on the coherence or accuracy of their accounts.

Rights acknowledged that, 'Given the sophistication of modern legal systems, many adults of normal intelligence are unable fully to comprehend all the intricacies and exchanges which take place in the courtroom.'[97] The situation is more severe in relation to children. In *V v UK*, a case concerning the trial of two 11 year olds charged with murder, the European Court recognised that the 'formality and ritual of the Crown Court must at times have seemed incomprehensible and intimidating for a child of 11'.[98]

In addition, the defendant may feel unable to relate to those who are running the case, in part due to variations in their backgrounds, as demonstrated by the available statistics. For example, in 2014, 19 per cent of those proceeded against in court for indictable offences were from a black, Asian, mixed or 'other' ethnic background,[99] whereas just 6 per cent of all judges were categorised as being from a Black and Minority Ethnic (BME) background.[100] In 2012, only 5.5 per cent of Queen's Counsel barristers and 11 per cent of all practising barristers in England and Wales were categorised as BME.[101] In terms of education, in 2011/12, 28.4 per cent of pupil barristers had attended the University of Oxford or the University of Cambridge.[102] This can be compared to 2 per cent of all students at a higher education institution in England and Wales who attended Oxbridge in 2011/12.[103] Racial, social and economic differences could heighten the defendant's feelings of alienation and discomfort.

During the trial, the defendant sits in the dock. The courtroom in the Crown Court is typically designed such that the attention is directed towards the lawyers in the centre of the courtroom, who face the judge and have their backs turned to the defendant. Miller notes that the courtroom is arranged hierarchically, and that while the positions reserved for lawyers for the defence and prosecution are equivalent, the position reserved for defendants is comparatively marginal and inferior.[104] The physical separation between the defence barrister and the defendant is such that the defendant is ordinarily unable to communicate with his barrister during the court proceedings. Consequently, there is little opportunity for him to draw the attention of his barrister to inaccuracies during a witness's testimony, or to suggest questions for cross-examination. Confinement to the dock effectively prohibits free and uninterrupted consultation and suggestion during the trial.[105]

97 *SC v UK* (2005) 40 EHRR 10 [29].
98 *V v UK* (2000) 30 EHRR 121 [88].
99 Ministry of Justice, *Statistics on Race and the Criminal Justice System 2014* (Ministry of Justice, November 2015) 44–45.
100 ibid 94.
101 Bar Standards Board, *Bar Barometer: Trends in the Profile at the Bar* (The General Council of the Bar of England and Wales, June 2014) 18, 44.
102 ibid 89.
103 Higher Education Statistics Agency, *Students in Higher Education Institutes 2011/12* (Higher Education Statistics Agency, 2013) Table 1.
104 J Miller, 'A Rights-Based Argument Against the Dock' [2011] *Crim LR* 216, 220.
105 ibid 221.

Feelings of discomfort, intimidation and isolation can prohibit the defendant from following the proceedings and inhibit him from taking an active role. It is unfortunate that the current conditions so blatantly discourage participation. In order to respect the individual dignity and autonomy of the defendant, he should not only be free to choose to take an active role in the criminal process, if he so wishes, but he should actually be able to take that role. Moreover, the defendant's voluntary participation is valuable to the pursuit of accurate fact-finding. It can help to avoid errors by, for example, ensuring that weaknesses or inaccuracies in the prosecution's case, including the testimony of prosecution witnesses, are made known. Further, defendants, as well as the wider community, may be more willing to accept guilty verdicts if the defendant is able to participate.[106] There may be some straightforward means of improving the current situation. For example, there could be adjustments to the language normally used in court. In addition, the defendant could be allowed to sit in a place which permits easy informal communication with his legal representatives, as is the case in relation to vulnerable defendants.[107] However, any reforms or adjustments to the trial structure or process, aimed at facilitating participation, must not occur at the expense of fair trial rights, including those which permit non-participation. In the meantime, the bars to effective communication between the defendant and the court provide an additional reason not to require the active participation of the defendant and penalise non-cooperation.

Despite the barriers to communication, the defendant holds rights to participate in the criminal process, as provided for by Article 6(3) of the ECHR. Article 6(3) grants the defendant the rights to be informed promptly, and in detail, of the nature and cause of the accusation against him; to have adequate time and the facilities for the preparation of his defence; to defend himself in person or through legal assistance; to examine or have examined witnesses against him and to obtain the attendance and examination of witnesses on his behalf under the same conditions as witnesses against him; and to have the free assistance of an interpreter if he cannot understand or speak the language used in court. If the defendant does choose to participate during his trial, he has the right to do so effectively.[108] In *SC v UK*, the European Court explained that 'the right of an accused to effective participation in his or her criminal trial generally includes, *inter alia*, not only the right to be present, but also to hear and follow the proceedings'.[109] The Court went on to explain that:

> 'effective participation' in this context presupposes that the accused has a broad understanding of the nature of the trial process and of what is at stake

106 J Jackson and S Summers, *The Internationalisation of Criminal Evidence: Beyond the Common Law and Civil Law Traditions* (Cambridge, Cambridge University Press, 2012) 24–25.

107 Criminal Practice Directions 2015 [2015] EWCA Crim 1567 para 3G.8.

108 *Stanford v UK* App no 16757/90 (ECHR, 23 February 1994).

109 *SC v UK* (2005) 40 EHRR 10 [28].

> for him or her, including the significance of any penalty which may be imposed. It means that he or she, if necessary with the assistance of, for example, an interpreter, lawyer, social worker or friend, should be able to understand the general thrust of what is said in court. The defendant should be able to follow what is said by the prosecution witnesses and, if represented, to explain to his own lawyers his version of events, point out any statements with which he disagrees and make them aware of any facts which should be put forward in his defence.[110]

In order to participate effectively, the defendant may require special measures to be put in place. The Criminal Practice Directions stipulate that 'the court is required to take "every reasonable step" to encourage and facilitate the attendance of witnesses and to facilitate the participation of any person, including the defendant'.[111] The steps which can be taken to assist vulnerable defendants include, specially chosen and adapted courtrooms, shortened sitting times and regular breaks, restricted attendance and removal of wigs and gowns. In addition, the Youth Justice and Criminal Evidence Act 1999 provides for the use of live link and intermediaries.[112] However, it should be noted that, for defendants, conditions of eligibility for special measures are strict, and they are not automatically entitled to the same range of special measures as other vulnerable witnesses.[113] Moreover, the effectiveness of special measures is uncertain. Even with the assistance of an intermediary, the defendant may feel that he is unable to meaningfully participate in his trial.[114]

The right to effective participation does not require that the defendant should understand or be capable of understanding every point of law or evidential detail, given the right to legal representation.[115] However, it is concerning that it also does not seem to include a more general requirement that the defendant himself be able to follow the proceedings and evidence of witnesses, so long as

110 ibid [29].

111 Criminal Practice Directions 2015 [2015] EWCA Crim 1567 para 3D.2. See also CrimPR r 3.9(3)(a) and (b).

112 YJCEA 1999, ss 33A–33C. The provisions in relation to intermediaries are not yet in force. However, the court has the power at common law to direct the use of intermediaries for the defendant. See *R v Cox* [2012] EWCA Crim 549, [2012] Cr App R 6.

113 This raises issues of compatibility with the principle of equality of arms. See L Hoyano, 'Striking a Balance Between the Rights of Defendants and Vulnerable Witnesses: Will Special Measures Directions Contravene Guarantees of a Fair Trial?' [2001] *Crim LR* 948; L Hoyano, 'Coroners and Justice Act 2009: Special Measures Directions Take Two: Entrenching Unequal Access to Justice?' [2010] *Crim LR* 345. On special measures for defendants, see generally J McEwan, 'Vulnerable Defendants and the Fairness of Trials' [2013] *Crim LR* 100.

114 See *R v D* [2013] EWCA Crim 465, [2014] 1 WLR 525. In this case, despite accepting that there had been shortcomings in the way the appellant's difficulties were handled at trial, the Court of Appeal held that he was able to meaningfully participate.

115 *SC v UK* (2005) 40 EHRR 10 [29].

his representatives can. In *Stanford v UK*,[116] the European Court held that, despite the defendant not being able to properly hear the proceedings, there had been no violation of Article 6. The Court suggested that the defendant's right to hear and follow the proceedings could be exercised by proxy through his lawyer. This argument is unconvincing. The right to follow proceedings should be a personal one which can be exercised by the defendant himself. Not only should respect for individual autonomy prohibit the defendant from being required to participate, it should also require that he be able to participate and that meaningful participation can be facilitated. Moreover, since the defendant is now expected to actively participate as an individual, it seems only fair that he be able to follow the proceedings as an individual.

Despite the numerous bars to effective communication and participation for many defendants, it is no longer accurate to state that, in England and Wales, 'It is regarded as a central principle of criminal trials that the defendant can sit back and wait for the prosecution to prove the case against him.'[117] The defendant can be faced with detrimental consequences for his failure to actively participate in the criminal process, such that he is effectively required to participate. Before the trial has even begun, the defence is expected to participate by disclosing its case to the prosecution. The Criminal Procedure and Investigations Act 1996 and the Criminal Justice Act 2003 extended the realm of defence participation by requiring the defendant to provide a statement setting out, *inter alia*, the nature of his defence and any points of law on which he wishes to rely. Failure to issue a defence statement, or departing from it, can result in adverse inferences of guilt being drawn against the defendant.[118] There are also statutory provisions which allow adverse inferences of guilt to be drawn from the defendant's silence, contained in the Criminal Justice and Public Order Act 1994.[119] These provisions, along with other reforms designed to secure the defendant's cooperation, have created a tension between adversarial ideologies and efficient fact-finding. The increasing emphasis on efficient fact-finding, at the expense of adversarial ideologies, has affected the defendant's capacity to choose whether or not to participate in the criminal process. This is particularly concerning given that defendants do not always feel able to participate effectively, even with the assistance of special measures.

Not only are defendants now expected to actively participate in the criminal process, but they are expected to do so constructively by, for example, alerting the prosecution to errors or oversights in its case.[120] The introduction of defence disclosure requirements and the case management regime set out in the Criminal Procedure Rules, as well as increasing concern for accurate fact-finding, has

116 App no 16757/90 (ECHR, 23 February 1994).

117 A Duff, L Farmer, S Marshall and V Tadros (eds), *The Trial on Trial 3: Towards a Normative Theory of the Criminal Trial* (Oxford, Hart Publishing, 2007) 199.

118 See ch 7.

119 See ch 6.

120 See CrimPR, r 1.2(1)(c). This is known as the 'grassing up' clause.

rendered 'ambush defences' unacceptable.[121] There has since been a number of cases upholding convictions where the defence had attempted to present a previously undisclosed defence at trial or purposely failed to point out prosecution errors until too late to rectify them.[122] The implications of this are dealt with in Chapter 7. Suffice to say here that, from an adversarial standpoint, in which the trial takes the form of a competition between two equal sides, a failure to mention or rectify a mistake made by the prosecution is not ordinarily objectionable. Nor is it objectionable within a conception of the trial as a means of calling the state to account for the accusations it makes, as the defendant should not be expected to assist the state in its duty to prove guilt. However, there is a distinction between passive and active obstruction of the opponent's case. While failing to point out mistakes made by the opposing side, particularly by the prosecution, would seem unobjectionable, deliberately sabotaging the opponent through, for example, tampering with evidence and, therefore, perverting the course of justice, distorts the appearance of fairness and undermines the legitimacy of the process.

As well as setting out the right to participate, Article 6 of the ECHR has been interpreted to recognise the right not to participate, principally in the form of the right to silence and the privilege against self-incrimination.[123] The right not to participate is, therefore, an implicit part of Article 6 and must be considered alongside the right to participate, and not as a bar to it. Duff *et al.* suggest that it is difficult to justify both the defendant's right to participate and his right not to participate.[124] But, if one considers that the right to participate is a choice which does not have to be exercised, rather than a normative expectation, then both can easily be accommodated. If active participation were an obligation, like the public trial requirement, it would be hard to recognise it as a 'right'. However, unlike the public trial requirement, obligatory participation is objectionable on other grounds, such as interference with principles of fairness. It is, therefore, unfortunate that the right to participate has increasingly become a requirement at the expense of the right not to participate.

4.4 Conclusion

Within a democratically liberal polity which accords importance to individual dignity and autonomy, and in which the state holds vast resources and criminal convictions come with far reaching consequences, defendants should not be

121 The Court of Appeal stated that ambush defences are 'no longer acceptable' in *R v Gleeson* [2003] EWCA Crim 3357, [2004] 1 Cr App R 29 [35] (Auld LJ).

122 See, for example, *R v Gleeson* [2003] EWCA Crim 3357, [2004] 1 Cr App R 29; *Malcolm v DPP* [2007] EWHC 363 (Admin), [2007] 1 WLR 1230; *R v Musone* [2007] EWCA Crim 1237, [2007] 1 WLR 2467; *Writtle v DPP* [2009] EWHC 236 (Admin), (2009) 173 JP 224; *R (on the application of Santos) v Stratford Magistrates' Court* [2012] EWHC 752 (Admin).

123 *Murray v UK* (1996) 22 EHRR 29.

124 A Duff, L Farmer, S Marshall and V Tadros (eds), *The Trial on Trial 3: Towards a Normative Theory of the Criminal Trial* (Oxford, Hart Publishing, 2007) 100.

required or expected to actively participate in the criminal process. Rather than calling the defendant to account, the trial should be viewed as a forum to hold the state to account. Citizens should be entitled to see that the state properly proves its accusations against them before subjecting them to condemnation and punishment. Placing the emphasis on the defendant's constructive cooperation, and providing incentives and penalties to secure it, signals a shift away from a voluntary approach to the defendant's participatory role in favour of a system of obligatory participation, and at the expense of England's adversarial history and the important legal norms it entails. The following chapters consider specific examples of the way in which defendants are now obliged to participate in the criminal process and penalised for their non-cooperation.

5 The privilege against self-incrimination

The privilege against self-incrimination means that a person cannot be legally compelled to provide the authorities with information which could reasonably lead to, or increase the likelihood of, that person's prosecution for a criminal offence, or which might be used against that person in criminal proceedings.[1] It applies to the provision of information during the investigative and pre-trial stages of the criminal process, as well as during the trial. In fact, it is the application of the privilege during the preliminary stages of the criminal process which has caused the most controversy and debate. The privilege has been described by the European Court of Human Rights as one of the 'generally recognised international standards which lie at the heart of the notion of a fair procedure under Article 6'.[2] Yet, within English law, there are many legislative provisions under which, contrary to the privilege, individuals can be compelled to provide information which can be used against them in a criminal prosecution. A failure to provide the necessary information can result in criminal prosecution for non-compliance with the participatory requirement.[3] This forms perhaps the most striking example of requiring defendant participation and penalising non-cooperation.

The privilege against self-incrimination is often considered together with the right to silence, since both are concerned with the legal significance of silence. However, the privilege and the right to silence can be distinguished on several grounds. First, the privilege is both a broader and narrower concept than the right to silence. It is broader in that it extends beyond speech. For instance, the privilege may apply to documents, physical objects and bodily samples.[4] At the same time,

1 See A L-T Choo, *The Privilege Against Self-Incrimination and Criminal Justice* (Oxford, Hart Publishing, 2013) 1. In *Beghal v DPP* [2015] UKSC 49, [2015] 3 WLR 344 [60], Lord Hughes refers to the privilege as an entitlement 'to refuse to answer questions or to yield up documents or objects if to do so would carry a real or appreciable risk of its use in the prosecution of that person or his spouse'.

2 *Murray v UK* (1996) 22 EHRR 29 [45].

3 See, for example, s 172 of the Road Traffic Act 1988, discussed in ch 5.3.3.

4 In practice, the scope of the privilege has been restricted in such a way that it does not ordinarily apply to material which has an 'existence independent of the will of the suspect'. See *Saunders v UK* (1997) 23 EHRR 313.

it is narrower because, unlike the right to silence, it covers only *self-incriminatory* information. Second, the source of the participatory requirement differs. The privilege has been abrogated by direct legal compulsion to participate, whereas the right to silence is inhibited through the threat of adverse inferences of guilt. Third, the sanctions for non-cooperation by way of exercising the right to remain silent and the privilege against self-incrimination differ. Whereas silence can lead to adverse inferences, reliance on the privilege can lead to criminal prosecution for non-cooperation. For these reasons, limitations to the privilege and the right to silence are presented as two separate examples of requirements to actively participate.

There are a number of contentious issues and uncertainties surrounding the privilege against self-incrimination. These include: the purpose of the privilege; the type of material, or information, covered by the privilege; the circumstances in which the privilege applies; whether the privilege is absolute or whether there should be recognised exceptions to it; and whether the unfairness targeted by the privilege lies in the compulsion to provide material, the use made of that material or in the penalty for failing to comply with a participatory requirement. Each of these issues will be addressed, to various extents, throughout this chapter.[5] However, the focus is on developing a defence for the privilege which can support a 'no-assistance' approach to the defendant's role in the criminal process, as well as evaluating the extent to which the privilege has been limited within English law, resulting in significant penalties for non-compliance.

5.1 Rationalising the privilege against self-incrimination

While the privilege against self-incrimination has long been recognised in English law, its precise origins have been disputed.[6] Some commentators believe that the privilege stems from the Latin maxim *nemo tenetur prodere seipsum,* loosely translated to mean 'no one is obliged to accuse himself', which was employed in the ecclesiastical and prerogative courts.[7] The belief is that the privilege became internalised in common law criminal procedure with the abolition of the courts of Star Chamber and High Commission in 1641.[8] Others believe that the privilege

5 For a more detailed exploration of these issues, see A L-T Choo, *The Privilege Against Self-Incrimination and Criminal Justice* (Oxford, Hart Publishing, 2013). See also A L-T Choo, '"Give Us What You Have" – Information, Compulsion and the Privilege Against Self-Incrimination as a Human Right' in P Roberts and J Hunter (eds), *Criminal Evidence and Human Rights: Reimagining Common Law Procedural Traditions* (Oxford, Hart Publishing, 2012).

6 See P McInerney, 'The Privilege Against Self-Incrimination from Early Origins to Judges' Rules: Challenging the "Orthodox View"' (2014) 18 *E&P* 101.

7 See RH Helmholz, 'The Privilege and the *Ius Commune:* The Middle Ages to the Seventeenth Century' in RH Helmholz, CM Gray, JH Langbein, E Moglen, HE Smith and AW Alschuler (eds), *The Privilege Against Self-Incrimination: Its Origins and Development* (Chicago, University of Chicago Press, 1997).

8 See, for example, LW Levy, *Origins of the Fifth Amendment: The Right Against Self-Incrimination* (New York, Oxford University Press, 1968).

did not become an enforceable right until the late eighteenth century,[9] as a result of the emerging adversarial system and as an extension of the privilege provided to witnesses in court.[10] Once defence counsel were able to address the jury and speak to issues of both law and fact, and once the presumption of innocence had been crystallised as a workable principle, the defendant was able to effectively claim a privilege against self-incrimination at trial. However, the privilege operated only in relation to sworn testimony.[11] Until the Criminal Evidence Act of 1898, the defendant was not a competent witness and, so, gave unsworn testimony. Consequently, one could argue that a right not to incriminate oneself did not formally exist during the period covered by incompetency rules.[12] Nonetheless, the practical silencing of the defendant during the emergence of the adversarial system meant that the defendant gained an indirect *de facto* privilege against self-incrimination. Developments in the trial process during the course of the eighteenth century gradually fed into the pre-trial stage of the criminal process in the nineteenth century.[13]

Like its origins, the precise scope of the modern privilege against self-incrimination is uncertain. It has been interpreted and applied inconsistently in a series of cases, particularly by the European Court of Human Rights. The lack of a consistent scope for the privilege may be attributable to the lack of a coherent rationale for it. A failure to appreciate the value of the privilege has arguably led to requirements being placed on suspects and defendants to supply information against themselves and, where this is not forthcoming, to the significant penalty of prosecution for non-cooperation. It would seem, then, that if a sound justification for the privilege could be identified, there would be less impetus to penalise non-cooperation in this way. We could then move closer to a system in which the defendant's participation is voluntary and the state is held to account for the accusations made against the defendant.

Yet, the privilege is as easily criticised as it is defended. Jeremy Bentham, one of the privilege's most prominent critics, felt that it was a product of irrational prejudice, for which no convincing justification could be advanced.[14] He believed

9 According to Langbein, it was not until the late 1780s that sources show the privilege being claimed by, or on behalf of, defendants in ordinary criminal trials. JH Langbein, *The Origins of the Adversary Criminal Trial* (Oxford, Oxford University Press, 2003) 280.

10 JH Langbein, 'The Historic Origins of the Privilege Against Self-Incrimination at Common Law' (1994) 92 *Michigan Law Review* 1047; HE Smith, 'The Modern Privilege: Its Nineteenth Century Origins' in RH Helmholz, CM Gray, JH Langbein, E Moglen, HE Smith and AW Alschuler (eds), *The Privilege Against Self-Incrimination: Its Origins and Development* (Chicago, University of Chicago Press, 1997) 146.

11 An extensive list of persons disqualified from giving sworn evidence by reason of presumed untrustworthiness developed in the early common law. These were gradually dismantled by legislation throughout the nineteenth century.

12 P McInerney, 'The Privilege Against Self-Incrimination from Early Origins to Judges' Rules: Challenging the "Orthodox View"' (2014) 18 *E&P* 101, 121.

13 ibid.

14 See J Bentham, *Rationale of Judicial Evidence, Specially Applied to English Practice* (London, Hunt & Clarke, 1827).

that an accurate verdict was likely to result from consideration of all relevant evidence, including self-incriminatory evidence.[15] By depriving the court of potentially reliable evidence of guilt, the privilege may also obstruct the efficient investigation and prosecution of criminals.[16] Consequently, the privilege may interfere with the aim of accurate fact-finding and the desire for an efficient criminal process. On the other hand, the privilege can act as a necessary constraint on the aims of the criminal process, for the sake of fairness and legitimacy. As explained in Chapter 2, the criminal process is legitimised not only through accurate verdicts, but also through respect for individual rights and fair procedures. In the absence of these latter considerations, even a factually accurate verdict should not be accepted as legitimate. We should, therefore, be prepared to accept that a loss of evidence may be a necessary consequence of exercising the privilege, and that legitimacy of the process must take precedence over efficiency concerns. However, it has proven difficult for courts and commentators to articulate exactly why there should be a right not to incriminate oneself in the first place.

In *Saunders v UK*, the European Court attempted to rationalise the privilege:

> [The] rationale lies, *inter alia*, in the protection of the accused against improper compulsion by the authorities thereby contributing to the avoidance of miscarriages of justice and to the fulfilment of the aims of Article 6. The right not to incriminate oneself, in particular, presupposes that the prosecution in a criminal case seek to prove their case against the accused without resort to evidence obtained through methods of coercion or oppression in defiance of the will of the accused. In this sense the right is closely linked to the presumption of innocence contained in Article 6(2) of the Convention.[17]

This important passage highlights a number of possible justifications for the privilege. Not least, it suggests that it can protect the innocent and uphold the presumption of innocence, thus linking the privilege to certain epistemic and due process concerns. The strength of these justifications is considered below, along with justifications based on the instrumental protection of privacy and the prevention of a cruel choice imposed by the state. Following brief examination of these commonly proposed justifications, the value of the privilege in its ability to reinforce and regulate the relationship between the citizen and the state is examined.

5.1.1 The presumption of innocence

The link between the privilege against self-incrimination and the presumption of innocence is relatively easy to identify. The interest in not being obliged to

15 A Lewis, 'Bentham's View of the Right to Silence' (1990) 43 *Current Legal Problems* 135, 151.

16 I Dennis, 'Instrumental Protection, Human Right or Functional Necessity? Reassessing the Privilege Against Self-Incrimination' (1995) 54 *Cambridge Law Journal* 342, 343.

17 *Saunders v UK* (1997) 23 EHRR 313 [68].

incriminate oneself is embodied in the fundamental principle that it is for the prosecution to prove the accused's guilt, and not for the accused to prove his innocence. If the accused is presumed to be innocent, it is wrong to compel him to be a source of incriminating information; he must be given the privilege of declining to cooperate in procedures designed to establish his guilt.[18] The strength of this link, however, depends on how one interprets the presumption of innocence. For instance, if the presumption is understood only in a very narrow sense, in terms of the prosecution's burden of proof at trial, the connection between the privilege and the presumption of innocence is not particularly strong. The presumption tells us only that the prosecution must prove guilt, and not where the evidence used to prove guilt can and cannot come from. One could also argue that the standard of proof is unaffected by the privilege;[19] the prosecution must prove guilt beyond a reasonable doubt regardless of the source of evidence. In response to this, it can be asserted that, by requiring the accused to provide incriminating information, it will inevitably become easier for the prosecution to reach the requisite standard and discharge the burden of proof. Arguably, the accused should not be co-opted into easing the prosecution's burden of proof, or helping to discharge it.

Redmayne notes a further way to link the presumption and the privilege.[20] The presumption can be understood as a rule requiring the state to treat citizens as innocent unless it has good reason to think otherwise. This argument is derived from Greenawalt's account of the right to silence which recognises a principle under which we should not be expected to respond to accusations unless they are supported with evidence.[21] However, when applying a wider interpretation of the presumption, as advocated in Chapter 1, and when approaching the issue from the perspective of a criminal process based on calling the state to account, it should not even be necessary for the citizen to respond when the accusations against him or her are backed up with evidence. In accordance with this wide interpretation, until guilt is proven, the state should treat citizens as if they had nothing to account for. Rather, the state should justify and account for the accusations of wrongdoing which it has brought against them, without their co-opted help.[22] A broad notion of the privilege against self-incrimination reinforces this 'no-assistance' principle.[23] The privilege can uphold the presumption

18 See I Dennis, 'Instrumental Protection, Human Right or Functional Necessity? Reassessing the Privilege Against Self-Incrimination' (1995) 54 *Cambridge Law Journal* 342, 353–354.

19 M Redmayne, 'Rethinking the Privilege Against Self-Incrimination' (2007) 27 *Oxford Journal of Legal Studies* 209, 218.

20 ibid 219.

21 K Greenawalt, 'Silence as a Moral and Constitutional Right' (1981) 23 *William & Mary Law Review* 15.

22 See S Greer, 'The Right to Silence, Defence Disclosure, and Confession Evidence' (1994) 21 *Journal of Law and Society* 102, 109; M Zander's note of dissent in Royal Commission on Criminal Justice, *Report* (Cm 2263, 1993) 221.

23 Assistance, in this context, refers only to assistance obtained through the active participation of the accused and not to information which may be obtained through passive participation or force.

of innocence by ensuring that the accused is not required to actively assist in establishing a case against himself. Limiting the scope of the privilege against self-incrimination operates so as to weaken the effect of the presumption of innocence.

In practice, the presumption of innocence is an over-inclusive justification for the privilege against self-incrimination.[24] It has the potential to account for all manner of evidence that the accused may be in a position to disclose, including confessions, fingerprints, breath or blood samples, documents and other real evidence. The scope of the privilege is not so encompassing. For example, it does not ordinarily apply to the collection of fingerprints, breath or blood samples. Even in the United States, where the privilege has express constitutional force, it has been limited to testimonial evidence.[25] This evidence must result from compulsion and must lead to self-incrimination.[26] Yet, if we approach the issue from a normative perspective, there is no compelling reason why the presumption of innocence should not prevent the privilege from allowing suspects to withhold any evidence that may incriminate them.[27] From this perspective, the presumption of innocence offers a sound justification for the privilege, as well as an argument against penalising those who rely on it. Given the reluctance to interpret the privilege broadly, however, the presumption of innocence will remain an over-inclusive justification in practice.

5.1.2 Protecting the innocent

As noted in *Saunders*, the privilege may have value in its ability to prevent wrongful convictions; to secure the acquittal of innocent suspects by preventing false confessions or the disclosure of unreliable information. This is most relevant in relation to police questioning, where the privilege might act as an inhibitor on overzealous police officers. The broader applicability of the privilege to non-testimonial, or material, evidence is unlikely to prevent wrongful convictions. Where, for example, the demand is for the handing over of a specific pre-existing document or the provision of a bodily sample, there is no danger of the suspect falsely confessing.[28] The contents of a document or sample will 'speak for itself'.[29]

24 I Dennis, 'Instrumental Protection, Human Right or Functional Necessity? Reassessing the Privilege Against Self-Incrimination' (1995) 54 *Cambridge Law Journal* 342, 355.

25 See, for example, *Schmerber v California* 384 US 757 (1966) where the use of a blood sample taken from the defendant against his will did not violate the Fifth Amendment of the United States Constitution.

26 *Fisher v United States* 425 US 391 (1976).

27 The normative response to certain policy arguments which have been advanced in order to limit the privilege are addressed in chs 5.3 and 5.4.

28 A L-T Choo, *The Privilege Against Self-Incrimination and Criminal Justice* (Oxford, Hart Publishing, 2013) 5.

29 *AT & T Istel Ltd v Tully* [1993] AC 45 (HL) 57 (Lord Griffiths).

In the context of preventing compelled false incrimination during police interrogation, the effectiveness of the privilege is questionable. On the one hand, a requirement to answer questions could put undue pressure on suspects, particularly vulnerable ones. On the other hand, in practice, the majority of suspects in the police station do not rely on the privilege,[30] and it is the frightened and vulnerable suspects who are most likely to succumb to pressure to confess,[31] despite having a privilege against self-incrimination. It has also been argued that such limited protection as the privilege may offer is unnecessary where the custodial regime is closely regulated by legislation, including the Police and Criminal Evidence Act 1984 (PACE 1984), and the willingness of courts to use exclusionary principles in the interest of securing legitimate verdicts.[32] Yet, these alternative safeguards do not render the privilege against self-incrimination as a potential means of protection redundant. The privilege has the benefit of offering a blanket protection, and its application does not depend on the discretion of any individual.

Seidmann and Stein offer an alternative way to link the privilege to protection of the innocent. They claim that allowing suspects to remain silent and not incriminate themselves discourages guilty defendants from giving false accounts.[33] With fewer false accounts being given, the claims of innocent suspects will be taken more seriously. One particular limitation of this argument is that fact-finders are likely to be more concerned with the nature of the account given and its fit with other evidence, than the bare fact that a suspect answered questions.[34] More convincingly, Schulhofer has argued that the absence of obvious examples in which the privilege has protected the innocent hardly shows that real cases involving harm to innocent suspects would not occur if the privilege were abolished.[35] However, since this justification for the privilege is most relevant in relation to official questioning of the suspect, and since its utility is far from certain, the protection of the innocent cannot be regarded as a particularly strong justification. It cannot account for a privilege which is broad enough in scope to prevent all, or even most, requirements of self-incriminatory participation on the part of the accused. The pressure put on suspects to speak during police questioning is addressed further in the following chapter on the right to silence.

30 See Royal Commission on Criminal Justice, *Report* (Cm 2263, 1993) 53–54.

31 See GH Gudjonsson, *The Psychology of Interrogations and Confessions: A Handbook* (Chichester, Wiley, 2003).

32 For example, the exclusionary discretion under the Police and Criminal Evidence Act 1984 (PACE 1984), s 78. See I Dennis, 'Instrumental Protection, Human Right or Functional Necessity? Reassessing the Privilege Against Self-Incrimination' (1995) 54 *Cambridge Law Journal* 342, 353.

33 DJ Seidmann and A Stein, 'The Right To Silence Helps the Innocent: A Game-Theoretic Analysis of the Fifth Amendment Privilege' (2001) 114 *Harvard Law Review* 430.

34 M Redmayne, 'Rethinking the Privilege Against Self-Incrimination' (2007) 27 *Oxford Journal of Legal Studies* 209, 220.

35 SJ Schulhofer, 'Some Kind Words for the Privilege Against Self-Incrimination' (1991) 26 *Valparaiso University Law Review* 311, 329.

5.1.3 Privacy

The process of obtaining self-incriminatory evidence, whether through questioning, physical searches or a requirement to provide documents and the like, can impede privacy. One could, therefore, argue that the privilege against self-incrimination is justified as a means of protecting the right to privacy. However, three limitations to this justification are immediately apparent. First, in practice, the privilege is primarily concerned with the use made of the evidence obtained rather than the nature of the disclosure. If information cannot be used against an individual in criminal proceedings, a requirement to provide the information may not engage the privilege.[36] Issues of privacy, on the other hand, will inevitably arise from the nature of the disclosure; privacy can be invaded by a compelled communication even if no evidential use is made of it.[37] Second, the privilege protects only against *self*-incrimination and not the disclosure of private information by others. Even if the notion of privacy is limited to the accused's consciousness, it is still possible to gather information about his thoughts, beliefs and feelings through other means, such as material evidence or through questioning other people.[38] Third, the privilege can only ensure the privacy of potentially *incriminating* information and not other potentially harmful information.[39] Thus, the privilege is hardly an effective protection of privacy.

Gerstein has advanced a novel rationale for the privilege based on privacy by claiming that it is a necessary part of a system of criminal law which is based on respect for individual dignity.[40] He links the idea of privacy to the control that we have over information about ourselves, with any compulsory self-incrimination being an obvious involuntary relinquishment of control over information.[41] Gerstein sees self-incriminatory information as particularly important for the individual to be able to control because a confession involves the admission of wrongdoing, self-condemnation and the revelation of remorse. He argues that 'a man ought to have absolute control over the making of such revelations as these'.[42] This line of reasoning shows concern for the preservation of individual dignity and autonomy, and it seems to solve the problem of why the privilege only covers incriminating information obtained from the suspect himself. However, it is open to criticism because the disclosure of incriminating information has no direct nor necessary link to feelings of wrongdoing, self-condemnation or remorse. Confessing to what one has done is not tantamount to confessing how one feels about these actions. It is entirely possible to rationalise and justify one's conduct

36 The concept of 'use immunity' is discussed in ch 5.3.1.

37 I Dennis, 'Instrumental Protection, Human Right or Functional Necessity? Reassessing the Privilege Against Self-Incrimination' (1995) 54 *Cambridge Law Journal* 342, 358.

38 D Dolinko, 'Is There a Rationale for the Privilege Against Self-Incrimination?' (1986) 33 *UCLA Law Review* 1063, 1110.

39 ibid 1108.

40 See RS Gerstein, 'Privacy and Self-Incrimination' (1970) 80 *Ethics* 87.

41 ibid 89.

42 ibid 90.

in such a way that a confession or other means of self-incrimination does not express feelings of wrongdoing, self-condemnation or remorse. Gerstein's approach protects against a very narrow range of intrusions upon privacy, not enough to claim the protection of privacy as a general justification for the privilege against self-incrimination.

5.1.4 Preventing cruel choices

Attempts have also been made to rationalise the privilege on the basis that it prevents suspects and defendants from facing the 'cruel trilemma' of having to choose between being penalised for non-cooperation, providing the authorities with incriminating evidence or lying and risking prosecution for perjury. Redmayne has referred to this as one of the most intuitive defences for the privilege.[43] However, not all commentators agree. Bentham, for example, labelled those who object to such harshness as 'old women'.[44] One problem with defending this justification is that it is only the guilty who suffer from the trilemma. This renders it inconsistent with a broad interpretation of the presumption of innocence, as the underlying premise is that the suspect is guilty. It could be argued that innocent people can face a similar dilemma For instance, innocent suspects in road traffic cases who are required to disclose the driver of their vehicle at a particular place or time may have a difficult choice in deciding whether to face sanctions for non-cooperation or incriminate a close friend or family member. Redmayne finds this duty to 'other-incriminate' disturbing, as it does not recognise affective bonds and may undermine a person's feelings of personal integrity.[45] This is not just an issue in regard to close relationships, but may also pose a difficult situation for a witness to a crime they believe is justified.

Proponents of the cruelty justification may also assert that an absence of the privilege does more than face the accused with a difficult choice; it requires him to inflict harm on himself by increasing the likelihood of conviction and punishment, as well as subjection to community condemnation and ridicule. However, Dolinko explains that conviction, punishment and condemnation are often the desired end results of the criminal justice system and, so, should not be labelled 'cruel'.[46] So long as we accept that the general practice of punishment is not inherently cruel, we are deprived of one possible basis for thinking it cruel to compel someone to help bring punishment on himself.[47] Yet, compelling persons

43 M Redmayne, 'Rethinking the Privilege Against Self-Incrimination' (2007) 27 *Oxford Journal of Legal Studies* 209, 221.

44 A Lewis, 'Bentham's View of the Right to Silence' (1990) 43 *Current Legal Problems* 135, 148.

45 M Redmayne, 'Rethinking the Privilege Against Self-Incrimination' (2007) 27 *Oxford Journal of Legal Studies* 209, 222–223.

46 D Dolinko, 'Is There a Rationale for the Privilege Against Self-Incrimination?' (1986) 33 *UCLA Law Review* 1063, 1103.

47 ibid 1104.

to inflict harm upon themselves aggravates the cruelty of simply inflicting it on them without their participation.[48] The cruelty does not necessarily lie in the consequence; it may lie in the circumstances that lead to that consequence. Self-incrimination (or other-incrimination) might be considered cruel because it forces people to make an exceptionally difficult choice. It is contrary to the basic human instinct of self-preservation that few of us could conform to.[49] For this reason, it is arguably wrong to punish people for failing to actively participate by disclosing self-incriminatory information when many of us would do the same.

Dolinko gets around this by noting that we punish people for other forms of 'self-preservation', such as destroying evidence or committing perjury.[50] It can be noted, however, that this latter type of 'self-preservation' requires the active involvement of the accused, whereas refusing to incriminate oneself (particularly in the face of direct questioning) is ordinarily a passive activity for which punishment for non-cooperation may seem particularly harsh. Nevertheless, the guilty suspect puts himself in that position by committing the crime. Dolinko finds no cruelty or hypocrisy in this.[51] Despite its intuitiveness, the limited applicability of this justification, and its incompatibility with a wide interpretation of the presumption of innocence, makes it difficult to advance.

5.2 The relationship between citizen and state

With the exception of the presumption of innocence, the justifications set out above suffer as self-contained rationales for the privilege against self-incrimination. While the presumption offers a rationale consistent with the theory put forward in this book, it is dependent on a wide interpretation and is hampered when applied to the privilege in practice. Like the presumption of innocence, the privilege against self-incrimination expresses some pivotal principles about the relationship between the citizen and the state. Normatively, the state ought to treat each citizen as if he or she were innocent until convicted of a criminal offence, and the accused should not be required or expected to actively assist the state in proving guilt. This is because, in a liberal democratic society, the state's powers in relation to the detection and prosecution of crime should be exercised according to certain standards that show respect for the dignity and autonomy of each individual.[52] The interest of all suspects in not being obliged to incriminate themselves derives from the values attached to autonomy, freedom and dignity of the individual.[53]

48 C Theophilopoulos, 'The Privilege Against Self-Incrimination and the Distinction Between Testimonial and Non-Testimonial Evidence' (2010) 127 *South African Law Journal* 107, 115.

49 D Dolinko, 'Is There a Rationale for the Privilege Against Self-Incrimination?' (1986) 33 *UCLA Law Review* 1063, 1095.

50 ibid 1106.

51 ibid 1100.

52 A Ashworth, 'Four Threats to the Presumption of Innocence' (2006) 10 *E & P* 241, 249.

53 I Dennis, 'Instrumental Protection, Human Right or Functional Necessity? Reassessing the Privilege Against Self-Incrimination' (1995) 54 *Cambridge Law Journal* 342, 353.

A basic minimum content of human dignity includes recognition that 'the state exists for the individual and not vice versa'.[54] Dignity requires that we are treated as subjects of state power, and not as mere objects for the extraction of evidence.[55] It also requires respect for autonomy.[56] Autonomy is respected by allowing freedom of choice, exhibited in the privilege against self-incrimination; the privilege affords the accused the choice of whether to participate in criminal proceedings. In Chapter 1, the importance of protecting dignity and autonomy was traced back to post-enlightenment ideals of the rights-bearing individual, and to social contract theories. According to such theories, we sacrifice a portion of our freedom so that we can enjoy what remains in peace. Since we give up some of our freedom by agreeing to abide by the laws of the state, arguably, the state should account for any allegation that we have breached those laws. This should be done without our coerced assistance.

The privilege against self-incrimination also provides a means of keeping the state's power in check, by placing limitations on what it can legitimately require of the accused. In so doing, it helps ensure that the state can be held to account without the active participation or assistance of the accused. By regulating the use of state power, the privilege can also protect those accused of criminal wrongdoing from abuses of that power. As noted by Dennis, in a system based on formal equality of parties, in which the state both investigates and adjudicates on the behaviour of citizens, there is an inherent danger of unfairness in the state exploiting its enforcement power to place an individual in a vulnerable position.[57] There is the risk that either investigative powers may be used to obtain evidence that is factually unreliable or they may be misused to compel the production of incriminating evidence by means inconsistent with the fundamental values of criminal law. If either of the risks materialises, the legitimacy of the criminal verdict may be compromised.[58] The role that the privilege plays in limiting the potential for abuse of state power is particularly apparent in the context of police interrogation, where there is also the most potential for the privilege to protect innocent suspects.

The privilege against self-incrimination may also regulate and reinforce the relationship between the citizen and the state by acting as what Redmayne has described as a 'distancing mechanism'.[59] A duty to cooperate creates a requirement to assist the state, suggesting identification with the state's goals. Although one

54 C McCrudden, 'Human Dignity and Judicial Interpretation of Human Rights' (2008) 19 *European Journal of International Law* 655, 679.

55 I Dennis, *The Law of Evidence,* 5th edn (London, Sweet & Maxwell, 2013) 207.

56 See, LR Barroso, 'Here, There, and Everywhere: Human Dignity in Contemporary Law and in the Transnational Discourse' (2012) 35 *Boston College International and Comparative Law Review* 331.

57 I Dennis, *The Law of Evidence,* 5th edn (London, Sweet & Maxwell, 2013) 207.

58 ibid.

59 M Redmayne, 'Rethinking the Privilege Against Self-Incrimination' (2007) 27 *Oxford Journal of Legal Studies* 209.

can give evidence reluctantly or defiantly, and the state cannot force us to agree with it, the fact remains that one is helping the state, and it then becomes difficult to distance oneself from the assistance. In this respect, the privilege allows us to disassociate ourselves from, or disavow, particular criminal prosecutions. This ability to keep some distance between us and the state is valuable when assisting a prosecution would conflict with deeply held commitments.[60] The privilege allows citizens to avoid what will often be a significant personal sacrifice; a sacrifice which could interfere with the citizen's autonomy and dignity.

As Redmayne notes, arguments surrounding the privilege are closely connected to difficult questions of political morality and liberalism.[61] These questions are about the extent to which autonomy can be restricted and citizens can be required to assist the state, and about when it is legitimate to sanction conduct. The complexity of these issues makes it difficult to coherently articulate the purpose of the privilege, and some have suggested that attempting to do so is a futile pursuit. Jackson, for example, has argued that it seems difficult to justify the privilege as a self-standing right that should exist independently of the absolute right not to be subjected to cruel, inhuman and degrading treatment and the qualified rights to privacy and the general right of silence.[62] He contends that if it is difficult to make a convincing case for such a substantive right on its own ground, it is equally difficult to make a convincing case for the need for such a privilege in order to safeguard other principles.[63] In his detailed analysis on the subject, Dolinko suggests that leading contemporary efforts to justify the privilege as more than a historical relic are uniformly unsatisfactory and that no efforts along similar lines are likely to succeed.[64] However, he goes on to acknowledge that a rule that lacks any principled justification may nevertheless come to serve important functions in the legal system as a whole.[65]

Despite these discouraging conclusions, the privilege against self-incrimination is, arguably, useful in its own right. It provides a means of reinforcing our relationship as individuals with the state, as well as reinforcing the role of the criminal process as a mechanism for calling the state to account for its accusations and request for condemnation and punishment of the accused. The privilege against self-incrimination operates as a restraint on the state's power, as a distancing mechanism, and as a means of protecting the accused's autonomy and dignity. If we can accept that we should respect the decision of defendants not to actively participate in proceedings against themselves, then we have a reason to recognise a privilege against self-incrimination. This line of reasoning can support a broad

60 ibid 225.

61 ibid 232.

62 J Jackson, 'Re-Conceptualizing the Right to Silence as an Effective Fair Trial Standard' (2009) 58 *International and Comparative Law Quarterly* 835, 846.

63 ibid.

64 D Dolinko, 'Is There a Rationale for the Privilege Against Self-Incrimination?' (1986) 33 *UCLA Law Review* 1063, 1064.

65 ibid.

interpretation of the privilege. When we limit the privilege by using state powers to require defendant participation, and by sanctioning those who do not cooperate, we are transforming the relationship of the state and the citizen as well as the nature of criminal procedure. A system in which non-compliant suspects are prosecuted for being non-compliant cannot be characterised as 'adversarial', or as a system of voluntary participation. Because the precise purpose of the privilege has proven difficult to identify or articulate, its scope has not readily been defined and, as we will see in the following section, this has led to confusion and inconsistency. It has led to judicial acceptance of demands on the defendant to actively participate and the imposition of penalties on those who refuse to do so.

5.3 Limiting the privilege against self-incrimination

Most commentators accept that, even if valuable, we should be prepared to restrict the scope of, or recognise exceptions to, the privilege against self-incrimination. Limiting the privilege inevitably results in requirements for the accused to actively participate and penalties for failure to comply. The scope of the privilege is not spelt out in the constitutional documents in which it is found. It has, therefore, been a matter of interpretation for the courts. Unfortunately, judgments from both the domestic courts and European Court have been confusing and inconsistent. As a result, the extent to which suspects and defendants can currently rely on the privilege against self-incrimination is unclear. Nonetheless, some understanding of the current scope of the privilege, and the extent to which it has been limited, can be discerned from an evaluation of the significant cases.

The European Court first recognised the privilege as an implicit Article 6 guarantee in the case of *Funke v France*.[66] The applicant had been suspected of tax evasion and required to provide customs authorities with statements of his overseas bank accounts. He was fined for not complying with this requirement. The Court held that the special features of customs law could not justify an infringement of the rights of anyone charged with a criminal offence to remain silent and not to contribute to incriminating themselves. This case is significant not only because it recognised the privilege as a right guaranteed by Article 6 of the European Convention on Human Rights, but also because the privilege's ability to obstruct the role of the suspect as an informational resource is at odds with the inquisitorial tendencies of many of the contracting States.[67] However, the decision did not specify whether the implied right to the privilege was absolute and, so, did little to set out a comprehensive scope for it.

The potentially broad recognition of the privilege in *Funke* was refined in a less than satisfactory way in *Saunders v UK*.[68] This case involved an administrative as opposed to a criminal inquiry which in itself does not engage Article 6. However,

66 (1993) 16 EHRR 297.
67 I Dennis, *The Law of Evidence,* 5th edn (London, Sweet & Maxwell, 2013) 161.
68 (1997) 23 EHRR 313.

the applicant's refusal to cooperate with the investigation under the Companies Act 1985 could have led to a finding of contempt of court and the imposition of a fine or committal to prison for up to two years. It was no defence to such refusal that the questions were of an incriminating nature.[69] Furthermore, any information gained from the inquiry could be used against the applicant in criminal proceedings. The Court found that there had been a violation of the privilege. In relation to the scope of the privilege, it held that:

> As commonly understood in the legal systems of the Contracting Parties to the Convention and elsewhere, it does not extend to the use in criminal proceedings of material which may be obtained from the accused through the use of compulsory powers but which has an existence independent of the will of the suspect such as, *inter alia*, documents acquired pursuant to a warrant, breath, blood and urine samples and bodily tissue for the purpose of DNA testing.[70]

In placing these limits on the breadth of the privilege, the Court made two important distinctions with regard to its application. These concern: the use made of the material obtained; and the type of material sought to be obtained.

5.3.1 Use of the material

The Court in *Saunders* was concerned not with the requirement to provide information, but the use made of that information in a subsequent criminal trial.[71] It is information which is obtained under compulsion,[72] and which may be *used against* an individual in criminal proceedings which engages the privilege. Following *Saunders*, 'use immunity' provisions were inserted into a large number of statutes. This was facilitated by section 59 and schedule 3 of the Youth Justice and Criminal Evidence Act 1999. In accordance with these provisions, information can be obtained under compulsion, but not subsequently used against a person. Such provisions are particularly prevalent in relation to administrative investigations into conduct such as fraud. For example, the Serious Fraud Office and the Department for Business, Innovation and Skills have compulsory powers to require people to answer questions and provide information with the threat of criminal sanction for non-compliance. The existence of such powers is thought to be essential for establishing how relevant enterprises were managed and for tracing the whereabouts of missing assets.[73]

69 ibid [70].
70 ibid [69].
71 ibid [67].
72 The privilege does not apply to information which is provided voluntarily. See *R v McGeough* [2015] UKSC 62, [2015] 1 WLR 4612.
73 I Dennis, 'Instrumental Protection, Human Right or Functional Necessity? Reassessing the Privilege Against Self-Incrimination' (1995) 54 *Cambridge Law Journal* 342, 369.

Where a compulsory power is not accompanied by a use immunity provision, it will be for the judge at any subsequent criminal trial to decide whether to exclude self-incriminatory evidence, applying the discretion in section 78 of PACE 1984.[74] In the recent case of *Beghal v DPP*,[75] the majority of the Supreme Court took the view that it was 'inevitable' that section 78 would be used to exclude any self-incriminating information obtained through compulsory questioning under schedule 7 of the Terrorism Act 2000. This view formed part of the basis for finding that the privilege does not appy to questioning under schedule 7.[76] Schedule 7 permits compulsory questioing of individuals at ports or borders for the purpose of determining whether they appear to be a person who is or has been concerned in the commission, preparation or instigation of acts of terrorism. The questioning itself does not form part of a criminal investigation, but it is possible that an investigation will commence following the questioning. In his dissenting judgment, Lord Kerr doubted that evidence obtained under schedule 7 would inevitably be excluded from a subsequent criminal trial. If, for example, there is significant other evidence which, alone, might establish the guilt of the accused, evidence of responses given during a schedule 7 investigation might be admitted to corroborate or reinforce that evidence.[77] Thus, in the absence of a specific use immunity provision, there is no guarantee that trial judges will exclude evidence obtained through the coerced particiation of the accused, no matter how likely exclusion may be.[78]

In accordance with the jurisprudence of the European Court, the privilege is not engaged during administrative inquiries; sanctions for failing to comply with a demand for information during such an inquiry will not breach Article 6, so long as the individual concerned had not been effectively *charged* with a criminal offence.[79] As such, use immunity can prevent the state from benefitting from the

74 See *R v K* [2009] EWCA Crim 1640, [2010] QB 343 [73].

75 [2015] UKSC 49, [2015] 3 WLR 344.

76 ibid [65]–[68].

77 ibid [117].

78 It is notable that the DPP had earlier declined to give an undertaking that answers to questions obtained by the exercise of schedule 7 powers would never form part of a subsequent prosecution case. The Court recommended that a use immunity provision be enacted to ensure the inevitability of exclusion of such evidence. *Beghal v DPP* [2015] UKSC 49, [2015] 3 WLR 344 [67]. *Beghal* can be compared to *R (on the application of DPP) v Leicester Magistrates' Court* [2015] EWHC 1295 (Admin), [2016] 1 Cr App R 5 [17], where it was held that a witness in criminal proceedings could be deposed, but that any evidence obtained from her under compulsion could not be used against her. Bean LJ took the view that, given the Crown's assurance that the witness would not be prosecuted, any attempt to prosecute her would be an abuse of process.

79 The term 'charged' has been used in an autonomous sense, referring to pending or anticipated criminal proceedings. See *Saunders v UK* (1997) 23 EHRR 313; *Allen v UK* (2002) 35 EHRR CD289; *King v UK* [2004] STC 911; *Weh v Austria* (2005) 40 EHRR 37; *Beghal v DPP* [2015] UKSC 49, [2015] 3 WLR 344. See generally A MacCulloch, 'The Privilege Against Self-Incrimination in Competition Investigations: Theoretical Foundations and Practical Implications' (2006) 26 *Legal Studies* 211.

compelled participation of an individual under administrative investigation in circumstances where that individual is later charged with a criminal offence. However, an important caveat of use immunity is that it protects answers and statements, but not pre-existing documents disclosed under compulsion. It is also noteworthy that England does not appear to have adopted a general principle of 'derivative use immunity', whereby all information discovered as a result of the original self-incrimination is excluded from subsequent criminal trials.[80]

A central proposition advanced in this book is that the accused should not be required to assist the state in establishing his guilt, whether by means of answering questions and providing statements, or through the provision of pre-existing documents. This ceases to be of concern if information obtained under compulsion cannot be used to assist the prosecution. One could argue that difficulties which surround establishing a precise scope for the privilege could be alleviated through greater reliance on use immunity. Suspects could be required to provide all manner of information during criminal investigations, as well as administrative investigations, with the fairness of the proceedings secured through exclusion of the compelled self-incriminatory information at the trial. An obvious weakness of this solution is the absence of derivative use immunity in English law. Even if the material provided by the suspect does not itself form part to the prosecution case, it may have led to the discovery of other incriminatory evidence, in which case the suspect's compelled participation will have assisted the prosecution.[81]

Unless all information discovered as a result of the original self-incrimination is excluded, the concept of use immunity becomes something of a legal fiction. Yet, distinguishing between information which would and would not have been obtained without the compelled self-incrimination could be difficult. Extending the concept of use immunity to all investigations would also be counterproductive. The primary purpose of requiring self-incrimination during criminal investigations is to equip the prosecution with evidence that can be used against the defendant. In other words, the purpose is to assist in establishing guilt. Use immunity provisions would defeat the very purpose of the participatory requirement. In many cases, it would be more advantageous for the prosecution to try to obtain the relevant evidence through other means, such that it could then be presented against the defendant in criminal proceedings.

80 In some jurisdictions, derivative use immunity has been granted to witnesses who are compelled to testify. See, for example, the decision of the Supreme Court of Canada in *R v S(RJ)* [1995] 1 SCR 451. See also A L-T Choo, *The Privilege Against Self-Incrimination and Criminal Justice* (Oxford, Hart Publishing, 2013) 35–39.

81 Under the current law on confessions, for example, the inadmissibility of a confession does not affect the admissibility of facts discovered as a result of that confession. However, evidence that the fact was discovered as a result of the confession is inadmissible. See PACE 1984, ss 76(4)–(6). See also *HM Advocate v P* [2011] UKSC 44, [2011] 1 WLR 2497, where it was held that evidence derived from impermissible questioning is not subject to an automatic exclusionary rule. In the context of the privilege, see *R v S(F)* [2008] EWCA Crim 2177, [2009] 1 WLR 1489, discussed in ch 5.3.2.

In addition to these limitations, use immunity does not prevent requirements to actively participate. The initial requirement to supply information raises issues surrounding respect for individual dignity and autonomy. The previous section of this chapter indicated that the privilege protects against compelled participation. Although the point of the protection is to prevent the state from using the accused as an object for the extraction of evidence, the core of the privilege is immunity from providing information.[82] Thus, to require the accused to provide self-incriminatory information, whether or not it becomes part of the prosecution case, acts to undermine the relationship between citizen and state. To summarise, the concept of use immunity has limited the extent to which an individual under certain types of investigation can be used as an evidential resource against him- or herself. However, it is hindered by the absence of derivative use immunity, and it cannot be an adequate replacement for the privilege against self-incrimination.

5.3.2 Type of material

In *Saunders*, the Court made a distinction as to the type of material which is covered by the privilege against self-incrimination. Material which falls outside of the scope of the privilege is that 'which has an existence independent of the will of the suspect'. This includes 'breath, blood and urine samples and bodily tissue for the purposes of DNA testing'.[83] The distinction essentially limits the applicability of the privilege to answers to questions and statements created at the request of the relevant authorities. The Court's explicit exclusion of pre-existing documents from the scope of the privilege was inconsistent with the previous decision in *Funke*, in which a requirement to provide documents was in breach of Article 6. It might have been expected that, following *Saunders*, documents would be excluded from the scope of the privilege. However, in *JB v Switzerland*,[84] a case which involved requirements to produce documents and declare a source of income, the Court found a breach of Article 6. The applicant, who had been the subject of tax evasion proceedings, was fined for non-compliance with the participatory requirements. The decision in this case was reached despite the Court relying on *Saunders* and citing the distinction between material having an existence independent of the will of the suspect and material obtained through defiance of the suspect's will. It has been described as a 'very poorly reasoned' judgment, with the Court failing to notice that the documents fell within the first category of material.[85]

Determining whether a particular type of material has an existence independent of the will of the suspect is not a straightforward task. In *R v S(F)*,[86] the appellants

82 A L-T Choo, *The Privilege Against Self-Incrimination and Criminal Justice* (Oxford, Hart Publishing, 2013) 115.
83 *Saunders v UK* (1997) 23 EHRR 313 [69].
84 App no 31827/96 (ECHR, 3 May 2001).
85 I Dennis, *The Law of Evidence,* 5th edn (London, Sweet & Maxwell, 2013) 168.
86 [2008] EWCA Crim 2177, [2009] 1 WLR 1489.

had been prosecuted under section 53(1) of the Regulation of Investigatory Powers Act 2000 for not complying with a requirement to disclose encryption keys to locked computer files. The Court of Appeal had to decide whether the encryption keys were covered by the privilege. The Court held that they were not. Even if the key was retained only in the appellant's memory, it had an existence of its own; it was thought to be no different to the key to a locked drawer. The Court also reasoned that the key itself is neutral, though *knowledge* of the key *may* be an incriminating fact if it unlocks incriminatory material. Where this is the case, it is open to the trial judge to use section 78 of PACE 1984 to exclude evidence of the means by which the prosecution gained access to the material.[87] To summarise, while the key, and the material obtained by means of the key, have an existence independent of the suspect's will, knowledge of the key *may* be covered by the privilege if the material obtained renders that knowledge incriminating. If this is the case, the judge can use her discretion to exclude evidence of such knowledge. If necessary to ensure fairness, the underlying material and the key may also be excluded.[88] Choo has noted that, although a detailed and interesting decision, it 'leaves one none the wiser as to the precise scope of the privilege as it pertains to information of the type in question'.[89]

In addition to the confusion created by the distinction, the courts have shown a willingness to depart from it. In *Jalloh v Germany*,[90] the European Court held that the privilege applied to the use of evidence obtained through the forcible administration of emetics. The relevant evidence was a bag of cocaine swallowed by the applicant. The bag of cocaine fell into the category of material having an existence independent of the will of the suspect, the use of which is generally not prohibited in criminal proceedings. However, there were several elements held to distinguish it from the examples of such material given in *Saunders*. These were: that the administration of emetics was used to retrieve real evidence in defiance of the applicant's will; that the degree of force used to obtain the evidence differed significantly from that normally required to obtain the types of material referred to in *Saunders* which can usually be produced through the normal functioning of the body; and that the evidence was obtained through a procedure which violated the applicant's right not to be subject to torture or inhuman or degrading treatment under Article 3.[91]

It was settled in *Jalloh* that incriminating evidence obtained through torture should never be relied on as proof of guilt, but the Court left open the question of whether the use of real evidence obtained through inhuman or degrading treatment always rendered a trial unfair. This question arose for consideration in

87 ibid [20]–[24].
88 ibid [25].
89 A L-T Choo, *The Privilege Against Self-Incrimination and Criminal Justice* (Oxford, Hart Publishing, 2013) 50.
90 (2007) 44 EHRR 32.
91 ibid [113]–[116].

Gafgen v Germany.[92] The applicant in this case had been accused of kidnap and murder, and had been subjected to real and immediate threats of torture by the police in order to gain a confession and acquire the location of the victim. This amounted to inhuman treatment. The Court confirmed that the use of confessions and statements obtained in breach of Article 3 would always render proceedings unfair. In relation to real evidence, however, it held that the fairness of the trial was only compromised by inhuman treatment if the admission of the impugned evidence had a bearing on the outcome of the proceedings against the defendant. In this case it did not, hence there was no violation of the privilege against self-incrimination.[93]

It is curious why there should be a distinction between material which does and does not have an existence independent of the will of the suspect. In *Brown v Stott*,[94] Lord Bingham noted that the distinction between answering questions and providing physical samples should not be pushed too far. Referring to the facts of the case, he maintained that while it is true that the answer to a question would create new evidence which did not exist previously, it may also be acknowledged that, although the percentage of alcohol in one's blood is a fact existing before being tested, the whole purpose of requiring a person to blow into a breathalyser is to obtain evidence not available until that has been done.[95] Moreover, providing physical samples can be more invasive than requiring answers to questions. It is not easy to comprehend why a requirement to answer a question is objectionable, whereas a requirement to undergo a breath test, or provide other incriminating evidence, is not.

Ward and Gardner went some way to finding logic in *Saunders*: as a result of the distinction, the privilege would serve to prevent the use at trial of material obtained 'through the *active co-operation* of the accused'.[96] Applying this logic, documents discovered by investigating authorities 'pursuant to a warrant' would fall outside of the scope of the privilege, whereas requiring a suspect to hand over documents would fall within the scope of the privilege.[97] However, in order to obtain bodily samples, the suspect may have to take positive steps. For this interpretation of the privilege to be consistent with a 'no-assistance' approach, all independently existing material would need to be obtained by force.

92 (2011) 52 EHRR 1.

93 ibid [173]–[188]. On the relationship between Article 6 and Article 3, see A Ashworth, 'The Exclusion of Evidence Obtained by Violating a Fundamental Right: Pragmatism Before Principle in the Strasbourg Jurisprudence' in P Roberts and J Hunter (eds), *Criminal Evidence and Human Rights: Reimagining Common Law Procedural Traditions* (Oxford, Hart Publishing, 2012).

94 [2003] 1 AC 681 (PC).

95 ibid 705.

96 T Ward and P Gardner, 'The Privilege Against Self-Incrimination: In Search of Legal Certainty' [2003] *European Human Rights Law Review* 388, 392. Original emphasis.

97 M Redmayne, 'Rethinking the Privilege Against Self-Incrimination' (2007) 27 *Oxford Journal of Legal Studies* 209, 214–215.

To obtain material by force would be consistent with the normative perspective advanced in this book. From this perspective, the scope of the privilege should be interpreted broadly, such that it applies to all manner of information, including that which has an existence independent of our will. In accordance with this position, the privilege is means, not material based.[98] It applies to a certain means of obtaining information, a means that requires active cooperation, rather than a particular type of information.[99] If real evidence, including documents and physical samples, are forcibly taken then the privilege is not breached. This is not to condone the use of force, but to regard it as an issue which falls outside of the scope of the privilege. Indeed, while there may be no objection to forcibly taking fingerprints,[100] the use of emetics would remain contrary to Article 3.[101] In accordance with this position, the privilege is breached when material is obtained by threatening suspects with prosecution for non-cooperation, and not when that material can be obtained without cooperation. However, this is not the practical reality. Post-*Saunders* cases have upheld requirements for active cooperation of the suspect in providing both pre-existing material and material dependent on his will.

5.3.3 A proportionality approach

In the case of *Brown v Stott*, the Privy Council declined to follow the distinction drawn by the European Court, regarding the type of material sought to be obtained. Instead, the Privy Council took a proportionality approach to the privilege against self-incrimination, finding that it is not absolute and can be balanced against the general interests of the community. The applicant, who had been suspected of drink-driving, had been compelled, under section 172 of the Road Traffic Act 1988, to incriminate herself by telling the police who had been driving her car. She was also required to provide a breath sample which proved positive for alcohol. The Privy Council held that there would be no violation of Article 6 if the evidence obtained were used against her at a criminal trial. Ultimately, the privilege was limited on the same proportionality basis as qualified Convention rights; namely that the single simple question put to the applicant was proportionate to the legitimate aim of road safety.[102] Lord Bingham summed up his position as follows:

> If, viewing this situation in the round, one asks whether section 172 represents a disproportionate legislative response to the problem of maintaining road

98 ibid 215.

99 ibid.

100 The police have powers to obtain fingerprints, footwear impressions and non-intimate bodily samples by force under PACE 1984, ss 61–63A.

101 However, this position is contrary to the decision in *Jalloh*, where the use of force actually engaged the privilege.

102 *Brown v Stott* [2003] 1 AC 681 (PC) 704–706.

> safety, whether the balance between the interests of the community at large and the interests of the individual is struck in a manner unduly prejudicial to the individual, whether (in short) the leading of this evidence would infringe a basic human right of the defendant, I would feel bound to give negative answers.[103]

This type of public interest reasoning had previously been dismissed by Strasbourg in *Funke,* as well as in *Saunders* where the Court rejected an argument that the public interest in the investigation of corporate fraud could justify a departure from the privilege.[104] In *Heaney and McGuinness v Ireland,*[105] the applicants were suspected of involvement in a terrorist bombing which resulted in several deaths and injuries. They had been required to account for their movements during a specific 24 hour period. Failure to meet this requirement was a criminal offence of which the applicants were convicted. The European Court held that the requirement to provide the information could not be justified on security and public order grounds. It was also held that any interference with the privilege must not destroy its 'very essence'.[106] However, the Court gave no clear indication of what constitutes the 'very essence' of the privilege against self-incrimination.[107]

More recent cases have seen the European Court open up to a proportionality approach, rather than focus on the type of material sought to be obtained. The turning point appears to be the case of *Jalloh,* in which the Court set out four factors to determine violations of the right. These were: 1) the nature and degree of compulsion used to obtain the evidence; 2) the weight of the public interest in the investigation and punishment of the offence in question; 3) the existence of any relevant safeguards in the procedure; and 4) the use to which any material so obtained is put.[108] Most significant is the reference to the public interest in the investigation and punishment of the offence. It contradicts the decisions in *Funke, Saunders* and *Heaney,* but it does follow Lord Bingham's approach to the issue in *Brown v Stott.* Taken together, the factors presented in *Jalloh* draw significant parallels with the *Brown v Stott* judgment, and show the European Court leaning towards a very limited scope for the privilege, based on proportionality.

This new proportionality approach was evident in *O'Halloran and Francis v UK.*[109] This case involved the same provision of the Road Traffic Act 1988 as *Brown v Stott.* Under section 172 of the Act, failure of a car owner to declare who

103 ibid 705–706.
104 *Saunders v UK* (1997) 23 EHRR 313 [74].
105 (2001) 33 EHRR 12.
106 ibid [55].
107 See L Hoyano, 'What is Balanced in the Scales of Justice? In Search of the Essence of the Right to a Fair Trial' [2014] *Crim LR* 4; A L-T Choo, *The Privilege Against Self-Incrimination and Criminal Justice* (Oxford, Hart Publishing, 2013) ch 4.
108 *Jalloh v Germany* (2007) 44 EHRR 32 [117].
109 (2008) 46 EHRR 21.

was driving their car at a specific time is a criminal offence punishable by a fine and penalty points. The vehicles registered to the two applicants in *O'Halloran* had been caught speeding. They were each asked to provide the name and address of the driver of the vehicle at the relevant time and were informed that failure to comply was a criminal offence. Mr O'Halloran named himself as the driver and, as a result, was convicted of the driving offence. Mr Francis, on the other hand, refused to supply the information and was convicted for his failure to comply. As this was a case of direct compulsion in a criminal investigation to provide information dependent on the will of the suspect, and was subject to criminal prosecution for non-compliance, it fell squarely within the scope of the privilege as set out in *Saunders*.

In finding that the privilege had not been breached, the Court considered three of the factors set out in *Jalloh*. As to the nature and degree of compulsion, the Court found that, although the compulsion was direct and criminal, it was limited in nature.[110] As to the existence of relevant safeguards, the Court relied on section 172(4), which provides that no offence is committed if the keeper of the vehicle did not know and could not with reasonable diligence have known who the driver of the vehicle was.[111] As to the use to which the information is put, the Court reasoned that, although the statement can be used against a defendant, the identity of the driver is only one element of the offence and cannot in itself found a conviction.[112] This reasoning, which was also presented in *Brown v Stott*, is particularly unconvincing. It is obvious that, in certain circumstances, for an individual to state that they were the driver of a car will be tantamount to a confession of an offence.

The Court did not have explicit regard for the public interest. However, the approach seems to be one of proportionality in all but name, being based on a weighting of various factors in the particular context.[113] Of particular significance is the fact that the Court followed a line of reasoning presented in *Brown v Stott*, namely that although there was direct compulsion, this flowed from the regulatory regime to which car owners and drivers are subject:

> Those who choose to keep and drive motor cars can be taken to have accepted certain responsibilities and obligations as part of the regulatory regime relating to motor vehicles, and in the legal framework of the United Kingdom these responsibilities include the obligation, in the event of suspected commission of road-traffic offences, to inform the authorities of the identity of the driver on that occasion.[114]

110 ibid [56]–[59].
111 ibid [59].
112 ibid [60]–[62].
113 I Dennis, *The Law of Evidence*, 5th edn (London, Sweet & Maxwell, 2013) 167.
114 *O'Halloran and Francis v UK* (2008) 46 EHRR 21 [57].

In a powerful dissent, Judge Pavlovschi found that the majority decision in *O'Halloran* was not only wrong, but also 'an extremely dangerous approach'.[115] He stated that:

> [I]n the particular circumstances of the case, compelling an accused to provide self-incriminating evidence contrary to his will under the threat of criminal prosecution amounts to a kind of compulsion which runs counter to the notion of a fair trial and, accordingly, is incompatible with the Convention standards.[116]

As to the 'regulatory regime' imposed on car owners, this new criterion is incompatible with the established case law on the privilege. In addition, applying public interest considerations to one particular context paves the way for further limitation to the privilege, in relation to other types of crime. Judge Pavlovschi fears that:

> [I]f one begins seeking to justify departures from the basic principles of modern criminal procedure and the very essence of the notion of a fair trial for reasons of policy, and if the Court starts accepting such reasons, we will face a real threat to the European public order as protected by the Convention.[117]

In their dissenting opinion in *Weh v Austria*,[118] Judges Lorenzen, Levits and Hajiyev also expressed concern about balancing the public interest in road safety against the privilege against self-incrimination. They submitted that provisions requiring car owners, on pain of penalty, to admit driving their car at the time of a specific offence will require them to provide the prosecution with a major element of evidence, leaving them with limited possibilities of defence in the subsequent criminal proceedings. Seen in this light, the infringement of the privilege does not appear proportionate to the aim of road safety. They felt that the vital public interest in the prosecution of traffic offences could not justify a departure from the basic principles of a fair procedure.[119]

A number of academics have also commented on the merit and consequences of founding decisions on public interest arguments. Ashworth, for example, fears that, having stepped away from key points in its *Saunders* judgment, the European Court will come to regard the privilege as capable of being traded off against the

115 ibid [O-II20].
116 ibid [O-II53].
117 ibid [O-II66].
118 (2005) 40 EHRR 37.
119 ibid [O-I4].

public interest.[120] Once the privilege is opened up to a broad balancing exercise, every case in which it is engaged should be decided according to the balance between the privilege and the interests of the public.[121] If this position is reached, the privilege might lose its symbolic significance and become devalued.[122]

One cannot deny that the prosecution of road traffic offences would be difficult without the cooperation of the accused. Throughout Europe, various legislative techniques have been adopted in order to prosecute road traffic offences effectively. These include drawing inferences from a failure to provide the requested information, and statutory rebuttable presumptions of fact that the registered owner of the vehicle was the driver in question. Neither of these methods can provide an adequate alternative to limiting the privilege; the latter engages the right to silence and the former compromises the presumption of innocence.[123] Nevertheless, there is a degree of international consensus as to the necessity of defendant participation in order to effectively prosecute road traffic offences. Within England and Wales, restrictions to the privilege might, therefore, be justified as a practical necessity rather than as proportionate to a legitimate aim.

Before settling on this conclusion, however, one could look to whether there are any practical measures that could be put in place during the investigative stage of the criminal process, such that the accused's participation is not necessary. For example, rather than rely solely on speed cameras, police officers could routinely patrol roads. The officer would be able to identify the driver of the vehicle at the time of commission of an offence. Alternatively, the quality of speed cameras could be improved, such that they capture the face of the individual driving the car. These measures are unlikely to appeal in practice, as they would require a significant amount of resources from a system currently focused on efficient criminal justice. Moreover, they would be an inadequate means of obtaining evidence for certain offences. For example, if an individual is suspected of drink-driving, it is only possible to know the level of alcohol in their system if a breath test is conducted. Given the obvious difficulties in obtaining a breath sample by force, this would continue to require the active cooperation of the accused.

120 A Ashworth, 'Case Comment: Human Rights: Article 6(1) – Privilege Against Self-Incrimination – Offence Under the Road Traffic Act 1988 s.172 of Failing to Furnish Information' [2007] *Crim LR* 897, 900.

121 ibid 899. This concern was also raised by Judge Pavlovschi in his dissenting opinion in *O'Halloran and Francis v UK*, and by Redmayne in his discussion of *Brown v Stott*. See M Redmayne, 'Rethinking the Privilege Against Self-Incrimination' (2007) 27 *Oxford Journal of Legal Studies* 209, 229.

122 A L-T Choo, *The Privilege Against Self-Incrimination and Criminal Justice* (Oxford, Hart Publishing, 2013) 67.

123 A Ashworth, 'Case Comment: Human Rights: Article 6(1) – Privilege Against Self-Incrimination – Offence Under the Road Traffic Act 1988 s.172 of Failing to Furnish Information' [2007] *Crim LR* 897, 898.

Owing to the difficulties that would inevitably be encountered in the absence of compelled participation, there may be strength in the argument that road traffic offences constitute a special class of offences which should be singled out as an exception to the privilege. Such an argument could be founded on the courts' logic that those who own or drive motor cars knowingly enter into a regulated regime, which includes requirements to provide certain information which may be incriminating.[124] As it stands, however, individuals cannot truly be said to have entered into this aspect of the regime ***knowingly***. They are not given notice that owning or driving a vehicle includes a requirement to relinquish the fundamental right not to incriminate oneself. If drivers, upon receiving or applying for their licence, or vehicle owners, upon purchase of a vehicle, were to be informed that they may be required to incriminate themselves, the argument would be stronger. The individual could decide whether he or she is willing to sacrifice his or her Article 6 right in return for the benefits of owning or driving a vehicle. In all likelihood, the vast majority of individuals would accept this condition. An exception to the privilege against self-incrimination could, therefore, be justified under the following conditions:

1) the individual made a voluntary decision to enter into a particular regulated activity;
2) the regulation of the activity is enforced through criminal laws which it would be impracticable to prosecute without the individual's cooperation;
3) before making their decision to enter into the activity, the individual was expressly informed that, as part of a regulatory regime, he or she may be required to incriminate him- or herself on some later occasion.

These conditions have been developed with road traffic offences in mind. They could, however, be extended to other regulated regimes that pose a serious risk to public safety and which are enforced through the criminal law. However, any extension should be approached cautiously, and apply only to regulated activities where there is a degree of international consensus that defendant cooperation is necessary for effective prosecution.

5.4 Reconsidering the scope of the privilege against self-incrimination

As a result of cases such as *Jalloh* and *O'Halloran*, it has become increasingly difficult to determine when, in practice, it is considered acceptable to penalise a failure to participate in the criminal process. As it stands, the privilege does not seem to apply to information obtained during administrative investigations where

124 *Brown v Stott* [2003] 1 AC 681 (PC) 705; *O'Halloran and Francis v UK* (2008) 46 EHRR 21 [57].

that information may not subsequently be used in criminal proceedings. In relation to criminal proceedings, it does not seem to apply to the gathering or use of information which has an existence independent of the will of the suspect, except sometimes where obtaining that information would violate the suspect's Article 3 rights. This is subject, however, to the persistent confusion as to when pre-existing documents fall within the scope of the privilege. In addition, an exception to the privilege has been recognised in relation to information dependent on the will of the suspect which it is necessary to obtain in the public interest of road safety (but not for the prevention of terrorism or fraud).

Although the European Court initially granted the privilege status as an Article 6 right in a decision which left it open to a broad interpretation, it has since been upholding restrictions to its application in confusing and inconsistent judgments. The continuation of such an approach leaves little hope for a process in which the use of state power to compel the participation of the accused is viewed as unacceptable. Moreover, despite the fact that the core of the protection afforded by the privilege is immunity from providing information, there has been a tendency to focus on unfairness at the trial stage. In other words, in determining breaches of Article 6, the courts have been less concerned with requirements to participate and more concerned with whether reliance on compulsorily obtained evidence would cause unfairness at trial.[125] This could lead to the conclusion that, even where the privilege is applicable, the right to a fair trial is not violated by requiring information (or penalising a failure to comply) because the fairness of the trial can be ensured through the exclusion of that information, applying section 78 of PACE 1984.

Taking this further, one might question the merit of having a privilege against self-incrimination in the first place. Given the availability of use immunity provisions and section 78, as well as the proportionality approach adopted by the courts, the privilege, as it currently applies, can have little impact on the prosecution of criminal offences. One possible counter argument is that the privilege is necessary compensation for the absence of sufficient safeguards for the defence at the investigative stage of the criminal process. These safeguards apply principally during police questioning and should include access to legal advice, disclosure of the evidence against the accused and a guarantee of an authenticated recording of any interview, *before* questioning or compulsion takes place.[126] Such safeguards could facilitate informed defence participation. With this in place, one could argue that the privilege would no longer be necessary as partial compensation for inadequately regulated evidence-gathering.[127] However, the privilege does more

125 See, for example, *Saunders v UK* (1997) 23 EHRR 313; *R v S(F)* [2008] EWCA Crim 2177, [2009] 1 WLR 1489; *Beghal v DPP* [2015] UKSC 49, [2015] 3 WLR 344. See also A L-T Choo, *The Privilege Against Self-Incrimination and Criminal Justice* (Oxford, Hart Publishing, 2013) 50, 115.

126 J Jackson and S Summers, *The Internationalisation of Criminal Evidence: Beyond the Common Law and Civil Law Traditions* (Cambridge, Cambridge University Press, 2012) 275.

127 A L-T Choo, *The Privilege Against Self-Incrimination and Criminal Justice* (Oxford, Hart Publishing, 2013) 118.

than replace insufficient pre-trial procedures. What seems most pertinent about the privilege is the impact that it can have on our relationship as individuals with the state; its ability to uphold certain elements of liberal democracy by ensuring our freedom to choose participation, rather than have it forced upon us, and by allowing us to disassociate ourselves from the goals of the state.

By restricting the breadth of the privilege in such a way that allows the state to compel its citizens to participate in the criminal process, English criminal procedure has shifted further away from its adversarial history, and the ideals which accompany voluntary participation. The value of the defendant's participation in acquiring evidence and contributing to efficient fact-finding has been afforded greater weight than concern for his fundamental rights. Conversely, in a system based on calling the state to account, the privilege must be afforded a broad scope. No distinction should be drawn between requirements to speak and requirements to provide the authorities with documents, blood samples and the like. Where these can be obtained without the active cooperation of the accused, no issues surrounding the privilege arise, as the accused has not been required to incriminate himself.

The key point is that the accused should not be required to actively participate or assist in proceedings against himself. This means that, in the context of the criminal process, the privilege should protect against both a requirement to supply information and the use of such information at a subsequent trial. Following this position, the privilege should not be abrogated on proportionality grounds. However, as outlined in the preceding section, limited exceptions may be justified where the accused had voluntarily entered into a regulated activity, with the knowledge that he may become required to incriminate himself. Adopting this very wide scope of the privilege is unlikely to have major practical consequences, as few suspects rely on the privilege and the majority of defendants plead guilty.[128] Far from providing a reason to abolish the privilege, this can support an argument in favour of its retention; we can take seriously a fundamental right without substantially constraining the aim of accurate fact-finding.[129]

The current scope of the privilege against self-incrimination has resulted, at least in part, from the weakness of the main justifications for it.[130] Without having a clear understanding of what the privilege is for, it is difficult to know where to draw the line. Likewise, without a clear scope of the privilege, it will remain difficult to determine just what purpose it is intended to serve. Yet, if we can take value in the privilege as a mechanism for reinforcing the boundaries of the state's relationship with its citizens, and accept that these boundaries include the notion that the state should not compel the active participation of the accused, then not only does the privilege have a purpose, but there is also a means for determining

128 See Royal Commission on Criminal Justice, *Report* (Cm 2263, 1993) 53–54.

129 A L-T Choo, *The Privilege Against Self-Incrimination and Criminal Justice* (Oxford, Hart Publishing, 2013) 119.

130 I Dennis, 'Instrumental Protection, Human Right or Functional Necessity? Reassessing the Privilege Against Self-Incrimination' (1995) 54 *Cambridge Law Journal* 342, 373.

its scope. This scope should be broad, prohibiting any requirement on the accused to take active steps to incriminate himself, unless previously agreed to as a condition of a regulated activity. Such a conception of the privilege would help ensure that the process aims of accurate fact-finding and conflict resolution are pursued without interfering with the necessary constraints which legitimise the process.

6 The right to silence

Like the privilege against self-incrimination, the right to silence can protect the accused's autonomy; it provides the freedom to choose whether or not to respond to official questioning in relation to a criminal offence. It can also prevent co-opted assistance to the state. Responses to questions may assist the state by providing, or leading to the discovery of, incriminating or falsely incriminating evidence. The right to silence can, therefore, be rationalised on similar grounds as the privilege against self-incrimination, namely that it can regulate and reinforce the proper relationship between citizen and state, while protecting against abuse of power and affording some protection against wrongful conviction.[1] The right to silence is, however, more specific than the privilege, as it does not apply in relation to the production of information through means other than speaking, such as documentary evidence.[2] Yet, there is little consensus regarding what the right to silence specifically entails or what the legal significance of silence should be. It has changed over time and has a variety of applications.[3]

If defined as an absolute right, the right to silence would protect suspects and defendants from being adversely affected by their refusal to answer questions or give testimony in criminal proceedings. This would grant the accused maximum freedom to decide whether to actively participate by speaking. Although there has never been an absolute right to silence, it has been substantially curtailed by sections 34 through 38 of the Criminal Justice and Public Order Act 1994 (CJPOA 1994). These provisions have qualified the right to silence by providing that, subject to certain requirements, adverse inferences may be drawn from: a failure to mention to the police a fact later relied on;[4] a failure to account to the police for certain suspicious circumstances;[5] and silence in court.[6] The provisions

1 See chs 5.1 and 5.2.

2 In practice, the privilege against self-incrimination has been interpreted such that it does not apply to evidence which exists independent of the will of the accused. *Saunders v UK* (1997) 23 EHRR 313. See ch 5.3.

3 See the six immunities identified by Lord Mustill in *R v Director of Serious Fraud Office, ex p Smith* [1993] AC 1 (HL) 30–31.

4 Criminal Justice and Public Order Act 1994 (CJPOA 1994), s 34.

5 ibid ss 36 and 37.

6 ibid s 35.

penalise both suspects and defendants who refuse to participate by expressly allowing, if not encouraging, silence to be used as evidence of guilt.[7] This creates an 'indirect compulsion' to speak.[8] The CJPOA 1994 is incompatible with a 'no-assistance' approach to the defendant's role in the criminal process; the defendant is expected to assist the state by speaking or else risk his silence being used to assist the state, as evidence of guilt.

The CJPOA 1994 does not place the accused under a legal obligation to answer questions. Since it is not an offence or contempt to remain silent, one can maintain that the right to silence continues to exist.[9] Yet, by attaching a significant consequence to silence, the decision to speak cannot be described as truly voluntary. This chapter begins with a brief explanation of the pre-1994 approach to silence and the debate which led to the enactment of the CJPOA 1994. It then examines the applicability of the individual statutory provisions and their impact on defendant participation. Finally, the right to silence is considered from a normative perspective, in the light of the impact which the CJPOA 1994 has had on fairness norms and the nature of criminal procedure.

6.1 Silence at common law

6.1.1 Pre-trial silence

The right to silence became an enforceable right with the rise of adversarialism during the eighteenth century.[10] However, it has never been an absolute right. At common law, silence in the face of accusations from other citizens could be treated as acceptance of those accusations, since the accuser and accused are assumed to be on equal terms.[11] Silence in the face of accusations from police, before caution,[12] could also be treated as acceptance, again because the police and the accused are thought to be on equal terms, particularly when a solicitor is present.[13] Silence as a response to police questioning after caution could never warrant comment from the prosecution, but sometimes could from the judge or co-accused. However, the precise scope for judicial comment on post-caution silence was uncertain.[14]

Broadly speaking, the fact of silence could sometimes be used by the jury to affect the weight which should be attached to a defence put forward at trial, but juries could not explicitly be invited to draw an inference of guilt from the earlier

7 Silence can provide 'additional support' for the prosecution case. Judicial Studies Board, *Crown Court Bench Book: Directing the Jury* (Judicial Studies Board, 2010) 393.

8 See *Murray v UK* (1996) 22 EHRR 29 [50].

9 CJPOA 1994, s 35(4). See also *Murray v UK* (1996) 22 EHRR 29 [48]; *Condron v UK* (2001) 31 EHRR 1 [59].

10 See ch 4.2.

11 *R v Christie* [1914] AC 545 (HL); *Parkes v R* [1976] 1 WLR 1251 (PC).

12 The police are required to caution a person when they have grounds to suspect him or her of committing an offence. The caution includes a statement of the right to silence. See Police and Criminal Evidence Act 1984 (PACE 1984), Code C, paras 10.1 and 10.5.

13 *R v Chandler* [1976] 1 WLR 585 (CA).

14 See *R v Gilbert* (1978) 66 Cr App R 237 (CA).

silence.[15] The distinction between silence as evidence of guilt and silence as affecting the weight of other evidence is not obvious. The latter may sometimes amount to no more than an indirect way of inferring the former.[16] Nonetheless, the defendant's pre-trial silence was afforded greater protection at common law than it is under the CJPOA 1994. Sections 34, 36 and 37 of the 1994 Act have explicitly increased the evidential significance of silence after caution. When evidence of silence falls outside of the scope of the CJPOA 1994, the common law still applies.[17] This preserves the principle that inferences can be drawn from a suspect's failure to deny accusations put to him by other citizens or put to him by the police prior to caution, where they are speaking on equal terms.[18]

6.1.2 Trial silence

The defendant became a competent witness on his own behalf by virtue of section 1 of the Criminal Evidence Act 1898. The 1898 Act was one of the final developments in the emergence of the adversarial system which had been gradually increasing the competency of defence witnesses. Prior to the 1898 Act, the defendant could only give an unsworn statement. The reason for this is unclear, but possible explanations include, concern about the reliability of the defendant as a witness, preventing the defendant from committing perjury and protection of the integrity of the oath as a guarantor of truth.[19] Until the establishment of full defence counsel in the nineteenth century, the defendant was expected to give unsworn evidence, refuting the charges against him. The precise evidential status of unsworn statements was obscure and they probably carried less weight than sworn statements. However, they allowed the defendant to tell his side of the story without being subject to cross-examination. The practice continued until its abolition by the Criminal Justice Act 1982.[20]

Section 1(a) of the Criminal Evidence Act 1898 granted the defendant competency as a witness, while section 1(b) prevented the defendant's silence from being the subject of any comment by the prosecution. The Act did not expressly prevent the judge or co-defendant from passing comment. Co-defendants were provided with a right to comment,[21] but the judicial position was less clear and a good deal of inconsistent case law ensued.[22] Shortly before the CJPOA 1994

15 *R v Ryan* (1966) 50 Cr App R 144 (CA); *R v Sullivan* (1966) 51 Cr App R 102 (CA); *R v Gilbert* (1978) 66 Cr App R 237 (CA).

16 *R v Gilbert* (1978) 66 Cr App R 237 (CA) 244–245.

17 CJPOA 1994, ss 34(5), 36(6) and 37(5).

18 See, for example, *R v Collins* [2004] EWCA Crim 83, [2004] 1 WLR 1705.

19 See P McInerney, 'The Privilege Against Self-Incrimination from Early Origins to Judges' Rules: Challenging the "Orthodox View"' (2014) 18 *E&P* 101, 114–117.

20 Criminal Justice Act 1982, s 78 and sch 16.

21 *R v Wickham* (1971) 55 Cr App R 199 (CA).

22 See *R v Rhodes* [1899] 1 QB 77 (CCR); *Waugh v R* [1950] AC 203 (PC); *R v Bathurst* [1968] 2 QB 99 (CA); *R v Sparrow* [1973] 1 WLR 488 (CA); *R v Mutch* [1973] 1 All ER 178 (CA).

came into force, the Court of Appeal reviewed the position. In the case of *Martinez-Tobon*, the Court summarised the principles that applied at common law where a defendant did not testify as follows:

> (1) The judge should give the jury a direction along the lines of the Judicial Studies Board specimen direction based on *R v Bathurst* [1968] 2 QB 99, 107. (2) The essentials of that direction are that the defendant is under no obligation to testify and the jury should not assume he is guilty because he has not given evidence. (3) Provided those essentials are complied with, the judge may think it appropriate to make a stronger comment where the defence case involves alleged facts which (a) are at variance with prosecution evidence or additional to it and exculpatory, and (b) must, if true, be within the knowledge of the defendant. (4) The nature and strength of such comment must be a matter for the discretion of the judge and will depend upon the circumstances of the individual case. However, it must not be such as to contradict or nullify the essentials of the conventional direction.[23]

If directed properly, it would have been clear to the jury that the defendant is under no obligation to actively participate at his trial and that it is the state, through the prosecution, that must account for the allegations against him. Adverse judicial comment could only be made in 'confession and avoidance' cases, meaning that a positive defence was raised which had a factual basis within the defendant's knowledge. However, even in cases that only called for the traditional *Bathurst* direction, a defendant might have been inhibited from remaining silent for fear that the jury would hold it against him. Whether this fear went beyond what one would experience in the absence of any judicial comment or direction is questionable. On the one hand, the *Bathurst* direction may have drawn the jury's attention to something they would otherwise have thought to be inconsequential. On the other hand, it may have acted to restrict how they took account of silence, by emphasising the existence of the right to silence and the fact that silence is not evidence of guilt. Since the disclosure or solicitation of information about jury deliberations is prohibited in England and Wales,[24] there is no available research on the impact of silence on jurors. While it is difficult to determine the impact of judicial comment on the defendant, the boundaries of acceptable comment were significantly more restricted at common law than they are under section 35 of the CJPOA 1994.

6.2 Reform to the right to silence

Prior to enactment of the CJPOA 1994, reform to the law on the right to silence had been considered by numerous committees, commissions and working

23 *R v Martinez-Tobon* [1994] 1 WLR 388 (CA) 397.
24 Juries Act 1974, s 20D.

groups.[25] Under consideration was whether greater account should be taken of an accused's silence in determinations of guilt. This issue was also raised in public speeches by politicians, legal professionals and senior police officers who believed the right was being exploited by 'professional criminals'.[26] Those in favour of amending the right to silence included the police service, Crown Prosecution Service (CPS) and many judges.[27] Their criticisms of the right echoed those of Jeremy Bentham from nearly 200 years ago. Bentham famously proclaimed that, 'Innocence claims the right of speaking, as guilt invokes the privilege of silence.'[28] Following this line of reasoning, silence in the face of accusations might be thought to constitute evidence of guilt;[29] denying consideration of such evidence could impede accurate fact-finding. More cautiously, one could argue that silence is an indicator of guilt, capable of undermining the defence's case at trial. Among other arguments in favour of reform was a view that silence operates as a barrier to the efficient progression of a case. Many police officers took the view that, by remaining silent, suspects seriously impede efforts to investigate crime.[30] In accordance with this line of reasoning, by encouraging suspects to talk at an early stage, police questioning can be more productive.

As these arguments show, reform to the right to silence was largely in pursuit of efficient fact-finding. To this end, reform was also intended to curb the use of ambush defences. There is no official definition of an ambush defence, but the term generally refers to the production of defence evidence at a time which hinders the prosecution. An ambush defence may take the form of a previously undisclosed positive defence, such as self-defence or an alibi, which is put forward at trial, catching the prosecution off guard. Alternatively, an ambush defence may take the form of a failure to point out mistakes of law or prosecution errors, such as mistakes on the indictment, until too late to rectify them.[31] Reform to the right

25 See, for example, Criminal Law Revision Committee, *Eleventh Report, Evidence (General)* (Cmnd 4991, 1972); Royal Commission on Criminal Procedure, *Report* (Cmnd 8092, 1981); Home Office Working Group on the Right of Silence, *Report* (London, HMSO, 1989); Royal Commission on Criminal Justice, *Report* (Cm 2263) (London, HMSO, 1993). See also S Easton, *Silence and Confessions: The Suspect as the Source of Evidence* (Basingstoke, Palgrave Macmillan, 2014) ch 2.

26 See, for example, the Dimbleby Lecture in 1973 by then Metropolitan Police Commissioner Sir Robert Mark and the 1987 Police Foundation Lecture by then Home Secretary Douglas Hurd.

27 Royal Commission on Criminal Justice, *Report* (Cm 2263, 1993) 50.

28 J Bentham, *Rationale of Judicial Evidence, Specially Applied to English Practice* (London, Hunt & Clarke, 1827).

29 This reasoning was relied on by the Criminal Law Revision Committee. The Committee took the view that silence should be capable of amounting to corroboration of other evidence. See Criminal Law Revision Committee, *Eleventh Report, Evidence (General)* (Cmnd 4991, 1972).

30 Royal Commission on Criminal Justice, *Report* (Cm 2263, 1993) 51.

31 See, for example, *R v Gleeson* [2003] EWCA Crim 3357, [2004] 1 Cr App R 29.

to silence was primarily aimed at the former type of ambush defence.[32] Ambush defences, one could argue, both impede accurate fact-finding and slow down the trial process. The threat of inferences being drawn from silence at the pre-trial stage might encourage a defendant to adopt a consistent account of events.

However, ambush defences were not as significant a problem as suggested by pro-reformers. In a study undertaken on behalf of the Royal Commission on Criminal Justice, Leng found that the proportion of contested cases in which ambush defences were raised was at most 5 per cent.[33] Similarly, in the Crown Court Study, Zander and Henderson found that prosecution counsel and the CPS saw ambush defences in 7 to 10 per cent of cases, and that these cases were more likely to end in conviction than acquittal.[34] Arguably, the very small minority of cases in which silence could lead to a successful ambush did not justify fundamental reform to the law on the right to silence, particularly as there are a number of negative consequences of reform, as explained below and in the final section of this chapter. Moreover, if the prosecution is satisfied that there is sufficient evidence to proceed against an individual, it should be capable of addressing, or overcoming, the lines of defence that can arise in a particular case. In some cases, a successful 'ambush' may be attributable to a failure to properly investigate an alleged offence or prepare a case for trial,[35] rather than a deliberate ploy on the part of the defence to evade a rightful conviction.

Those who opposed reform to the right to silence included the Bar Council, the Law Society, the Criminal Bar Association and many academic commentators. There was concern that, by equating silence with guilt, innocent suspects and defendants would be put at risk of wrongful conviction.[36] They pointed to the many innocent explanations for silence. Pre-trial silence might be a response to, *inter alia*: an emotional and highly suggestible state of mind; ignorance of some vital facts which could explain away otherwise suspicious circumstances; confusion and liability to make mistakes which could be interpreted as deliberate lies; ill health; a poor understanding of English; seeking to protect others; a reluctance to admit to having done something discreditable but not illegal; fear of reprisal; or a generally negative conception of the police and thus a reluctance to cooperate with them.[37] Innocent explanations for silence at trial include: an unsympathetic

32 Royal Commission on Criminal Justice, *Report* (Cm 2263, 1993) 51; S Easton, *Silence and Confessions: The Suspect as the Source of Evidence* (Basingstoke, Palgrave Macmillan, 2014) 23.

33 R Leng, *The Right to Silence in Police Interrogation: A Study of Some of the Issues Underlying the Debate*, Royal Commission on Criminal Justice Research Study No. 10 (London, HMSO, 1993) 58.

34 See M Zander and P Henderson, *The Crown Court Study*, Royal Commission on Criminal Justice Research Study No. 19 (London, HMSO, 1993).

35 See M Zander, 'Consultation on Proposals for Advance Disclosure of Defence Witness Lists and Unused Defence Expert Witness Reports' (2002) 4–8. Available at <www.lse.ac.uk/collections/law/staff%20publications%20full%20text/zander/adv.discl..pdf> accessed 1 April 2016.

36 See S Greer, 'The Right to Silence: A Review of the Current Debate' (1990) 53 *MLR* 709.

37 ibid 727. See also Royal Commission on Criminal Justice, *Report* (Cm 2263, 1993) 52.

character; being vulnerable or suggestible; sensitive or embarrassing subject matter; a physical or mental condition falling short of that required to be unfit to plead; an inability to recall the incident in question; stress or anxiety; fear of undermining a co-defendant's case; or fear of reprisals.[38]

There was concern that reform would weaken the protection which the right to silence affords to innocent suspects, particularly during police interrogations. The threat of adverse inferences has the potential to increase the pressure on suspects in the police station to offer a false confession or disclose information that may be used against them. Those who resist the pressure to speak then face the risk of their silence being used against them as evidence of guilt. For these reasons, in 1993, the Royal Commission on Criminal Justice advised against reforming the right to silence. The majority of the Commission felt that:

> the possibility of an increase in the convictions of the guilty is outweighed by the risk that the extra pressure on suspects to talk in the police station and the adverse inferences invited if they do not may result in more convictions of the innocent.[39]

While the arguments against reform were focused on protecting the innocent,[40] they highlight the role which the right to silence can play in protecting all suspects against the abuse of power. The right can constrain the state's power by limiting the opportunity to coerce or compel accused persons to cooperate in procedures against themselves. The potential for abuse of law enforcement powers is at its greatest in relation to custodial interrogations, where there is also considerable physical and psychological pressure to cooperate. If taken to extremes, this pressure may produce confessions that are unreliable.[41] Those who succumb to the pressure may be misrepresented or misunderstood, may panic or get confused, and the police, whether maliciously or not, may take advantage of that.

Owing to the vulnerability of some suspects and the risk of abuse of power associated with custodial interrogation, there was, and continues to be, greater academic objection towards curtailing the right to silence in the police station than in court.[42] Yet, silence in the police station was the primary target of those in favour of reform. Reform to the right to silence at trial can have little impact on the efficient investigation of crime or on the prevalence of ambush defences. At the same time, reforming the right to silence in court was intended to do more than clarify the common law's position on judicial discretion to comment on

38 See Royal Commission on Criminal Justice, *Report* (Cm 2263, 1993) 52; T Bucke, R Street and D Brown, *The Right to Silence: The Impact of the Criminal Justice and Public Order Act 1994* (Home Office Research Study No. 199) (London, Home Office, 2000) 54–55.

39 Royal Commission on Criminal Justice, *Report* (Cm 2263, 1993) 54.

40 See R Leng, 'The Right to Silence Reformed: A Re-appraisal of the Royal Commission's Influence' (2001) 6 *Journal of Civil Liberties* 107.

41 I Dennis, *The Law of Evidence,* 5th edn (London, Sweet & Maxwell, 2013) 208.

42 ibid 208–209.

silence.[43] As will become clear, the purpose was to increase defendant participation, or else to provide the prosecution with additional evidence of guilt.

Arguably, the position of those opposed to reform was stronger than those in favour of it. Moreover, there appeared to be no practical need for reform. In summarising the pre-1994 research evidence on silence in the police station, the Royal Commission found that the right was exercised only in a minority of cases, and those who remained silent were more likely to plead guilty or be found guilty.[44] The research evidence neither confirmed nor refuted the suggestion that silence is used by a disproportionate number of experienced criminals who exploit the system in order to obtain an acquittal.[45] Ultimately, however, the arguments against reform to the right to silence were either ignored or thought to be unpersuasive. The CJPOA 1994 introduced provisions which have created an expectation of defendant participation and, as such, have had a substantial impact on the defendant's role in the criminal process, as well as the nature of criminal procedure. The provisions within the CJPOA 1994 are equivalent to those which had earlier been enacted in Northern Ireland, following concern that terrorist suspects were utilising the right to silence.[46]

6.3 Section 34

Section 34 Effect of accused's failure to mention facts when questioned or charged:

> (1) Where, in any proceedings against a person for an offence, evidence is given that the accused —
>
> > (a) at any time before he was charged with the offence, on being questioned under caution by a constable trying to discover whether or by whom the offence had been committed, failed to mention any fact relied on in his defence in those proceedings; or
> >
> > (b) on being charged with the offence or officially informed that he might be prosecuted for it, failed to mention any such fact
>
> . . .

43 *R v Cowan* [1996] QB 373 (CA) 378.

44 Research conducted prior to the CJPOA 1994 found that between 6 and 10 per cent of suspects outside of the Metropolitan police district remained silent in the police station to some extent. Within the Metropolitan police district the figure rose to between 14 and 16 per cent. See Royal Commission on Criminal Justice, *Report* (Cm 2263, 1993) 53–54. In a later study, also conducted prior to the CJPOA 1994, Phillips and Brown found that a total of 23 per cent of suspects refused to answer some or all of police questions. See C Phillips and D Brown, *Entry into the Criminal Justice System: A Survey of Police Arrests and their Outcomes* (Home Office Research Study No. 185) (London, Home Office, 1998) 75.

45 Royal Commission on Criminal Justice, *Report* (Cm 2263, 1993) 53.

46 However, the reforms were not restricted to alleged terrorist cases. See Criminal Evidence (Northern Ireland) Order 1988; J Jackson, 'Recent Developments in Criminal Evidence' (1989) 40 *Northern Ireland Legal Quarterly* 105.

being a fact which in the circumstances existing at the time the accused could reasonably have been expected to mention when so questioned, charged or informed, as the case may be, subsection (2) below applies.

(2) Where this subsection applies —

. . .

(c) the court, in determining whether there is a case to answer;

and

(d) the court or jury, in determining whether the accused is guilty of the offence charged,

may draw such inferences from the failure as appear proper.

Section 34 permits inferences to be drawn from a defendant's failure to mention to the police, when questioned under caution, a fact relied on at trial. However, if the fact is accepted by the prosecution to be true, an inference should not be drawn.[47] A broad approach has been taken to what constitutes a 'fact', such that it covers any alleged fact which is in issue and is put forward as part of the defence case, whether by the defendant, defence counsel or elicited from a witness.[48] The fact could be, for example, the nature of a defence, such as duress or self-defence, the defendant's whereabouts at a particular time or the defendant's affiliation with a particular witness. The fact must be one which, in the circumstances existing at the time of questioning, the defendant could reasonably have been expected to mention. When determining reasonableness, all of the circumstances in relation to the particular defendant, at the time he was questioned, can be taken into account. The broad nature of these circumstances include, *inter alia*, time of day, age, experience, mental capacity, state of health, sobriety, tiredness, knowledge, personality and legal advice.[49] It is for the jury to make the assessment of reasonableness. While the courts have the power to withdraw inferences from the jury, they have been reluctant to do so on the grounds that the defendant's silence was reasonable because, for example, he had acted on legal advice[50] or was suffering from drug withdrawal.[51]

The inferences that can be drawn are those that 'appear proper'.[52] In the context of section 34, this is likely to be an inference that the fact not mentioned during police questioning, but relied on at trial, was recently fabricated or could not

47 *R v Wisdom and Sinclair* (CA, 10 December 1999); *R v Webber* [2004] UKHL 1, [2004] 1 WLR 404. However, see *R v Panchal* [2012] EWCA Crim 2327, where a misdirection on s 34 in relation to true facts did not affect the safety of the conviction.

48 See *R v Nickolson* [1999] Crim LR 61 (CA); *R v Betts and Hall* [2001] EWCA Crim 224, [2001] 2 Cr App R 16; *R v Milford* [2001] Crim LR 330 (CA); *R v Webber* [2004] UKHL 1, [2004] 1 WLR 404; *R v Smith* [2011] EWCA Crim 1098.

49 *R v Argent* [1997] 2 Cr App R 27 (CA) 33.

50 The relationship between s 34 and legal advice is examined below, at ch 6.3.1.

51 See *R v Condron and Condron* [1997] 1 WLR 827 (CA).

52 CJPOA 1994, s 34(2).

withstand scrutiny. The inference could then contribute to a finding of guilt. When summing up to the jury, the judge must give a direction in line with the Judicial College directions. The direction should include the following:

> 1. The facts which the accused failed to mention but which are relied on in his defence should be identified.
> 2. The inferences . . . which it is suggested might be drawn from failure to mention such facts should be identified, to the extent that they may go beyond the standard inference of late fabrication.
> 3. The jury should be told that, if an inference is drawn, they should not convict 'wholly or mainly on the strength of it'.
> 4. The jury should be told that an inference should be drawn 'only if you think it is a fair and proper conclusion'.
> 5. . . . the inference canvassed should only be drawn if there is no other sensible explanation for the failure.
> 6. An inference should only be drawn if, apart from the defendant's failure to mention facts later relied on in his defence, the prosecution case is 'so strong that it clearly calls for an answer by him'.
> 7. The jury should be reminded of the evidence on the basis of which the jury are invited not to draw any conclusion from the defendant's silence . . .
> 8. A special direction should be given where the explanation for silence of which evidence has been given is that the defendant was advised by his solicitor to remain silent.[53]

The direction is an attempt to limit the influence of silence on decision making. The direction is necessary to ensure compliance with the right to a fair trial under Article 6 of the European Convention on Human Rights (ECHR).[54] However, a defective direction will not necessarily render a trial unfair or a conviction unsafe.[55]

Although it was thought by some that section 34 might be found incompatible with the ECHR,[56] the European authorities have found inferences from silence to

53 For the direction in full, see Judicial Studies Board, *Crown Court Bench Book: Directing the Jury* (Judicial Studies Board, 2010) 264–265 and Appendix 2. As to the third point, see CJPOA 1994, s 38(3), which provides that an inference cannot form the sole basis for conviction. This has been supplemented by the European Court's decision that silence should not be a main decisive factor. *Murray v UK* (1996) 22 EHRR 29 [47].

54 *Condron v UK* (2001) 31 EHRR 1. See also the discussion in I Dennis, *The Law of Evidence*, 5th edn (London, Sweet & Maxwell, 2013) 178–180.

55 See *Adetoro v UK* App no 46834/06 (ECHR, 20 April 2010); *R v Chivers* [2011] EWCA Crim 1212. See also *R v Collins* [2014] EWCA Crim 773, in which the trial judge did not direct the jury on a 'no comment' interview, despite the prosecution pursuing the topic of adverse inferences in its closing speech. The absence of direction was 'unfortunate', but did not render the conviction unsafe.

56 See, for example, I Dennis, 'The Criminal Justice and Public Order Act 1994: The Evidence Provisions' [1995] *Crim LR* 4, 6.

be within the limits of Article 6, so long as certain safeguards are in place, including a careful direction to the jury.[57] In *Murray v UK*, a case concerning the Northern Irish equivalent to the CJPOA 1994, and a decision by a Diplock court, the European Court summed up the position as follows:

> On the one hand, it is self-evident that it is incompatible with the immunities under consideration to base a conviction solely or mainly on the accused's silence or on a refusal to answer questions or to give evidence himself. On the other hand, the Court deems it equally obvious that these immunities cannot and should not prevent that the accused's silence, in situations which clearly call for an explanation from him, be taken into account in assessing the persuasiveness of the evidence adduced by the prosecution.[58]

The Court went on to state that:

> Whether the drawing of adverse inferences from an accused's silence infringes Article 6 is a matter to be determined in the light of all the circumstances of the case, having particular regard to the situations where inferences may be drawn, the weight attached to them by the national courts in their assessment of the evidence and the degree of compulsion inherent in the situation.[59]

As explained in previous chapters, the courts have tended to take a narrower approach to the interpretation of fair trial rights than they are afforded under the theory of the criminal process as a process of calling the state to account. Thus, normatively, the jurisprudence of the European Court should not be taken as the defining standard of fairness. Namely, the reluctance to meddle in the applicability of the CJPOA 1994 does not render the provisions unobjectionable. The issue of whether drawing inferences from silence is, in principle, consistent with fairness is returned to later in this chapter.

Fairness aside, the logic of the European Court's approach is open to question, as expressed by Judge Wojtyczek in *O'Donnell v UK*, a case in which there had been strong circumstantial evidence against the accused:

> I am not able to understand this approach. The explanations of the accused are simultaneously seen as necessary, as the situation calls for an explanation, and unnecessary, as there is other strong evidence on which to base his conviction. If in a specific case there is sufficient evidence to decide a case without drawing any inferences from the accused's silence, then there is no need to resort to any adverse inferences from his silence in deciding the case.[60]

57 See *Condron v UK* (2001) 31 EHRR 1; *Beckles v UK* (2003) 36 EHRR 13.
58 *Murray v UK* (1996) 22 EHRR 29 [47].
59 ibid.
60 *O'Donnell v UK* [2015] ECHR 16667/10. Concurring opinion of Judge Wojtyczek [6].

Since the prosecution case must be 'so strong that it clearly calls for an answer',[61] before an inference can be drawn, it will usually be unnecessary to take account of silence in determining guilt; there will be other evidence on which to base a conviction. This, taken together with the requirement that silence cannot be the sole or main basis for conviction, means that silence should ordinarily be afforded little, if any, evidential value.[62] The same is true of inferences drawn under sections 35 through 37.

The weight which juries actually accord to silence is unknown, but the pressure on the accused to participate is substantial. As argued by Leng, an implicit function of section 34 is to establish and enforce a norm that suspects generally should answer questions in police interview.[63] Moreover, the assumption underlying the silence provisions is that an innocent person would want to explain their innocence at the first opportunity. The fact-finder is effectively invited to penalise the defendant's failure to do so. Consequently, whether logical or not, there is ample scope for silence to play a role in determinations of guilt. The Judicial College specimen direction makes it clear that the jury 'may take [silence] into account as some ***additional support*** for the prosecution's case'.[64] Thus, unlike at common law, silence in itself can be used as evidence of guilt. The fact that section 34 inferences can be drawn by the court in determining whether there is a case to answer,[65] before any evidence is adduced by the defence, also clarifies that silence can do more than merely affect the weight of other evidence. The implication may be that the fact-finder now feels encouraged to use silence against the defendant, as a means of penalising non-cooperation, despite the fact that the CJPOA 1994 has been interpreted in such a way that silence should have little evidential value.

Section 34 is a controversial provision which has generated an extensive and complex body of case law. Initially, there was some judicial reluctance to adopt an expansive approach to the CJPOA 1994.[66] In *Bowden*, the Court of Appeal stated that 'since [the provisions] restrict rights recognised at common law as appropriate to protect defendants against the risk of injustice they should not be construed more widely than the statutory language requires'.[67] This reflects a view that the silence provisions should be approached carefully, perhaps because they contradict a procedural tradition of adversarialism, within which the defendant is not obliged

61 Judicial Studies Board, *Crown Court Bench Book: Directing the Jury* (Judicial Studies Board, 2010) 264.

62 R Leng, 'The Right to Silence Reformed: A Re-appraisal of the Royal Commission's Influence' (2001) 6 *Journal of Civil Liberties* 107, 110.

63 R Leng, 'Silence Pre-trial, Reasonable Expectations and the Normative Distortion of Fact Finding' (2001) 5 *E & P* 240, 242.

64 Judicial Studies Board, *Crown Court Bench Book: Directing the Jury* (Judicial Studies Board, 2010) 393. Emphasis added.

65 This could occur where the defence rely on a previously undisclosed fact during cross-examination of prosecution witnesses.

66 See I Dennis, 'Silence in the Police Station: The Marginalisation of Section 34' [2002] *Crim LR* 25.

67 *R v Bowden* [1999] 1 WLR 823 (CA) 827 (Lord Bingham CJ).

to participate. However, section 34 itself invites an expansive interpretation and the effect of the legislation as a whole has been to greatly inhibit the defendant's free choice to remain silent under police questioning. As the case law developed, a broader understanding of section 34 has emerged than that envisaged in *Bowden*. This has been particularly acute in regard to legal advice to remain silent at the police station.

6.3.1 Silence and legal advice

The case law in respect of legal advice to remain silent is revealing of both the assumptions behind section 34 and the expectation of defendant participation.[68] The defendant has a right to legal advice in the police station.[69] If he is not afforded the opportunity to exercise this right, no inference can be drawn from his silence.[70] If he declines legal representation, as many suspects do,[71] inferences may be drawn from his silence. There are good reasons why a legal representative might advise a suspect to remain silent. Such advice may, for example, stem from inadequate disclosure by the police.[72] However, as it stands, genuine reliance on legal advice to remain silent is not sufficient to circumvent section 34. It is, according to the Court of Appeal, the 'true reason' for silence which is important. As stated by Auld LJ in *Hoare*:

> The section 34 inference is concerned with flushing out innocence at an early stage or supporting other evidence of guilt at a later stage, not simply with whether a guilty defendant is entitled, or genuinely or reasonably believes that he is entitled, to rely on legal rights of which his solicitor has advised him. Legal entitlement is one thing. An accused's reason for exercising it is another. His belief in his entitlement may be genuine, but it does not follow that his reason for exercising it is . . .[73]

68 See, for example, *R v Condron and Condron* [1997] 1 WLR 827 (CA); *R v Betts and Hall* [2001] EWCA Crim 224, [2001] 2 Cr App R 16; *R v Howell* [2003] EWCA Crim 1, [2005] 1 Cr App R 1; *R v Hoare* [2004] EWCA Crim 784, [2005] 1 WLR 1804; *R v Beckles* [2004] EWCA Crim 2766, [2005] 1 WLR 2829. For a detailed examination of the relationship between the right to silence and legal advice, see H Quirk, 'Twenty Years On, the Right of Silence and Legal Advice: The Spiralling Costs of an Unfair Exchange' (2013) 64 *Northern Ireland Legal Quarterly* 465.

69 See PACE 1984, s 58; European Convention on Human Rights, Article 6; *R v Samuel* [1988] QB 615 (CA).

70 CJPOA 1994, s 34(2A).

71 See L Skinns, 'The Right to Legal Advice in the Police Station: Past, Present and Future' [2011] *Crim LR* 19.

72 On the very limited disclosure requirements at the stage of police interview, see PACE 1984, Code C, paras 11.1A and Note 11ZA. The courts have been reluctant to accept inadequate police disclosure as a basis for precluding adverse inferences. See, for example, *R v Argent* [1997] 2 Cr App R 27 (CA); *R v Roble* [1997] Crim LR 449 (CA); *DPP v Ara* [2001] EWHC Admin 493, [2002] 1 WLR 815.

73 *R v Hoare* [2004] EWCA Crim 784, [2005] 1 WLR 1804 [54].

In the earlier case of *Howell*,[74] Laws LJ placed section 34 in the context of a general change in the way that criminal cases are prepared and processed. As part of this change, the defendant is expected to participate by responding to police questions:

> It seems to us that this provision is one of several enacted in recent years which has served to counteract a culture, or belief, which had long been established in the practice of criminal cases, namely that in principle a defendant may without criticism withhold any disclosure of his defence until the trial. Now, the police interview and the trial are to be seen as part of a continuous process in which the suspect is engaged from the beginning . . .
>
> This benign *continuum* . . . is thwarted if currency is given to the belief that if a suspect remains silent on legal advice he may systematically avoid adverse comment at his trial. And it may encourage solicitors to advise silence for other than good objective reasons.[75]

This passage conveys the intent of the CJPOA 1994 as discouraging ambush defences. In addition, legal advice is perceived as a challenge to the norm that suspects should speak at interview.[76] The passage suggests that legal advice, and perhaps legal representatives more generally, should not be permitted to disturb the shift in the nature of English criminal procedure away from adversarialism, and away from the accompanying notions of voluntary participation, as outlined in Chapter 3. This is in contrast to the significant role which lawyers played in the development of adversarialism in the eighteenth and nineteenth centuries.[77]

There is an inconsistency between directing the jury to only draw an inference if the only sensible explanation for silence is that the defendant had no answer to give, or none that would withstand scrutiny, and allowing inferences to be drawn where a defendant has relied on legal advice to remain silent. Legal advice can always constitute an explanation for silence. While the courts have found that legal advice is not in itself a sufficient explanation for silence, when silence is advised, it is likely done so for reasons beyond the accused's entitlement to remain silent.[78] As Redmayne points out, the lawyer 'will presumably explain that, while silence carries certain risks, she thinks that silence is in the suspect's best interests'.[79] For the jury to determine the 'true reason' for silence would be an entirely speculative exercise. In *Beckles*, the Court of Appeal approved *Hoare*, and emphasised that the ultimate question is the reasonableness of the defendant's decision to remain

74 [2003] EWCA Crim 1, [2005] 1 Cr App R 1.

75 ibid [23]–[24]. Original emphasis.

76 R Leng, 'Silence Pre-trial, Reasonable Expectations and the Normative Distortion of Fact Finding' (2001) 5 *E & P* 240, 242.

77 See JH Langbein, *The Origins of the Adversary Criminal Trial* (Oxford, Oxford University Press, 2003).

78 M Redmayne, 'English Warnings' (2008) 30 *Cardozo Law Review* 1047, 1069.

79 ibid.

silent.[80] However, as noted by Quirk, 'it is unclear how it can be "unreasonable" for a suspect to follow legal advice, other than by the implication that it is being used as a pretext to evade conviction'.[81] Thus, while juries cannot rationally draw an inference from silence where it has been legally advised, they are nevertheless told that they can. Redmayne describes this area of section 34 case law as a 'sad mess'.[82]

Further inconsistency arises from the fact that the applicability of section 34, in respect of silence at the police station, depends on the accused being afforded access to legal advice; yet, to rely on that advice, in so far as it is to remain silent, can be detrimental to the accused.[83] This challenges the position taken by the European Court of Human Rights in *Condron v UK*; that access to legal advice and the physical presence of a solicitor during police interview 'must be considered a particularly important safeguard for dispelling any compulsion to speak which may be inherent in the terms of the caution'.[84] The legal advisor is clearly thought to play a protective role. Yet, at the same time, the presence of a legal advisor has been used as a justification for requiring participation. Even before the CJPOA 1994 was enacted, instead of legal advice justifying silence, the Court of Appeal construed the presence of a solicitor as legitimising the evidential significance of silence.[85] This occurred in *Chandler*,[86] where the presence of a solicitor was thought to put the police and suspect on equal terms. However, the presence of a legal advisor will not necessarily enhance the position of the accused. In *Paris*,[87] for example, one suspect had, in the presence of a solicitor, been intimidated and bullied into giving a false confession after denying involvement in an offence over 300 times.

The value of legal advice has been eroded. As Cape argues, as a matter of principle, a suspect should be able to rely on legal advice without fear of being penalised for doing so.[88] 'If defendants can never be sure that they are acting reasonably in relying on the advice of their lawyer, then they can never be sure that they should accept their lawyer's advice.'[89] This unfortunate situation has arisen due to one of the rationales of the CJPOA 1994. The legislation was, in part, a trade-off against the improved right to legal advice provided for by the

80 *R v Beckles* [2004] EWCA Crim 2766, [2005] 1 WLR 2829 [46].
81 H Quirk, 'Twenty Years On, the Right of Silence and Legal Advice: The Spiralling Costs of an Unfair Exchange' (2013) 64 *Northern Ireland Legal Quarterly* 465, 474.
82 M Redmayne, 'English Warnings' (2008) 30 *Cardozo Law Review* 1047, 1071.
83 See S Cooper, 'Legal Advice and Pre-Trial Silence – Unreasonable Developments' (2006) 10 *E & P* 60, 67.
84 *Condron v UK* (2001) 31 EHRR 1 [60].
85 See S Easton, 'Legal Advice, Common Sense and the Right to Silence' (1998) 2 *E & P* 109, 119–120.
86 [1976] 1 WLR 585 (CA).
87 (1993) 97 Cr App R 99 (CA).
88 E Cape, 'Sidelining Defence Lawyers: Police Station Advice After Condron' (1997) 1 *E & P* 386, 398.
89 ibid 402.

Police and Criminal Evidence Act 1984 (PACE 1984). The silence provisions were based on what Quirk describes as the 'extraordinary syllogism' that, if legal advisors were recommending that suspects exercise their rights, or were inhibiting the police from infringing these rights, then one of the most symbolic protections for suspects should be curtailed in order to 'rebalance' the system.[90] This occurred despite there being 'no evidential basis for these claims but much to contradict them'.[91]

One tactic devised by legal advisors to avoid inferences is to present the police with a prepared written statement, before a 'no comment' interview. This will be successful if the statement gives full details of the defence.[92] However, an omission or deviation from the statement, such that the defendant is seen to have relied on a new fact at trial, can lead to adverse inferences being drawn, even if the defence overall remains consistent.[93] Adopting a fastidious approach to prepared statements (prepared at a time when the solicitor is unlikely to have had much, if any, disclosure of the police case), and to the relevance of legal advice more generally, pushes the application of section 34 beyond ensuring the early disclosure of defence cases. It is revealing of the desire to secure defendant participation and, as noted by Leng, the courts willingness to sanction non-cooperation through adverse inferences.[94]

To avoid adverse inferences, it may be necessary for the defendant to convince the court or jury that silence was the result of genuine and reasonable reliance on legal advice. In doing so, the grounds for that advice may need to be disclosed. Likewise, to rebut a claim of recent fabrication, the defendant may be obliged to disclose both that he had told his solicitor of the facts on which he now relies and the broader details of their conversation. This is likely to entail a waiver of legal professional privilege. In *Seaton*,[95] the Court of Appeal analysed the previous case law regarding the relationship between silence, legal advice and legal privilege,[96] and came to some important conclusions. The Court held that a defendant cannot be asked whether he told his solicitor or counsel that what he now says is true unless he has waived privilege. However, the defendant is perfectly entitled to open up his communication with his lawyer.[97] If the defendant does give evidence of what passed between him and his solicitor:

90 H Quirk, 'Twenty Years On, the Right of Silence and Legal Advice: The Spiralling Costs of an Unfair Exchange' (2013) 64 *Northern Ireland Legal Quarterly* 465, 471.

91 ibid.

92 *R v Knight* [2003] EWCA Crim 1977, [2004] 1 WLR 340; *R v McKnight* [2013] EWCA Crim 937.

93 See *R v Mohammad* [2009] EWCA Crim 1871; *R v Parradine* [2011] EWCA Crim 656.

94 See R Leng, 'Silence Pre-trial, Reasonable Expectations and the Normative Distortion of Fact Finding' (2001) 5 *E & P* 240; R Leng, 'The Right to Silence Reformed: A Re-appraisal of the Royal Commission's Influence' (2001) 6 *Journal of Civil Liberties* 107.

95 [2010] EWCA Crim 1980, [2011] 1 WLR 623.

96 See *R v Wilmot* (1989) 89 Cr App R 341 (CA); *R v Bowden* [1999] 1 WLR 823 (CA); *R v Loizou* [2006] EWCA Crim 1719, (2006) 150 SJLB 1187.

97 *R v Seaton* [2010] EWCA Crim 1980, [2011] 1 WLR 623 [43].

> [H]e is not thereby waiving privilege entirely and generally, that is to say he does not automatically make available to all other parties everything that he said to his solicitor, or his solicitor to him, on every occasion. He may well not even be opening up everything said on the occasion of which he gives evidence, and not on topics unrelated to that of which he gives evidence. The test is fairness and/or the avoidance of a misleading impression. It is that the defendant should not, as it has been put in some of the cases, be able both to 'have his cake and eat it'.[98]

While a defendant may not need to waive privilege in relation to the entire pre-interview communication, the effect of section 34 is to subject the defendant to 'indirect compulsion'[99] to waive privilege in order to avoid a penalty for non-cooperation. This places undue pressure on the defendant not only to actively participate at the trial, but also to offer an explanation for his earlier silence, thus reflecting a view that participation is expected throughout the criminal process and that non-participation requires justification. Faced with a difficult choice between inferences of guilt or waiving privilege and disclosing potentially damaging information, defendants find themselves on the horns of a dilemma.

Section 34 has given rise to many difficulties such that its benefits, if any, do not outweigh the burdens imposed by its retention.[100] A vast amount of time and resources have been put into clarifying the provision. In addition, the focus on the defendant's participation undermines the defendant's ability to exercise his fundamental right to silence and to legal advice. As Leng argues, the judicial interpretation of section 34 has 'signalled its allegiance to the political objective of the legislation: to establish the norm that suspects should speak in police interview'.[101] Leng goes on to note that section 34 places the normative question of whether the accused should have disclosed a relevant fact at the heart of the jury's decision making.[102] Since inferences should only be drawn where there is no plausible explanation for silence, and where the case is strong enough to clearly call for an explanation, silence should have little evidential value. However, the current approach inevitably creates risks that a guilty verdict may be used to sanction uncooperative defendants.[103]

98 ibid (Hughes LJ).

99 *Condron v UK* (2001) 31 EHRR 1 [60].

100 See D Birch, 'Suffering in Silence: A Cost-Benefit Analysis of Section 34 of the Criminal Justice and Public Order Act 1994' [1999] *Crim LR* 769.

101 R Leng, 'Silence Pre-trial, Reasonable Expectations and the Normative Distortion of Fact Finding' (2001) 5 *E & P* 240, 250.

102 ibid 255.

103 ibid.

6.4 Sections 36 and 37

Section 36 Effect of accused's failure or refusal to account for objects, substances or marks:

(1) Where —

(a) a person is arrested by a constable, and there is —

(i) on his person; or
(ii) in or on his clothing or footwear; or
(iii) otherwise in his possession; or
(iv) in any place in which he is at the time of his arrest,

any object, substance or mark, or there is any mark on any such object; and

(b) that or another constable investigating the case reasonably believes that the presence of the object, substance or mark may be attributable to the participation of the person arrested in the commission of an offence specified by the constable; and
(c) the constable informs the person arrested that he so believes, and requests him to account for the presence of the object, substance or mark; and
(d) the person fails or refuses to do so,

then if, in any proceedings against the person for the offence so specified, evidence of those matters is given, subsection (2) below applies.

(2) Where this subsection applies —

. . .

(c) the court, in determining whether there is a case to answer; and
(d) the court or jury, in determining whether the accused is guilty of the offence charged,

may draw such inferences from the failure or refusal as appear proper.

Section 37 Effect of accused's failure or refusal to account for presence at a particular place:

(1) Where —

(a) a person arrested by a constable was found by him at a place at or about the time the offence for which he was arrested is alleged to have been committed; and
(b) that or another constable investigating the offence reasonably believes that the presence of the person at that place and at that time may be attributable to his participation in the commission of the offence; and
(c) the constable informs the person that he so believes, and requests him to account for that presence; and

> (d) the person fails or refuses to do so,
>
> then if, in any proceedings against the person for the offence, evidence of those matters is given, subsection (2) below applies.
>
> (2) Where this subsection applies—
>
> . . .
>
> (c) the court, in determining whether there is a case to answer; and
> (d) the court or jury, in determining whether the accused is guilty of the offence charged,
>
> may draw such inferences from the failure or refusal as appear proper.

Section 36 allows inferences to be drawn from an arrested person's failure to account for suspicious objects, substances and marks which are found in his possession or at the scene of his arrest. Section 37 permits inferences to be drawn from an arrested person's failure to account for his suspicious presence at a particular place around the time that an offence was committed. The inference most likely to be drawn by the court or jury is that the accused's silence is an indicator of guilt; that he failed to account for the circumstances because he had no account to give or none that would withstand scrutiny. Unlike section 34, these two provisions have received little academic attention;[104] also they have generated very little case law. Nonetheless, they warrant attention, as they associate silence with guilt, and penalise those who do not cooperate, in much the same way as section 34, albeit in more specific circumstances. Moreover, despite the lack of case law, a significant number of suspects are given a warning by the police under sections 36 and 37.[105]

In order for sections 36 and 37 to apply, the investigating constable must explain to the accused why the particular circumstances are suspicious and that inferences may later be drawn from a refusal or failure to account for them.[106] Additionally, the investigating constable must reasonably believe that the circumstances may be attributable to the accused's participation in the commission of the offence and advise the accused that he so believes. As with section 34, silence cannot be the sole or main evidence against the defendant at trial, and the jury must be given a direction in line with the Judicial College specimen

104 For further exploration of ss 36 and 37, see A Owusu-Bempah, 'Silence in Suspicious Circumstances' [2014] *Crim LR* 126. On s 36 in relation to expert evidence of drug traces, see A Marks, 'Evidence of Drug Traces: Relevance, Reliability and the Right to Silence' [2013] *Crim LR* 810.

105 See PACE 1984, Code C 10.11. Early research indicates that 39 per cent of suspects exercising their right to silence (amounting to 5 per cent of all suspects) were given a warning under ss 36 or 37. The majority of those given a warning failed to provide an account, or gave one which police officers considered unsatisfactory. T Bucke, R Street and D Brown, *The Right to Silence: The Impact of the Criminal Justice and Public Order Act 1994* (Home Office Research Study No. 199) (London, Home Office, 2000) 39.

106 CJPOA 1994, ss 36(4) and 37(3).

directions.[107] Crucially, the jury must be told that they can only hold against the defendant a failure to give an explanation if they are sure that he had no acceptable explanation to offer.[108]

As with section 34, the accused must have been afforded access to legal advice before inferences can be drawn under sections 36 or 37.[109] However, this condition appears to apply only to questioning at an authorised place of detention, namely a police station. The same is true of section 34.[110] It is conceivable that sections 36 and 37 are particularly useful outside of the police station, such as when the accused is arrested at the scene of a crime. In such cases, the threat of adverse inferences could be used to put pressure on the accused to offer an explanation, regardless of the fact that he may be largely ignorant of the circumstances surrounding the offence, his arrest, the criminal process, or his rights as a suspect. The effect of Code C 11.1A and C 11.1 of PACE 1984 is that questioning of an arrested suspect should normally take place in the police station. Moreover, Code C 11.4 requires that, during formal interview at a police station, the suspect must be asked if he wishes to confirm or deny any earlier significant silence. Yet, there is nothing in the CJPOA 1994 or PACE 1984 that explicitly prevents an accused from being questioned outside of the police station. Nor does the legislation prohibit inferences from silence at this stage.

This calls into the question the compatibility of sections 36 and 37 (and section 34) with Article 6 of the ECHR. In *Murray v UK*, access to a lawyer was held to be of paramount importance for the rights of the defence at the initial stage of police interrogation, where the accused faces a fundamental dilemma relating to his defence.[111] Such a dilemma arises where exercising the right to silence may lead to adverse inferences. That the initial stage of police interrogation occurs outside of a police station is unlikely to diminish the magnitude of the dilemma faced by the accused. In *Cadder*,[112] the Supreme Court, following the Strasbourg ruling in *Salduz v Turkey*,[113] held that, under Article 6, the suspect must have access to legal advice before being subjected to police questioning, unless, in the particular circumstances, there are compelling reasons to restrict this right. Although the Court referred only to questioning in police custody, it is submitted that the same should apply to questioning outside of the police station, where the compulsion to speak might be greater; the accused is unlikely to have had an adequate opportunity to consider the situation in which he has found himself or the best

107 See Judicial Studies Board, *Crown Court Bench Book: Directing the Jury* (Judicial Studies Board, 2010). In *Milford*, it was held that the direction laid down in *R v Cowan* [1996] QB 373 (CA) 'related to a case involving section 35 but it is common ground that the same principles apply when dealing with section 36'. *R v Milford* [2002] EWCA Crim 1528 [25] (Pill LJ).

108 *R v Compton* [2002] EWCA Crim 2835, (2003) 147 SJLB 24 [37].

109 CJPOA 1994, ss 36(4A) and 37(3A).

110 ibid s 34(2A).

111 *Murray v UK* (1996) 22 EHRR 29 [66]. See also *Condron v UK* (2001) 31 EHRR 1.

112 [2010] UKSC 43, [2010] 1 WLR 2601.

113 (2008) 49 EHRR 421.

course of action and, so, may be particularly susceptible to pressure or coercion. The applicability of sections 36 and 37, as well as section 34, outside of the police station requires clarification.[114]

Sections 36 and 37 are concerned with the accused's failure or refusal to 'account for' suspicious objects, substances or marks, or presence at the scene of a crime. Complete silence clearly constitutes a failure to account for the circumstances. However, the statute does not specify how detailed or comprehensive an account must be before section 36 or 37 will cease to apply. In *Compton*,[115] the Court of Appeal had to decide whether, for the purpose of section 36, the appellants had failed or refused to account for the presence of large sums of money contaminated with heroin which were found in their homes. Upon being cautioned, two of the appellants had stated that the money had come from legitimate means, with one also pointing out that he was a heroin addict. The third appellant, when interviewed before the heroin had been detected, said that his wife was a heroin addict and that the money had come from his father and the sale of a vehicle. When re-interviewed after the heroin had been detected he exercised his right to silence. The Court of Appeal held that the appellants had not accounted for the presence of the heroin-contaminated money. It was not enough to refer to other states of fact, from which it could be inferred what the account might be.[116] For example, in the case of the third appellant, it was insufficient that it could have been inferred from the earlier interview that the heroin came from his father who was a known drug dealer, his wife or the purchaser of the vehicle. He had not accounted for a specific state of fact.

The implication of the Court of Appeal's approach is that the accused must not only cooperate with the police by offering a possible explanation, but must do so in a specific and detailed way. This approach goes beyond allowing inferences to be drawn from silence; it allows inferences to be drawn from unsatisfactory explanations. Thus, sections 36 and 37 not only hinder the accused's freedom to choose whether or not to respond to questioning, but they also shape the response that he must give. This is unfortunate given that, during the stressful experience of police interrogation, the accused may be under a great deal of psychological pressure, may be confused and uninformed and, despite having been cautioned, may not fully understand the implications of his decisions. There will also be instances where the accused does not have the requisite knowledge to provide a satisfactory account, such as cases in which not even experts can offer a definitive explanation for the presence of traces of drugs.[117]

Sections 36 and 37 have generated much less controversy than section 34. This may be due to the fact that they apply only in relation to very specific circumstances. However, their applicability within those circumstances is broad, and they lack

114 A Owusu-Bempah, 'Silence in Suspicious Circumstances' [2014] *Crim LR* 126, 134.

115 [2002] EWCA Crim 2835, (2003) 147 SJLB 24.

116 ibid [34].

117 A Marks, 'Evidence of Drug Traces: Relevance, Reliability and the Right to Silence' [2013] *Crim LR* 810, 823.

two of the important triggering conditions of section 34. As a result, sections 36 and 37 can sometimes be utilised where section 34 is not available.[118] First, unlike section 34, the operation of the provisions does not depend on the defence case put forward at trial. The sole question is whether the defendant did account for the particular circumstances, as put to him by the police officer.[119] It is immaterial whether, at trial, the defendant puts forward a positive defence, relies on a previously unmentioned fact or provides a full account of the circumstances. The purpose of the provisions seems to be to focus attention on the answers that are given at the time of questioning, and the inferences which may be drawn appear to relate directly to guilt rather than to the credibility of any defence put forward at trial. Such inferences may be extremely tenuous, particularly where the defendant provides an insufficiently detailed account to the police, but goes on to provide a consistent and more comprehensive account of the circumstances at trial. Given the stressful nature of police interrogations, it is difficult to see how the initial 'failure to account' could be used as a reliable indicator of guilt in such cases.

Second, unlike section 34, sections 36 and 37 include no requirement that it be reasonable to expect the defendant to provide an account of the relevant circumstances to the police. As stated in *Roble,* reasonableness 'is not a concept which finds place in section 36'.[120] There will, therefore, be situations in which it would be unreasonable to expect an accused to account for certain suspicious circumstances; yet, failure to do so can be construed as an indication of guilt. For example, the accused might lack a sufficient understanding of English to deal with difficult legal concepts or provide a coherent account.[121] A reasonable reliance on legal advice is also irrelevant. Since genuine reliance on legal advice is not enough to prevent inferences, it will ordinarily be open to a jury to infer guilt under sections 36 and 37 in cases where the accused received legal advice to remain silent. One would hope that, if the court or jury is aware of a particular reason why the accused failed or refused to account for the circumstances, no inferences would be drawn, as inferences should only be drawn if there is no acceptable explanation for silence. However, the possibility of drawing inferences remains open and an unsympathetic jury may take advantage of this. By failing to take account of the circumstances at the time of questioning, the accused becomes more susceptible to coercion to actively participate at the police station and to tenuous inferences being drawn at trial. To avoid this, where, in the circumstances, it would be unreasonable to expect the accused to provide an account, the judge could use the exclusionary discretion under section 78 of PACE 1984 to prevent the prosecution from relying on evidence of silence.[122]

118 See *R v Abbas* [2010] EWCA Crim 161, [2010] All ER (D) 79 (Jan).
119 *R v Compton* [2002] EWCA Crim 2835, (2003) 147 SJLB 24 [32].
120 *R v Roble* [1997] Crim LR 449 (CA) (Rose LJ).
121 This did not affect the applicability of s 36 in *Roble.*
122 A Owusu-Bempah, 'Silence in Suspicious Circumstances' [2014] *Crim LR* 126, 135.

As well as reinforcing the suspiciousness of certain circumstances, sections 36 and 37 have contributed to a change in the role of the defendant in the criminal process. Although they apply only to specific circumstances, the provisions have been interpreted such that their applicability within those circumstances is broad, going beyond what was permissible at common law, and increasing the evidential significance of silence.[123] Sections 36 and 37 impose a participatory burden on the accused, affecting not only the freedom to choose whether or not to respond to police questioning, but also shaping the response that should be given. Like section 34, they focus the attention of the fact-finder on whether, and how, the defendant responded to accusations, rather than the strength of the prosecution case. Those who do not respond adequately may be penalised by having their failure to participate linked to guilt.

6.5 Section 35

Section 35 Effect of accused's silence at trial:

> (1) At the trial of any person for an offence, subsections (2) and (3) below apply unless —
>
> > (a) the accused's guilt is not in issue; or
> > (b) it appears to the court that the physical or mental condition of the accused makes it undesirable for him to give evidence; . . .
>
> (2) Where this subsection applies, the court shall, at the conclusion of the evidence for the prosecution, satisfy itself (in the case of proceedings on indictment, in the presence of the jury) that the accused is aware that the stage has been reached at which evidence can be given for the defence and that he can, if he wishes, give evidence and that, if he chooses not to give evidence, or having been sworn, without good cause refuses to answer any question, it will be permissible for the court or jury to draw such inferences as appear proper from his failure to give evidence or his refusal, without good cause, to answer any question.
> (3) Where this subsection applies, the court or jury, in determining whether the accused is guilty of the offence charged, may draw such inferences as appear proper from the failure of the accused to give evidence or his refusal, without good cause, to answer any question.

The CJPOA 1994 repealed section 1(b) of the Criminal Evidence Act 1898,[124] which had prevented the prosecution from commenting on the defendant's

123 There is a general common law proposition that guilt may be inferred from the unreasonable behaviour of a defendant when confronted with facts which seem to accuse. See *R v Raviraj* (1987) 85 Cr App R 93 (CA). Sections 36 and 37 have a broader applicability, as they apply after arrest, allow evidential significance to be attached to silence itself and allow inferences to be drawn from unsatisfactory accounts.

124 CJPOA 1994, s 168(3) and sch 11.

failure to give evidence in court. Section 35 allows comment to be made and inferences to be drawn from a defendant's silence, unless a physical or mental condition makes it undesirable for him to testify. Before an inference can be drawn, the defendant must have been made aware, at the end of the prosecution's case, that the stage has been reached at which he can give evidence and the possible consequences of not doing so. Implicit in section 35 is the requirement that the prosecution present a *prima facie* case, based on its own evidence. In the absence of a *prima facie* case, the judge should find that the defence has no case to answer and the defendant will not be called upon to give evidence.

Where inferences can be drawn under section 35, the jury must be directed in a certain manner. The essential elements of the direction were set out by the Court of Appeal in *Cowan*:

> (1) The judge will have told the jury that the burden of proof remains upon the prosecution throughout and what the required standard is. (2) It is necessary for the judge to make clear to the jury that the defendant is entitled to remain silent. That is his right and his choice. The right of silence remains. (3) An inference from failure to give evidence cannot on its own prove guilt. That is expressly stated in section 38(3) of the Act. (4) Therefore, the jury must be satisfied that the prosecution have established a case to answer before drawing any inferences from silence. Of course, the judge must have thought so or the question whether the defendant was to give evidence would not have arisen. But the jury may not believe the witnesses whose evidence the judge considered sufficient to raise a prima facie case. It must therefore be made clear to them that they must find there to be a case to answer on the prosecution evidence before drawing an adverse inference from the defendant's silence. (5) If, despite any evidence relied upon to explain his silence or in the absence of any such evidence, the jury conclude the silence can only sensibly be attributed to the defendant's having no answer or none that would stand up to cross-examination, they may draw an adverse inference.[125]

Although appearing to place some limit on a potentially broad discretion to equate silence with guilt, a departure from an essential element of the judicial direction will not necessarily result in a successful appeal.[126] Once satisfied that the defendant has a case to answer, the jury is entitled to infer guilt from his

125 *R v Cowan* [1996] QB 373 (CA) 381.

126 *Adetoro v UK* App no 46834/06 (ECHR, 20 April 2010); *R v Birchall* [1999] Crim LR 311 (CA). However, in *Birchall* the Court held that it was essential to the interest of justice that a jury should not consider whether to draw an adverse inference until they had concluded that there was a case to answer and, as such, the trial judge's omission of this point constituted a reason for finding in favour of the appellant.

failure to testify or answer any question, if it appears proper to do so.[127] As with section 34, the underlying assumption is that the innocent, with nothing to hide, will want to speak.

The defendant is not a compellable witness.[128] Yet, the overall effect of section 35 is to penalise defendants who do not actively participate, by allowing their failure to do so to be treated as evidence of guilt. Section 35 arguably has a more corrosive effect on the defendant's autonomy than the other provisions. This is because it is the only provision in the CJPOA 1994 which treats silence alone as suspicious and deserving of adverse treatment. Whereas sections 34, 36 and 37 require some triggering condition on the part of the defendant before inferences can be drawn, namely reliance on a previously unmentioned fact or silence in the face of certain suspicious circumstances, section 35 merely requires a competent defendant to exercise the right to silence. Moreover, like sections 36 and 37, the application of section 35 does not depend on the defence case at trial. Even in the absence of a positive defence, where the defence simply deny the allegations and put the prosecution to proof, silence can lead to an inference of guilt.[129] As Redmayne notes, in such cases, the section 35 inference 'appears to be extremely tenuous'.[130]

In *Cowan*, the Court of Appeal held that it would be inappropriate for a judge to embark or invite the jury to embark on possible speculative reasons consistent with innocence which might prompt a defendant to remain silent.[131] In order to convince a court or jury not to draw inferences, the defence need to produce independent evidence to explain the silence.[132] It is, therefore, the responsibility of the defence to justify a lack of participation. Pattenden argues that the need to produce evidence for an innocent explanation places a new evidential burden on the defendant which is irreconcilable with the traditional theory that the defendant can contest the case against him without calling evidence.[133] This, Pattenden claims, is a subtle subversion of the burden of proof and a 'misguided, new development in the law of evidence'.[134]

127 In *Murray v DPP* [1994] 1 WLR 1 (HL) 11, the House of Lords made clear that, in an appropriate case, an inference that the defendant was guilty might properly be drawn from his refusal to testify.

128 CJPOA 1994, s 35(4).

129 See, for example, *R v Whitehead* [2006] EWCA Crim 1486, (2006) 150 SJLB 888. Allowing inferences to be drawn in the absence of a positive defence appears to contradict the approach taken by the House of Lords in its initial determination of the Northern Irish equivalent to s 35. The Court did not seem to envisage inferences under the legislative regime going beyond what was permitted at common law, namely where a positive defence is raised which is within the defendant's knowledge. See *Murray v DPP* [1994] 1 WLR 1 (HL) 5 and 11.

130 M Redmayne, 'English Warnings' (2008) 30 *Cardozo Law Review* 1047, 1075.

131 *R v Cowan* [1996] QB 373 (CA) 386.

132 ibid 380. The Court of Appeal expressed the need for exceptional circumstances or an 'evidential basis' before a jury should be directed against drawing an inference from silence at trial.

133 R Pattenden, 'Silence: Lord Taylor's Legacy' (1998) 2 *E & P* 141, 157.

134 ibid 156.

It is not always possible to produce evidence to explain silence. It would, therefore, be more consistent with fairness to routinely take into account the fact that innocent explanations do exist. Jackson notes that:

> [N]o matter how strong the evidence, the court or jury is in a position to draw the 'proper' inference from silence only where it knows the reason for silence. Without knowledge of the reason, it would only seem safe to draw an inference of guilt when the trier of fact is already convinced of guilt on the basis of existing proof beyond reasonable doubt. But the inference then becomes merely an *ex post facto* rationalisation of what the trier of fact is already convinced of and the provision becomes redundant. If the trier of fact has become convinced on the basis of lesser proof than this, then the provision is being used to do what in many cases it cannot do, namely provide the necessary evidence to bring the proof up to the standard.[135]

Thus, while the jury can only be sure that the defendant's explanation for silence is false or that his silence stems from guilt where other evidence proves him guilty, section 35 allows silence to contribute to a finding of guilt. As with the other provisions, if section 35 were applied correctly, silence would have little to no evidential value. If silence lacks evidential value, the primary purpose of the provisions must be to increase participation and sanction non-cooperation.

In order to address some of the unfairness inherent in equating silence directly with guilt, the trial judge could be under a duty to remind the jury that silence is not necessarily an indicator of guilt, and that there could be an explanation for which the defence has not adduced evidence. This would assist the jury in making an informed assessment of whether to infer guilt from silence.[136] If applied to all of the silence provisions, it could decrease the risk of wrongful conviction and go some way to reasserting a strong right to silence. Among those advocating such a direction is Greer, who maintains that 'The basic principle should be that, in trials on indictment, judges should be obliged to point out to jurors that silence . . . may be entirely innocent', with possible grounds for an innocent explanation being listed by trial judges.[137] Likewise, Pattenden suggests something similar to the *Lucas* direction which is given in relation to lies.[138] This includes in appropriate cases that the jury be reminded that 'people sometimes lie, for example, in an attempt to bolster up a just cause, or out of shame or out of a wish to conceal disgraceful behaviour from their family'.[139] In the conception of the criminal

135 J Jackson, 'Interpreting the Silence Provisions: The Northern Ireland Cases' [1995] *Crim LR* 587, 600.

136 A Owusu-Bempah, 'Judging the Desirability of a Defendant's Evidence: An Unfortunate Approach to s.35(1)(b) of the Criminal Justice and Public Order Act 1994' [2011] *Crim LR* 690, 703.

137 S Greer, 'The Right to Silence: A Review of the Current Debate' (1990) 53 *MLR* 709, 730.

138 R Pattenden, 'Silence: Lord Taylor's Legacy' (1998) 2 *E & P* 141, 154.

139 *R v Lucas* [1981] QB 720 (CA) 724 (Lord Lane CJ).

process based on calling the state to account, as advanced in this book, the direction would be taken further. The jury would be instructed not to use the fact of silence against the defendant, who should not be penalised for exercising an established right.

The argument for a *Lucas*-type direction, indicating to the jury that there may have been innocent reasons for failure to give evidence, was rejected by the House of Lords on the basis that it might mislead the jury as to the reason for silence, and result in unfounded speculation.[140] This overlooks the fact that the jury is already being invited to speculate guilt from the defendant's decision not to testify. Ignoring the possibility of innocent reasons for silence can damage the aim of accurate fact-finding rather than promote it. This unfortunate situation might occur where, for example, the defendant has failed to testify due to fear of reprisals from a co-defendant. It would be difficult, if not impossible, for the defence to adduce evidence of this fear without exposing the defendant to that of which he was afraid. It is a fundamental problem that section 35 makes such a strong connection between silence and guilt; it effectively forces the defendant to participate if he wishes to prevent this link.

6.5.1 Vulnerable defendants

Trial judges may withdraw from the jury the issue of adverse inferences from silence. In *Lancaster*, the Court of Appeal warned that, without individual consideration of the circumstances, the routine application of section 35 'can lead to unnecessary problems, whilst not necessarily contributing to the achievement of justice'.[141] However, it has also been made clear that the operation of section 35 is not to be reduced or marginalised,[142] and the appellate courts have declined to anticipate or speculate on circumstances where inferences may or may not be drawn.[143] In *Cowan*, the Court of Appeal rejected a submission that the provision should be used only exceptionally and confirmed that the CJPOA 1994 was intended by Parliament to alter the law on the right to silence.[144] The courts have since appeared reluctant to minimise the scope of section 35 by reference to asserted excuses, such as memory loss,[145] or fear of a co-accused.[146]

The one substantive barrier to drawing inferences is section 35(1)(b), when it appears to the court that the physical or mental condition of the accused makes it

140 *R v Becouarn* [2005] UKHL 55, [2005] 1 WLR 2589 [24].
141 *R v Lancaster* [2001] EWCA Crim 2836 [17] (Gibbs J).
142 *R v Becouarn* [2005] UKHL 55, [2005] 1 WLR 2589 [23].
143 *R v Cowan* [1996] QB 373 (CA) 381; *Murray v UK* (1996) 22 EHRR 29 [56].
144 *R v Cowan* [1996] QB 373 (CA) 378.
145 *R v Napper* (1997) 161 JP 16 (CA).
146 *R v Rafik* [2014] EWCA Crim 2544, [2015] Crim LR 235. See also *R v Cowan* [1996] QB 373 (CA); *R v Becouarn* [2005] UKHL 55, [2005] 1 WLR 2589; *R v Barry* [2010] EWCA Crim 195, [2010] 2 All ER 1004; *R v Hamidi* [2010] EWCA Crim 66, [2010] Crim LR 578.

undesirable for him to give evidence.[147] This provision has the potential to act as a safeguard for vulnerable defendants against the indiscriminate drawing of adverse inferences, linking silence directly to guilt, notwithstanding a legitimate explanation for silence. Unfortunately, the provision is applied very restrictively and is failing to fulfil its potential. In *Friend*,[148] the first reported case to examine section 35(1)(b), the trial judge gave a section 35 direction, despite the defendant's young age (15 years), low IQ and mental age of around nine. The Court of Appeal held that the judge had acted within his discretion. The Court went on to state that, for the purposes of section 35(1)(b), a physical condition might include a risk of an epileptic attack, and a mental condition might include latent schizophrenia where the experience of giving evidence might trigger a florid state.[149] 'Undesirable' was, thus, interpreted narrowly and in terms of the impact that testifying would have on a defendant's immediate health. Little consideration was given to the quality of the defendant's evidence or the fact that he may create a highly unfavourable impression through no fault of his own.

Consequent upon the restrictive approach taken by the courts, all but those defendants who are borderline unfit to plead are expected to testify, even if they can do no more than deny the accusations.[150] The *Pritchard* test,[151] which is used to determine unfitness to plead, focuses on the intellectual ability of the defendant. It does not account for the likely harm which testifying will cause to the defendant or impairments to the defendant's ability to give evidence effectively. In order to safeguard those who are fit to plead, yet suffer from a mental or physical condition which may affect their testimony, the notion of 'undesirable' should be afforded a wider scope. In *Friend's* second appeal, the Court opened up to this possibility by quashing the conviction in the light of new expert evidence that Friend suffered from Attention Deficit Hyperactivity Disorder (ADHD).[152] Yet, the judicial approach to section 35(1)(b) has remained narrow.[153] This is particularly worrying for young defendants whose age is unlikely to be taken into account when determining whether it is 'desirable' for them to testify.[154]

147 See A Owusu-Bempah, 'Judging the Desirability of a Defendant's Evidence: An Unfortunate Approach to s.35(1)(b) of the Criminal Justice and Public Order Act 1994' [2011] *Crim LR* 690.

148 [1997] 1 WLR 1433 (CA).

149 ibid 1442.

150 M Redmayne, 'English Warnings' (2008) 30 *Cardozo Law Review* 1047, 1087. See also *R v Friend* [1997] 1 WLR 1433 (CA) 1440.

151 *R v Pritchard* (1836) 7 C & P 303. See also *R v M* [2003] EWCA Crim 3452, [2003] All ER (D) 199.

152 *R v Friend* [2004] EWCA Crim 2661.

153 See, for example, *R v LH* [2001] EWCA Crim 1344; *R (on the application of DPP) v Kavanagh* [2005] EWHC 820 (Admin), [2006] Crim LR 370; *R v Ensor* [2009] EWCA Crim 2519, [2010] 1 Cr App R 18.

154 See, for example, *R v Friend* [1997] 1 WLR 1433 (CA); *R v AC* [2001] EWCA Crim 713; *R v LH* [2001] EWCA Crim 1344.

In *D*, the Court of Appeal explicitly rejected a submission that a blanket approach of generosity should be taken in relation to those who are young or have mental difficulties.[155] In this case, expert evidence showed that the defendant, who was 17 years old at the time of the offence, had: ADHD; a full scale IQ of 68; low non-verbal abilities; poor working memory; a lack of knowledge and concepts normally gained through education; a limited vocabulary and semantic knowledge; a severe stammer; language levels around the equivalent of a seven to eight year level; was compliant and easily led; and did not know the meaning of 'jury', 'defence', 'evidence', 'oath' or 'alleged'.[156] Nonetheless, the Court upheld the conviction for murder, finding that the trial judge had been entitled to give a section 35 direction. The judge was 'entitled to look beyond the expert material' and consider other factors, such as the conduct of the accused after the event, the nature of the account given by the defence and, optimistically, the anticipated approach of a fair-minded jury.[157]

One particular factor which influenced the decision in *D* was the availability of a registered intermediary. The defence argued that this special measure had not been sufficient to enable D to participate effectively. The Court disagreed and remained of the opinion that it was desirable for D to testify. However, it seems that if it can be established that a defendant cannot effectively participate, section 35(1)(b) should apply.[158] A similar approach was taken by the European Court in *O'Donnell v UK*,[159] a case which concerned the Northern Irish equivalent of section 35(1)(b). Although the applicant had an IQ of 62 and a 6-year-old's understanding of spoken English, the Court held that the adverse inference direction did not violate Article 6. This decision was reached, in part, because questions could have been put to the defendant in a controlled manner. The current approach is such that even defendants with severe intellectual disabilities are expected to testify. Whereas eligibility for special measures should signal that a defendant will have particular difficulty in giving evidence, in practice, the availability of special measures has contributed to finding that a defendant should give evidence. There is, thus, an expectation of defendant participation, despite the difficulties in securing effective participation.

Following the Court of Appeal's ruling in the case of *Tabbakh*,[160] it seems also that, for the purpose of section 35(1)(b), the extent to which the defendant's well-being might be affected, if he were to give evidence, should be considered in the light of the importance of the evidence that he can provide;[161] the greater the

155 *R v D* [2013] EWCA Crim 465, [2014] 1 WLR 525 [57].

156 ibid [13].

157 ibid [55].

158 A Roberts, 'Case Comment: R v Dixon: Evidence – Failure to Give Evidence - Adverse Inference' [2014] *Crim LR* 141, 143.

159 [2015] ECHR 16667/10. See A Owusu-Bempah, 'Vulnerable Defendants and the Right to Silence: *O'Donnell* v *United Kingdom* [2015] ECHR 16667/10' (2015) 79 *Journal of Criminal Law* 322.

160 [2009] EWCA Crim 464, (2009) 173 JP 201.

161 See also *R v D* [2013] EWCA Crim 465, [2014] 1 WLR 525.

importance of the evidence, the more desirable it is for him to testify. Determining the desirability of a defendant's testimony in relation to the importance of his evidence seems superfluous, as the defendant's testimony will always be significant. It has the potential to influence the jury's assessment of the case, even where he is simply denying the allegations against him. The manner of giving evidence could have just as significant an impact as the content of that evidence.

As it now stands, in order to fall within section 35(1)(b), the defendant will likely need to show, with evidence, that he is suffering from a physical or mental condition that will be triggered or worsened by giving evidence, and that his evidence will be of relatively little importance to the case.[162] Thus, even where vulnerable, the onus is on the defendant to justify a lack of participation. Practitioners worry about the vulnerability of defendants who are not considered 'undesirable' witnesses for the purpose of section 35(1)(b). A post-CJPOA study found that there was concern that such defendants, having been effectively forced into the witness box, may come across poorly and damage their case; this may, in turn, increase the possibility of wrongful conviction.[163] Unfortunately, however, the defendant's participation in the trial process is perceived as of paramount importance, above other considerations, including his well-being.

6.6 The impact of the CJPOA 1994 on participation

Not long after the CJPOA 1994 came into force, Bucke, Street and Brown conducted empirical studies into the practical effects of the legislation.[164] Although they produced a detailed and useful report, some 20 years later, the situation might be quite different. This was the experience in Singapore where provisions similar to those in the CJPOA 1994, and inspired by the Criminal Law Revision Committee's 1972 report, had little effect initially, but saw greater use in later years.[165] The same is true of Northern Ireland.[166] It is possible that, within England and Wales, the growing focus on efficient fact-finding through increased participation has led to greater influence of the silence provisions.

A principal conclusion from Bucke *et al.*'s research was that the silence provisions did not have a major impact on the outcome of cases, with no discernible

162 See, A Owusu-Bempah, 'Judging the Desirability of a Defendant's Evidence: An Unfortunate Approach to s.35(1)(b) of the Criminal Justice and Public Order Act 1994' [2011] *Crim LR* 690.

163 T Bucke, R Street and D Brown, *The Right to Silence: The Impact of the Criminal Justice and Public Order Act 1994* (Home Office Research Study No. 199) (London, Home Office, 2000) 56.

164 ibid.

165 A Tan, 'Adverse Inferences and the Right to Silence: Re-examining the Singapore Experience' [1997] *Crim LR* 471. See also HL Ho, 'The Privilege Against Self-Incrimination and Right of Access to a Lawyer: A Comparative Assessment' (2013) 25 *Singapore Academy of Law Journal* 826.

166 See J Jackson, 'Silence Legislation in Northern Ireland: The Impact After Ten Years' (2001) 6 *Journal of Civil Liberties* 134.

increase in the conviction rate or the rate of guilty pleas. One must bear in mind, however, that to try to isolate the effect of the CJPOA 1994 on juries' decision making would be problematic. In the absence of research into jury deliberations, the impact of silence on the outcome of cases can only be speculative. Nevertheless, the incentive element of the CJPOA 1994 may have encouraged more suspects and defendants to speak. Bucke *et al.*'s research points to a significant reduction in the extent to which suspects rely on their right to silence during police questioning, with the proportion of suspects refusing to answer some or all police questions falling from 23 to 16 per cent.[167] Still, there was no change in the proportion of suspects providing admissions.[168] This is consistent with a police perception that more suspects are lying. As to the use of silence in court, the impression of practitioners is that more defendants have been testifying.[169]

The incentivising function of the CJPOA 1994 has had a particularly acute impact on certain groups of people. Like sentence discounts for guilty pleas,[170] allowing inferences to be drawn from silence disproportionally affects black defendants. In a Home Office study conducted prior to implementation of the CJPOA 1994, Phillips and Brown found that black suspects were significantly more likely than either white or Asian suspects to exercise their right to silence in the police station.[171] This could be, in part, due to the lower levels of confidence in the police among black people than among white or Asian people.[172] In Bucke *et al.*'s post-CJPOA study, which is directly comparable to that of Phillips and Brown, there was a steep decline in the number of black suspects refusing to answer questions, in comparison to the decline among white and Asian suspects.[173] However, the number of black suspects refusing to answer all, or some, questions remained higher than that of Asian and white suspects.[174] Thus, black defendants appear to have been particularly susceptible to legislative pressure to

167 T Bucke, R Street and D Brown, *The Right to Silence: The Impact of the Criminal Justice and Public Order Act 1994* (Home Office Research Study No. 199) (London, Home Office, 2000) 31.

168 ibid 34.

169 ibid 52.

170 See ch 3.2.2.

171 Twenty-one per cent of black suspects refused to answer all questions, compared with 13 and 8 per cent respectively of Asian and white suspects. C Phillips and D Brown, *Entry into the Criminal Justice System: A Survey of Police Arrests and Their Outcomes* (Home Office Research Study No. 185) (London, Home Office, 1998) 78.

172 ibid.

173 Seven per cent of black suspects refused to answer all questions, compared with 6 and 5 per cent respectively of Asian and white suspects. T Bucke, R Street and D Brown, *The Right to Silence: The Impact of the Criminal Justice and Public Order Act 1994* (Home Office Research Study No. 199) (London, Home Office, 2000) 34.

174 Twelve per cent of black suspects refused to answer some questions, compared with 8 and 9 per cent respectively of Asian and white suspects. T Bucke, R Street and D Brown, *The Right to Silence: The Impact of the Criminal Justice and Public Order Act 1994* (Home Office Research Study No. 199) (London, Home Office, 2000) 34.

cooperate and, at the same time, face a disproportionate risk of being penalised as a result of exercising the right to silence and putting the prosecution to proof. This is the case despite their reliance on silence being, at least partially, attributable to poor relationships with the police, and not indicating a greater likelihood of guilt.

Bucke *et al.* concluded that the CJPOA 1994 has had a marked impact on: suspects' use of silence at the police station; police practices in relation to interviewing and disclosure; the advice given at the police station by legal advisors; the proportion of defendants testifying at trial; the way in which cases are prosecuted and defended at trial; and on judge's directions to the jury.[175] Perceptions of increased participation point to the conclusion that the pressure imposed on defendants to participate, and the inferences that may be drawn if they do not, has affected the voluntary nature of participation, particularly among black people. As Hodgson notes, the defendant is 'systematically restrained from behaving in an adversarial way, with penalties attaching to the exercise of the right to put the prosecution to proof'.[176] On the one hand, the lack of change in plea, charge and conviction rates indicates that the legislation has failed to further the aim of accurate fact-finding. On the other hand, the CJPOA 1994 has had an impact on the working of the criminal process, particularly the role of the defendant as a participant.

6.7 Reconsidering the right to silence

Both the domestic courts and Strasbourg have taken a 'silence is an indicator of guilt' approach in their assessments of the CJPOA 1994. They have, for the most part, adopted an expansive interpretation of the provisions, based on the belief that drawing inferences from silence is a matter of 'common sense'.[177] However, as Easton points out, common sense can be 'unreliable, impressionistic and unsystematic'.[178] Common sense may wrongly equate silence with guilt and fail to consider other possible factors underlying silence, such as fear and anxiety.[179] Juries may not be able to distinguish suspicious silence from innocent silence; they are currently being asked to speculate. This is unlikely to further the desired end of truth-finding. On the contrary, it creates greater potential for wrongful convictions. Although there is no evidence that the CJPOA 1994 has affected the conviction rate, it is possible that it is now easier for the prosecution to obtain convictions and that the conviction rate now includes more innocent defendants,

175 ibid xiii.

176 J Hodgson, 'The Future of Adversarial Criminal Justice in 21st Century Britain' (2010) 35 *North Carolina Journal of International Law and Commercial Regulation* 319, 332.

177 *Murray v DPP* [1994] 1 WLR 1 (HL); *R v Webber* [2004] UKHL 1, [2004] 1 WLR 404 [33].

178 S Easton, 'Legal Advice, Common Sense and the Right to Silence' (1998) 2 *E & P* 109, 114.

179 ibid.

particularly since it is frightened and vulnerable suspects who are most likely to succumb to pressure to confess.[180]

The danger of wrongful conviction and the risk of abuse of power is most prevalent in relation to police interrogations. For this reason, Dennis has submitted that section 34 'ought to be repealed as a matter of principle'.[181] This argument can be extended to sections 36 and 37. Suspects who are given a warning under one of these provisions may find themselves under even greater compulsion to speak than those whose silence can attract a section 34 inference. This is because they are expected to provide the police with a detailed account of the circumstances, even if this is not a reasonable expectation. Yet, it is precisely the isolating, intimidating and coercive nature of police interrogation which may make it unrealistic to expect many suspects to provide a full and accurate account.

Circumstances change at the trial stage, where the defendant knows the precise charges against him, has heard the evidence against him, has had the opportunity to challenge it and is participating in a public hearing before an impartial tribunal.[182] Although silence at the trial may offer some protection against wrongful conviction, it is difficult to justify a strong right to silence in court on the same policy basis as silence in the police station. However, from the perspective of a criminal process based on calling the state to account for the accusations against the accused, in-court silence can be justified. From this standpoint, an absolute right to silence should exist, such that no adverse consequences should flow from an accused person's decision to remain silent as a response to official questioning. This position expresses greater concern for the broader normative implications of limiting the right to silence, including implications for the presumption of innocence and the burden of proof. Unfortunately, at the time of reform to the right to silence, the focus on fact-finding and the risk to the innocent overshadowed broader issues of principle.[183]

One's view of the implications which allowing inferences to be drawn from silence has on the presumption of innocence will depend on how one interprets the presumption. On the one hand, it could be argued that inferences are a natural consequence of the defendant's silence and merely an application of common sense which has no bearing on the state's obligation to prove guilt. On the other hand, it could be argued, and it is submitted here, that the presumption of innocence should extend beyond the prosecution's burden of proof at trial; it should operate as a direction to treat the defendant as if he were innocent at all stages of the criminal process, until guilt is proved. In consequence, the defendant should not be required to play an active role in the state's obligation to prove guilt by answering questions, nor should his silence be used against him by the

180 See GH Gudjonsson, *The Psychology of Interrogations and Confessions: A Handbook* (Chichester, Wiley, 2003).

181 I Dennis, *The Law of Evidence,* 5th edn (London, Sweet & Maxwell, 2013) 208.

182 ibid 540.

183 See R Leng, 'The Right to Silence Reformed: A Re-appraisal of the Royal Commission's Influence' (2001) 6 *Journal of Civil Liberties* 107.

prosecution. Adherence to the presumption of innocence indicates that it is wrong to require an individual to supply evidence against himself.[184] On this basis, it can be argued that treating silence as evidence of guilt is at odds with the presumption of innocence.

At the very least, the CJPOA 1994 reduces the force of the presumption of innocence by implying that if an accused cannot, or does not, account for allegations against him, then those allegations must be true. As Auld LJ has stated:

> The whole basis of section 34, in its qualification of the otherwise general right of an accused to remain silent and to require the prosecution to prove its case, is an assumption that an innocent defendant . . . would give an early explanation to demonstrate his innocence.[185]

In the case of sections 36 and 37, it is also implied that failure to provide a full and adequate explanation of certain suspicious circumstances renders the suspicion well-founded, and that the failure can, therefore, be attributed to guilt, along with those circumstances. These types of implication are reminiscent of the pre-adversarial 'accused speaks' trial under which the onus was on the defendant to explain away any incriminating or suspicious circumstances.[186] Within the 'accused speaks' trial, the assumption was that if the defendant were innocent, he ought to be able to demonstrate it by the quality and character of his reply to the prosecutor's evidence.[187] The same assumption now seems to apply in relation, not only to the courtroom, but also to the accused's response to police questioning. The CJPOA 1994 clearly places the emphasis on the defendant's participation, rather than the prosecution's case. When the emphasis is on the defendant's participation, the presumption of innocence is much less pronounced.

In *O'Donnell v UK*, Judge Wojtyczek expressed the view that:

> A restriction on the right to silence affects the way in which the presumption of innocence operates in practice and entails a *de facto* reallocation of the burden of proof, even if such reallocation is not explicitly recognised in the legal system.[188]

In reviewing the impact of the CJPOA 1994, Bucke *et al.* found a difference in opinion amongst criminal justice practitioners as to whether the provisions had,

184 A Ashworth, 'Self-Incrimination in European Human Rights Law – A Pregnant Pragmatism?' (2008) 30 *Cardozo Law Review* 751, 768.

185 *R v Hoare* [2004] EWCA Crim 784, [2005] 1 WLR 1804 [53].

186 JH Langbein, *The Origins of the Adversary Criminal Trial* (Oxford, Oxford University Press, 2003). See ch 4.2.

187 JM Beattie, *Crime and the Courts in England 1660–1800* (Oxford, Clarendon Press, 1986) 341.

188 *O'Donnell v UK* [2015] ECHR 16667/10. Concurring opinion of Judge Wojtyczek [3].

in practice, if not in law, shifted the burden of proof onto the defendant. Those who felt that it did so argued that the defendant now has to effectively prove his innocence by accounting for his silence. Those who thought the opposite argued that the prosecution still has to prove its case beyond reasonable doubt.[189] Setting a high standard of proof encourages the jury to probe the prosecution case, rather than focusing on whether the defendant offered an adequate response to questioning. However, the participatory burden now placed on the defendant can detract from the prosecution's general burden of proof. Where the defendant neither participates, nor offers an adequate explanation for silence, the burden which the prosecution must discharge is eased by permitting the trier of fact to draw a direct inference of guilt on the basis that the defendant was not prepared to assert his innocence because he was not innocent.[190] This would appear to allow the trier of fact to raise the prosecution case up to the standard of proof beyond reasonable doubt when the case standing alone cannot reach this standard.[191]

The appropriate limits of state-induced pressure on the accused to respond to questioning may depend on one's view of the proper relationship between state and citizen. A strong libertarian view, as expressed here, holds that citizens must be accorded maximum freedom in deciding whether to cooperate with state investigations designed to establish guilt and inflict punishment. As noted in previous chapters, regard for suspects and defendants as autonomous citizens of a liberal polity, who should be protected from the state's potentially oppressive penal power, should prevent the state from requiring accused persons to participate in proceedings against themselves. By attaching a legal consequence to silence, the CJPOA 1994 places a participatory requirement on the defendant which undermines their autonomy. The choice now faced by the defendant is not simply between speaking and not speaking, but between answering questions, knowing that the response may be used against them in some way, or facing the prospect of silence being presented as evidence of guilt.

A less rigorous approach, such as that of Greenawalt, would hold that it is not, in principle, unfair to expect citizens to respond to well-founded accusations, where substantial evidence of wrongdoing exists.[192] The jurisprudence surrounding the CJPOA 1994 seems to correspond to this approach. Yet, even if one subscribes to this view, it should be acknowledged that the accusations which trigger the 1994 Act will not necessarily be well-founded. For example, in relation to sections 36 and 37, it is not obvious that being in possession of an object, substance or mark, or being at a place at or about the time an offence is alleged to have been

189 T Bucke, R Street and D Brown, *The Right to Silence: The Impact of the Criminal Justice and Public Order Act 1994* (Home Office Research Study No. 199) (London, Home Office, 2000) 57–58.

190 J Jackson, 'Interpreting the Silence Provisions: The Northern Ireland Cases' [1995] *Crim LR* 587, 600.

191 ibid.

192 K Greenawalt, 'Silence as a Moral and Constitutional Right' (1981) 23 *William & Mary Law Review* 15, 43.

committed will necessarily amount to substantial evidence of wrongdoing. The applicability of the provisions does not appear to depend on the existence of evidence of wrongdoing beyond the circumstances themselves. The police must reasonably believe that the relevant circumstances are attributable to the accused's participation in an offence, but what constitutes a 'reasonable belief' has not been tested.[193]

On the other end of the spectrum is the view that direct compulsion in the form of criminal sanctions for non-cooperation should be imposed to secure participation where it is not forthcoming. This is the approach that has been taken in regards to certain information that should ordinarily fall within the scope of the privilege against self-incrimination.[194] It is, therefore, not too far-fetched to envisage such an approach being taken in regard to the right to silence, if doing so was believed to further the aims of the criminal process.

It is important that we do not reach this extreme position. Ideally, a strong right to silence would exist, whereby the defendant can remain silent free from consequence. In order to achieve this, the relevant provisions of the CJPOA 1994 would need to be repealed. The prosecution would, once again, be prohibited from commenting on silence, and judicial comment to the effect that silence constitutes evidence of guilt would be considered a misdirection. Such an approach would be similar to that taken in other Anglo-American jurisdictions. In Canada, for example, to use silence as evidence of guilt is thought to be 'inimical to the dignity of the accused'.[195] Additionally, to ensure that erroneous 'common sense' inferences are not drawn, the judiciary would need to be placed under an obligation to direct the jury that innocent explanations for silence do exist, that silence can protect against misinterpretations and abuses of power, that the defendant has a right to remain silent and that silence should not be used as evidence of guilt.

Each of the silence provisions within the CJPOA 1994 is objectionable on the grounds that it has: eroded the right to silence; undermined the rationales behind it, including protection from wrongful conviction and abuse of power; and reduced the force of the presumption of innocence and burden of proof. In addition, the CJPOA 1994 forces the defendant to second guess his solicitor's

193 A Owusu-Bempah, 'Silence in Suspicious Circumstances' [2014] *Crim LR* 126, 130–131.

194 See *O'Halloran and Francis v UK* (2008) 46 EHRR 21, discussed in ch 5.3.

195 *R v Noble* [1997] 1 SCR 874 [75]. See also *R v Chambers* [1990] 2 SCR 1293; *R v Prokofiew* [2012] 2 SCR 639. In the United States, a strong right to silence exists under the Fifth Amendment of the Constitution, so long as it is specifically invoked by the accused. See *Griffin v California* 380 US 609 (1965); *Salinas v Texas* 133 S Ct 2174 (2013). Most states in Australia prohibit adverse prosecutorial and judicial comment on silence. See s 20 of the Uniform Evidence Act 1995. However, in 2013, legislative changes, based on s 34 CJPOA 1994, were made in New South Wales, allowing inferences to be drawn from silence in the police station under certain circumstances. See s 89A of the Evidence Act 1995 (NSW). In the international context, the Rome Statute of the International Criminal Court explicitly states that silence shall not be a consideration in the determination of guilt or innocence. See Article 55(2)(b) and Article 67(1)(g).

advice to remain silent and imposes an evidential burden on the defence to justify silence. It does all of this despite there being no demonstrated practical need for the legislation and without increasing the rate of confessions and convictions, or increasing efficiency. It has, however, increased participation, by putting the focus on the defendant and creating an expectation of cooperation. As Leng notes:

> In constitutional terms the reform represents a re-negotiation of the relationship between citizen and state under which the authority of the police is enhanced and the citizen, in the roles of suspect or defendant, is required to participate actively in the processes of investigation and trial.[196]

To penalise those who do not participate, through asserting the often tenuous link between silence and guilt, is counter to a system that allows the defence to test the prosecution case, while respecting defence rights and ensuring fairness. It is, thus, inconsistent with adversarial and rights based accounts of criminal procedure, as well as the normative theory which requires the state to account for the accusations it makes against the accused without his co-opted assistance.

196 R Leng, 'The Right to Silence Reformed: A Re-appraisal of the Royal Commission's Influence' (2001) 6 *Journal of Civil Liberties* 107, 132.

7 Disclosure

Prior to the trial, the prosecution and the defendant are under a duty to disclose to each other, and to the court, information about their case. Broad prosecution disclosure obligations are easy to justify; they are a means of ensuring fairness and redressing an inequality of arms. Without foreknowledge of the case against the accused, the defence may not know how to prepare for trial or what evidence to call.[1] Moreover, since they ordinarily lack the resources and statutory powers to carry out a full investigation, the defendant may be reliant on evidence uncovered by the police and prosecution in order to support their case. Consequently, the defendant has a strong interest in gaining access 'to all the fruits of the police investigation'.[2] The important position which prosecution disclosure holds in English criminal procedure can be traced back to the emergence of the adversarial system and, in particular, the Treason Trials Act of 1696 which included a provision granting treason defendants the right to obtain a copy of the indictment prior to the trial.[3]

It is difficult to advance an argument in favour of defence disclosure on similar grounds to that of prosecution disclosure. Prior to the Criminal Procedure and Investigations Act 1996 (CPIA 1996), the defendant was under no general duty to disclose his case before trial. The limited exceptions were: disclosure of alibi defences and alibi witnesses in trials on indictment;[4] disclosure of expert evidence in trials on indictment;[5] and a more general requirement to disclose a defence in some serious or complex cases of fraud.[6] The general position of non-disclosure can be justified as a reflection of the principle that the defendant need not respond until the prosecution has established a *prima facie* case in court.[7] As will be shown,

1 See M Redmayne, 'Criminal Justice Act 2003: (1) Disclosure and Its Discontents' [2004] *Crim LR* 441, 442.
2 I Dennis, *The Law of Evidence*, 5th edn (London, Sweet & Maxwell, 2013) 354.
3 On the development of the adversarial system, see ch 4.2.
4 Criminal Justice Act 1967, s 11.
5 Police and Criminal Evidence Act 1984 (PACE 1984), s 81.
6 Criminal Justice Act 1987, s 9(5).
7 R Leng, 'Losing Sight of the Defendant: The Government's Proposals on Pre-Trial Disclosure' [1995] *Crim LR* 704, 704.

supplying the prosecution with information about the nature and details of one's case prior to trial can assist in establishing a *prima facie* case, or otherwise establishing guilt. A non-disclosure norm thus reinforces a 'no-assistance' approach to the defendant's role in the criminal process, making voluntary the provision of information to the state, and ensuring that the state is able to account for the accusations brought against the defendant.

The CPIA 1996 restricted prosecution disclosure obligations and imposed new and radical duties on the defence. The most significant element of the legislation, for the purpose of this book, is the requirement to provide a defence statement which sets out the details of the defence case. Failure to comply with this requirement is penalised at trial through provisions which permit adverse comment to be made and adverse inferences to be drawn against the defendant. Such inferences may contribute to a finding of guilt. The disclosure requirements have been augmented by the case management provisions of the Criminal Procedure Rules (CrimPR) and judicial disdain for ambush defences. Taken together, the 'disclosure regime' imposes significant participatory requirements on both the defendant as an individual and the defence as a party.[8] However, it is the defendant who has the most to lose from disclosure failures, as the CPIA 1996 provides for penalties which can contribute to a conviction.[9] The disclosure regime has normative and practical implications for: the enforceability of certain fair trial rights; the defendant's role in the criminal process; and the nature of criminal procedure. Before exploring these implications, this chapter examines the rationale behind the CPIA 1996 and the participatory requirements imposed on the parties by the CPIA 1996 and the CrimPR.

7.1 Introduction of the CPIA 1996

Prosecution non-disclosure of exculpatory evidence can result (and has resulted) in wrongful convictions.[10] Yet, the CPIA 1996 was introduced partly as a response to complaints by the police that prosecution disclosure had become too generous.[11] Under the common law, and subject to public interest immunity, the defence had access to all possibly relevant prosecution material.[12] There was concern that this expansive approach to prosecution disclosure allowed the defence to go on 'fishing expeditions'; purposely wasting the time and resources

8 The Criminal Procedure and Investigations Act 1996 (CPIA 1996) imposes disclosure obligations directly on the accused. The Criminal Procedure Rules (CrimPR) impose duties and obligations on the 'participants' and the 'parties', which includes defence representatives.

9 Defence representatives can also be penalised for disclosure failures. For example, a wasted costs order can be made. See the discussion on penalties in ch 7.3.2.

10 See, for example, *R v Maguire* [1992] QB 936 (CA); *R v Ward* [1993] 1 WLR 619 (CA); *R v Taylor* (1994) 98 Cr App R 361 (CA).

11 See R Morgan, 'The Process is the Rule and the Punishment is the Process' (1996) 59 *MLR* 306.

12 *R v Keane* [1994] 1 WLR 746 (CA). See also *R v Ward* [1993] 1 WLR 619 (CA); *R v Brown* [1998] AC 367 (HL).

of the police and prosecution by requiring them to sort through large masses of material in the hope of either causing delay or finding something that would provoke the prosecution to drop the case. The defence could supposedly do this through successive requests for material, far beyond the stage at which it could reasonably be claimed that the information was likely to cast doubt upon the prosecution case.[13] However, there was a lack of evidence to support these assertions and, in response, one could argue that the defence is the best judge of what is relevant to its case.[14]

The limited disclosure obligations placed on the defence also caused concern to those considering reform,[15] particularly senior police officers who led a campaign for reform.[16] The general position of non-disclosure was thought to have provided an unwarranted advantage, allowing the defence to ambush prosecutors at trial with defences they were not prepared to address, resulting in unjust acquittals. This view persisted despite evidence that ambush defences were not a significant problem,[17] and despite section 34 of the Criminal Justice and Public Order Act 1994 (CJPOA 1994) having already been enacted to address the issue.

Although the reform campaign relied largely on anecdote, the Royal Commission on Criminal Justice responded to the concerns by recommending a disclosure regime based on two stages.[18] The prosecution would make primary disclosure, followed by the disclosure of a statement from the defence outlining the basics of its case. The prosecution would then make further disclosure of any information likely to assist the defence case. According to the Commission, the objective of the proposals was to 'bring forward the moment at which the issues which the jury will have to decide can be clearly and concisely laid out'.[19] The Commission believed that there were powerful reasons for extending disclosure obligations to the defence:

13 Royal Commission on Criminal Justice, *Report* (Cm 2263, 1993) 93.

14 M Redmayne, 'Criminal Justice Act 2003: (1) Disclosure and Its Discontents' [2004] *Crim LR* 441, 444.

15 Royal Commission on Criminal Justice, *Report* (Cm 2263, 1993) 97.

16 R Morgan, 'The Process is the Rule and the Punishment is the Process' (1996) 59 *MLR* 306, 307; M Redmayne, 'Process Gains and Process Values: The Criminal Procedure and Investigations Act 1996' (1997) 60 *MLR* 79, 84.

17 The majority of the Royal Commission on Criminal Justice recognised that ambush defences may cause 'no untoward practical disadvantages in the great majority of cases': Royal Commission on Criminal Justice, *Report* (Cm 2263, 1993) 98. Leng found that ambush defences were raised in 5 per cent of contested cases at the most. See R Leng, *The Right to Silence in Police Interrogation: A Study of Some of the Issues Underlying the Debate*, Royal Commission on Criminal Justice Research Study No. 10 (London, HMSO, 1993). Zander and Henderson found a rate of 7 to 10 per cent in a sample of Crown Court cases, with two fifths of these causing no problem for the prosecution. Moreover, these cases were more likely to end in conviction than acquittal. See M Zander and P Henderson, *The Crown Court Study*, Royal Commission on Criminal Justice Research Study No. 19 (London, HMSO, 1993). See also the discussion on ambush defences in ch 6.2.

18 Royal Commission on Criminal Justice, *Report* (Cm 2263, 1993) ch 6.

19 ibid 84.

> [T]his would not only encourage earlier and better preparation of cases but might well result in the prosecution being dropped in the light of the defence disclosure, an earlier resolution through a plea of guilty, or the fixing of an earlier trial date. The length of the trial could also be more readily estimated, leading to a better use of the time both of the court and of those involved in the trial; and there would be kept to a minimum those cases where the defendant withholds his or her defence until the last possible moment in the hope of confusing the jury or evading investigation of a fabricated defence.[20]

Not everyone was in agreement as to the benefits of the proposed reforms. Zander argued that a general requirement of defence disclosure would involve significant extra delays, costs and inefficiencies which, in practice, have been barriers to a smooth operation of the relevant provisions.[21] The disclosure regime has, in fact, led to significant delays, adjournments and ineffective trials, largely as a result of non-compliance by both parties, but particularly by the prosecution.[22]

The CPIA 1996, as originally enacted, was based on proposals set out in a Home Office Consultation Paper which was itself a response to the Royal Commission's recommendations.[23] However, the Act went further than the Commission had recommended; it introduced a more restrictive approach to prosecution disclosure and a broader approach to defence disclosure. It placed a greater emphasis on the alleged problems which disclosure causes to the prosecution than its importance as a safeguard against wrongful convictions. Initially, the disclosure regime did not work as intended.[24] It was not enforced with vigour and, unlike the CJPOA 1994, produced little case law on the applicability of adverse inferences for disclosure failures. In order to rectify this, amendments were made by part 5 of the Criminal Justice Act 2003 (CJA 2003). The amendments went some way towards expanding the prosecution's limited and subjective obligations. However, they also extended defence disclosure

20 ibid 97.

21 ibid 222. See also R Leng, 'Losing Sight of the Defendant: The Government's Proposals on Pre-Trial Disclosure' [1995] *Crim LR* 704.

22 A number of reviews have found that prosecution failures to comply with disclosure requirements have led to significant inefficiencies and generate far more concern than defence failures. See, for example, HM Crown Prosecution Service Inspectorate, *Disclosure: A Thematic Review of the Duties of Disclosure of Unused Material Undertaken by the CPS* (London, HMCPSI, 2008); Lord Justice Gross and Lord Justice Treacy, *Further Review of Disclosure in Criminal Proceedings: Sanctions for Disclosure Failure* (London, Judiciary of England and Wales, 2012); Lord Justice Gross, His Honour Judge Kinch and H Riddle, *Magistrates' Court Disclosure Review* (London, Judiciary of England and Wales, 2014).

23 Home Office, *Disclosure: A Consultation Document* (Cm 2864, 1995).

24 See HM Crown Prosecution Service Inspectorate, *Thematic Review of the Disclosure of Unused Material* (London, HMCPSI, 2000); J Plotnikoff and R Woolfson, *'A Fair Balance?' Evaluation of the Operation of Disclosure Law* (RDS Occasional Paper No. 76) (London, Home Office, 2001).

obligations, and made it easier to penalise defendant non-cooperation. Increased incentives and sanctions for defence non-disclosure were intended to increase convictions.[25] This demonstrates the twin-purpose of the disclosure regime as efficiently securing convictions.

Any practical improvements made by the CJA 2003 do not appear to have gone far enough in ensuring compliance or reducing inefficiencies, and a number of reviews have since been conducted with the aim of improving the operation of the current disclosure regime.[26] Quirk has contended that the disclosure regime cannot be made to work merely by amendment, because it lacks consideration for the working of cultures and practices of the key protagonists and, so, results in inappropriate allocations of responsibilities.[27] Quirk notes that:

> The statutory regime requires the culturally adversarial police to fulfil an effectively inquisitorial function; prosecutors to view material from a defence perspective; the defence to act in the interests of the administration of the justice system rather than of their clients; and defendants to cooperate with proceedings against themselves.[28]

These are all requirements which the respective parties are not necessarily well equipped to fulfil. Regardless of levels of compliance, however, the disclosure regime has promoted a change in both the role of the parties and the nature of criminal procedure.

7.2 Prosecution disclosure under the CPIA 1996

Section 3 Initial duty of prosecutor to disclose:

> (1) The prosecutor must-
>
> (a) disclose to the accused any prosecution material which has not previously been disclosed to the accused and which might reasonably be considered capable of undermining the case for the prosecution against the accused or of assisting the case for the accused, or
> (b) give to the accused a written statement that there is no material of a description mentioned in paragraph (a).

25 Home Office, *Justice for All* (Cm 5563, 2002) ch 3.

26 See Lord Justice Gross, *Review of Disclosure in Criminal Proceedings* (London, Judiciary of England and Wales, 2011); Lord Justice Gross and Lord Justice Treacy, *Further Review of Disclosure in Criminal Proceedings: Sanctions for Disclosure Failure* (London, Judiciary of England and Wales, 2012); Lord Justice Gross, His Honour Judge Kinch and H Riddle, *Magistrates' Court Disclosure Review* (London, Judiciary of England and Wales, 2014).

27 H Quirk, 'The Significance of Culture in Criminal Procedure Reform: Why the Revised Disclosure Scheme Cannot Work' (2006) 10 *E & P* 42.

28 ibid 46.

Section 7A Continuing duty of prosecutor to disclose:

> (2) The prosecutor must keep under review the question whether at any given time (and, in particular, following the giving of a defence statement) there is prosecution material which —
>
> (a) might reasonably be considered capable of undermining the case for the prosecution against the accused or of assisting the case for the accused, and
>
> (b) has not been disclosed to the accused.

This chapter is primarily concerned with the disclosure obligations imposed on the defendant and the defence. However, it is worth noting the duties of the prosecution, so that defence disclosure can be considered in the context of the disclosure regime as a whole. It is a fundamental principle that a defendant should not be tried without knowing the nature of the case against him.[29] As stated by the Court of Appeal: 'in our adversarial system, in which the police and prosecution control the investigatory process, an accused's right to fair disclosure is an inseparable part of his right to a fair trial'.[30] The right to disclosure is recognised in Article 6(3)(a) of the European Convention on Human Rights (ECHR), which provides that everyone charged with a criminal offence has the right to be informed promptly, in a language which he understands and in detail, of the nature and cause of the accusation against him. Prosecution disclosure is also an essential part of ensuring equality of arms between the parties.[31] To achieve this, Article 6(1) requires that 'the prosecution authorities should disclose to the defence all material evidence in their possession for or against the accused'.[32]

There has long been a general and uncontroversial principle that the prosecution should disclose the evidence it will rely on at trial. The CPIA 1996 is primarily concerned with the disclosure of material that does not form part of the prosecution case, commonly referred to as 'unused material'. The Act governs disclosure from the point at which a not-guilty plea is entered for a summary trial in the magistrates' court or the case arrives in the Crown Court for trial on indictment, and continues until the conclusion of the proceedings.[33]

29 See *Jespers v Belgium* (1981) 27 DR 61; *Edwards v UK* (1992) 15 EHRR 417; *Secretary of State for the Home Department v F* [2009] UKHL 28, [2010] 2 AC 269.

30 *R v Brown* [1994] 1 WLR 1599 (CA) 1606 (Steyn LJ).

31 *Rowe and Davis v UK* (2000) 30 EHRR 1 [60].

32 ibid [60]–[61]. This is subject to restrictions which are 'strictly necessary' and counterbalanced by the procedures followed by the judicial authorities.

33 CPIA 1996, ss 1 and 7A. During the period between arrest and application of the CPIA 1996, the police and prosecution have some duty to disclose the information necessary to enable the accused to receive informed advice from his solicitor. See *DPP v Ara* [2001] EWHC Admin 493, [2002] 1 WLR 815. The police are also under a duty to provide sufficient information to the accused and his solicitor before interview to enable them to understand the nature of the alleged offence, and why the accused is suspected of committing it. However,

The CPIA 1996 initially split the prosecution's duty of disclosure into two stages. The first stage was governed by section 3 which originally provided that the prosecution must disclose materials 'which in the prosecutor's opinion might undermine the case for the prosecution against the accused'. It now provides for the disclosure to the accused of 'any prosecution material . . . which might reasonably be considered capable of undermining the case for the prosecution against the accused or of assisting the case for the accused'.[34] This is a more objective standard. Assuming that the defence complied with the duty to provide a defence statement, the original CPIA 1996 then imposed upon the prosecution secondary disclosure obligations. Section 7 required the prosecution to 'disclose to the accused any prosecution material which has not previously been disclosed to the accused and which might be reasonably expected to assist the accused's defence'.

The original two stage procedure was highly subjective and dependent on defence disclosure. It was amended by the CJA 2003. Section 7A now puts the prosecution under a duty of continuous disclosure; they must keep under review whether there is any evidence capable of undermining the prosecution case or assisting the defence. The amended section 3 and the new section 7A effectively eliminated the distinction between primary and secondary disclosure, and make it difficult to regard prosecution disclosure as being conditional on the service of a defence statement. However, the two remain linked in a practical way: the more that is disclosed in the defence statement, the more likely it is to alert the prosecution to disclosable material in its possession.[35] Despite the amendments, it could be argued that the prosecution's disclosure obligations do not go far enough to ensure equality of arms. Whereas Article 6 requires that 'the prosecution authorities should disclose to the defence all material evidence in their possession for or against the accused',[36] sections 3 and 7A confine the obligation to disclosure of material which is capable of undermining the prosecution or assisting the defence. By limiting prosecution disclosure, the CPIA 1996 may put the parties in a less equal position, compromising the defendant's ability to have a fair trial.[37]

'this does not require the disclosure of details at a time which might prejudice the criminal investigation'. See PACE 1984, Code C, para 11.1A and Note 11ZA. Beyond this, there is no general duty to disclose material, and any disclosure that might be required cannot normally exceed the duty of disclosure under the CPIA 1996. The test for disclosure is what justice and fairness requires of the responsible prosecutor in the circumstances of each case. See *R v DPP ex p Lee* [1999] 1 WLR 1950 (QB) 1963. Following conviction, the prosecution's duty of disclosure is limited to the duty to disclose any material coming to light that might cast doubt upon the safety of the conviction. See *R (on the application of Nunn) v Chief Constable of Suffolk* [2014] UKSC 37, [2015] AC 225.

34 CPIA 1996, s 3(1)(a).

35 M Redmayne, 'Criminal Justice Act 2003: (1) Disclosure and Its Discontents' [2004] *Crim LR* 441, 445.

36 *Rowe and Davis v UK* (2000) 30 EHRR 1 [60]–[61].

37 However, it is unlikely that the CPIA 1996 would be found to be in breach of Article 6. See SD Sharpe, 'The Human Rights Act 1998: Part 3: Article 6 and the Disclosure of Evidence

In terms of enforcement, there is a clear imbalance in the 1996 Act.[38] Whereas defendant non-compliance may be penalised with adverse comment and adverse inferences, there are no such provisions within the Act to sanction prosecution non-disclosure. In some cases, the defendant may be the one who is penalised for prosecution failures to comply with disclosure obligations, as defence failures can be caused by prosecution delays.[39] However, specific penalties for prosecution non-compliance may be felt unnecessary, since the defence can apply for further disclosure under section 8 if there is reasonable cause to believe that there is prosecution material required to be disclosed by section 7A. Yet, section 8 only applies if the defendant has complied with the obligation to furnish a defence statement,[40] emphasising the perceived importance of defence cooperation. There is, also, the possibility of the judge using section 78 of the Police and Criminal Evidence Act 1984 (PACE 1984) to exclude prosecution evidence not previously disclosed, where its admission would have such an adverse effect on the fairness of the proceedings that the court ought not to admit it.[41] As a last resort, prosecution disclosure failures could lead to an application to stay the proceedings on grounds of abuse of process.[42] There is, however, very little evidence of any real sanction being imposed for defective prosecution disclosure.[43] Moreover, appeals against conviction on the basis of disclosure failures will only be successful

in Criminal Trials' [1999] *Crim LR* 273. On the uncertain scope of the right to disclosure, see J Jackson and S Summers, *The Internationalisation of Criminal Evidence: Beyond the Common Law and Civil Law Traditions* (Cambridge, Cambridge University Press, 2012) ch 9.

38 For a critique of the imbalance in sanctions, see C Taylor, 'The Disclosure Sanctions Review: Another Missed Opportunity?' (2013) 17 *E & P* 272.

39 That the prosecution may be the cause of defence failures was acknowledged in Lord Justice Gross and Lord Justice Treacy, *Further Review of Disclosure in Criminal Proceedings: Sanctions for Disclosure Failure* (London, Judiciary of England and Wales, 2012). However, the review did not recommend strengthening sanctions against the prosecution.

40 CPIA 1996, s 8(1).

41 See, for example, *R v Boardman* [2015] EWCA Crim 175, [2015] 1 Cr App R 33.

42 Applications to stay proceeding have been discouraged. See Lord Justice Gross and Lord Justice Treacy, *Further Review of Disclosure in Criminal Proceedings: Sanctions for Disclosure Failure* (London, Judiciary of England and Wales, 2012) 9. See also, *R v Salt* [2015] EWCA Crim 662, [2015] 1 WLR 4905, in which the Court of Appeal set aside a stay of proceedings following prosecution disclosure failures; *R v Asiedu* [2015] EWCA Crim 714, [2015] 2 Cr App R 8, in which it was held that prosecution non-disclosure was not, by itself, an abuse of court process; *R v TJC* [2015] EWCA Crim 1276, [2015] Crim LR 1018, in which the Recorder had been wrong to rule that it would be an abuse of process to try the defendant on a count that the Recorder felt was not properly particularised; *R v R* [2015] EWCA Crim 1941, [2016] 1 Cr App R 20, in which the trial judge had been wrong to stay proceedings as an abuse of process due to delay arising from disclosure of large quantities of electronic documents. The Court of Appeal found that the delay, of itself, was not sufficient to warrant a conclusion that there could not be a fair trial, serious prejudice must also be shown (at [66]).

43 C Taylor, 'The Disclosure Sanctions Review: Another Missed Opportunity?' (2013) 17 *E & P* 272, 277–279.

if the failure renders the conviction unsafe.[44] The CPIA 1996 demonstrates greater concern for the participation and cooperation of the defence than the prosecution, by expressly subjecting defence failures to specific penalties.

The CPIA 1996 is accompanied by a number of guidelines intended to ensure proper prosecution disclosure,[45] including the Code of Practice issued under part 2 of the Act. The Code provides, *inter alia*, that the investigating police officers have a duty to record all information received and to make disclosure of it to the prosecutor.[46] They are also required to pursue all reasonable lines of inquiry.[47] Yet, there is significant concern that disclosure is often inadequate, and appeals on the grounds of defective disclosure are not uncommon.[48] The institutional divide between the police and the prosecution is problematic. The police may not know enough about the legal elements of the case to appreciate the significance of some of the material, and the Crown Prosecution Service (CPS) is unable to disclose information to the defence which has not been disclosed to them by the police through schedules of material. The defence may, as a result, be deprived of material relevant to its case. In addition, the police may perceive themselves as agents of the prosecution and may know that undisclosed material will often not be discovered. Consequently, they may be reluctant to reveal information likely to damage the prosecution's case.[49]

Research on the operation of the CPIA 1996 has consistently found that schedules of material prepared by the police are poor, and that, due in part to inadequate resources, the CPS often make late or incomplete disclosure to the defence.[50] In addition, doubts have been expressed as to the motivation of

44 See, for example, *R v Kenedy* [2008] EWCA Crim 2817.

45 See, for example, *The Attorney General's Guidelines on Disclosure* (2013); *Judicial Protocol on the Disclosure of Unused Material in Criminal Cases* (2013).

46 Criminal Procedure and Investigations Act 1996 Code of Practice (Code of Practice), paras 4.1–4.4 and 7.1–7.5. The Code was revised in 2015 such that if a guilty plea is anticipated in a trial at the magistrates' court, a schedule of unused material need not be served. See the Code of Practice, paras 6.1–6.5. The revisions are the result of recommendations of the Magistrates' Court Disclosure Review. See Lord Justice Gross, His Honour Judge Kinch and H Riddle, *Magistrates' Court Disclosure Review* (London, Judiciary of England and Wales, 2014).

47 Code of Practice, para 3.5.

48 For a recent successful appeal, see *R v Joof* [2012] EWCA Crim 1475. In its 2014 Annual Report, the Criminal Cases Review Commission noted that 'We continue to see a number of cases involving the non-disclosure of significant information.' Criminal Cases Review Commission, *Annual Report and Accounts 2013/14* (London, HMSO, 2014) 7.

49 See, for example, *R v Maxwell* [2010] UKSC 48, [2011] 1 WLR 1837. See also H Quirk, 'The Significance of Culture in Criminal Procedure Reform: Why the Revised Disclosure Scheme Cannot Work' (2006) 10 *E & P* 42, 48.

50 See, HM Crown Prosecution Service Inspectorate, *Thematic Review of the Disclosure of Unused Material* (London, HMCPSI, 2000); J Plotnikoff and R Woolfson, '*A Fair Balance?' Evaluation of the Operation of Disclosure Law* (RDS Occasional Paper No. 76) (London, Home Office, 2001) ch 4; HM Crown Prosecution Service Inspectorate, *Disclosure: A Thematic Review of the Duties of Disclosure of Unused Material Undertaken by the CPS*

the prosecution when undertaking work of this nature, in particular whether they have the incentive to do a thorough job.[51] Yet, despite the difficulties which defective prosecution disclosure can, and does, cause for the defence and the overall fairness of the criminal process, official reports and reviews tend to emphasise the need for defence compliance with disclosure duties.[52]

7.3 Defence disclosure under the CPIA 1996

Section 5 Compulsory duty by accused:

> (5) Where this section applies, the accused must give a defence statement to the court and the prosecutor.

The CPIA 1996 imposed, for the first time in the history of English criminal procedure, a general duty on the defendant to make pre-trial disclosure. In its 1993 Report, the Royal Commission recommended the defence disclose sufficient information for the prosecution to understand the substance of its case. Section 5, however, requires disclosure of a much more detailed defence statement. Disclosure must be made once the prosecution has purported to have complied with the initial disclosure obligations under section 3.[53] The general duty to produce a defence statement is voluntary in the magistrates' court, but compulsory in the Crown Court.[54] This is significant because the vast majority of criminal cases are heard in the magistrates' court. However, since prosecution and defence disclosure remain linked in a practical way, the defendant may gain from disclosing his case in summary trials. In particular, the defence cannot request further disclosure under section 8 unless a defence statement has been provided to the court and prosecutor.[55]

(London, HMCPSI, 2008); Lord Justice Gross, *Review of Disclosure in Criminal Proceedings* (London, Judiciary of England and Wales, 2011) 38–42; Lord Justice Gross, His Honour Judge Kinch and H Riddle, *Magistrates' Court Disclosure Review* (London, Judiciary of England and Wales, 2014) 19.

51 Lord Justice Gross, *Review of Disclosure in Criminal Proceedings* (London, Judiciary of England and Wales, 2011) 38.

52 See, for example, Lord Justice Gross, *Review of Disclosure in Criminal Proceedings* (London, Judiciary of England and Wales, 2011); Lord Justice Gross and Lord Justice Treacy, *Further Review of Disclosure in Criminal Proceedings: Sanctions for Disclosure Failure* (London, Judiciary of England and Wales, 2012). See also C Taylor, 'The Disclosure Sanctions Review: Another Missed Opportunity?' (2013) 17 *E & P* 272.

53 Submission of the defence statement is subject to a 28 day time limit in the Crown Court and a 14 day time limit in the magistrates' court. See CPIA 1996, s 12 and the Criminal Procedure and Investigations Act 1996 (Defence Disclosure Time Limits) Regulations 2011/209.

54 CPIA 1996, ss 5 and 6.

55 ibid s 8(1).

7.3.1 Defence statements

Section 6A Contents of defence statement:

(1) For the purposes of this Part a defence statement is a written statement –

(a) setting out the nature of the accused's defence, including any particular defences on which he intends to rely,
(b) indicating the matters of fact on which he takes issue with the prosecution,
(c) setting out, in the case of each such matter, why he takes issue with the prosecution,
(ca) setting out particulars of the matters of fact on which he intends to rely for the purposes of his defence, and
(d) indicating any point of law (including any point as to the admissibility of evidence or an abuse of process) which he wishes to take, and any authority on which he intends to rely for that purpose.

As originally enacted, the CPIA 1996 required a defence statement which set out in general terms the nature of the accused's defence; indicated the matters on which he took issue with the prosecution; and set out, in the case of each such matter, the reason why he took issue with the prosecution. The statement also needed to include the particulars of any alibi. The current statutory regime for the content of defence statements was inserted by the CJA 2003 and can be found in section 6A(1), as set out above.[56] The provision requires the accused to 'specify his defence with particularity'.[57] Where the defendant has no positive case to advance at trial, the defence statement must say that the defendant does not admit the offence and calls the Crown to prove it. It should also say that he advances no positive case.[58] If the defendant is going to advance a positive case that must appear in the defence statement and notice must be given. However, where there has been no defence statement and no positive defence put forward at trial, the significance of the absent defence statement may be marginal.[59]

Section 6A(2) provides that a defence statement which discloses an alibi must give particulars of it, including the name, address and date of birth of any alibi witnesses. The obligation to give details of alibi witnesses is triggered by the defendant's belief that the witness could give evidence in support of the alibi.[60] The defendant is expected to disclose the details regardless of whether the witness can in fact give such evidence or whether they are willing to do so. Moreover,

56 On defence statements, see generally RL Denyer, 'The Defence Statement' [2009] *Crim LR* 340; C Taylor, 'The Evolution of the Defence Statement' (2010) 74 *Journal of Criminal Law* 214; A Owusu-Bempah, 'Defence Participation through Pre-Trial Disclosure: Issues and Implications' (2013) 17 *E & P* 183.

57 I Dennis, *The Law of Evidence*, 5th edn (London, Sweet & Maxwell, 2013) 362.

58 *R v Rochford* [2010] EWCA Crim 1928, [2011] 1 WLR 534.

59 *R v Essa* [2009] EWCA Crim 43 [22].

60 *Re Joseph Hill & Company Solicitors* [2013] EWCA Crim 775, [2014] 1 WLR 786 [34].

if the defendant will not be specific about his alibi, defence counsel are expected to disclose the identity of potential alibi witnesses.[61] In *Re Joseph Hill & Company Solicitors*, the Court of Appeal took the view that defence counsel should have identified the defendant's family members who were at home at the time of the alleged offence, as these were the persons who were able to give evidence in support of the defendant's claim to have been at home himself.[62] This case provides an example of the way in which defence lawyers are at times expected to act in the interests of the administration of justice rather than their client's interest in presenting a strong and consistent defence. The defendant might be criticised in court if a person identified by his lawyer does not, in fact, give evidence. Where this occurs, the disclosure obligations imposed on the defence can act to assist the prosecution in strengthening its case, or provide ammunition to undermine the defence case. Disclosure of information by defence counsel, including the identity of potential witnesses, may also conflict with the demands of client confidentiality.[63]

Section 6B (which is not yet in force) creates a duty of updated defence disclosure. It requires the defendant to provide an updated defence statement within a specific time period or a written statement that no changes have been made to the defence statement. Section 6C provides for the disclosure of the names, addresses and dates of birth of all defence witnesses. This provision came into force in 2010. Disclosure under section 6C is mandatory in both the magistrates' court and the Crown Court. Where the defendant wishes to call a witness who was not included in the original notice under section 6C, he must serve an amended notice. In many cases, the witness list will be tentative, as the defence may not be sure of whom to call until after completion of the prosecution evidence. This raises questions about the enforceability of section 6C in practice.[64] Section 6C takes the defence disclosure obligations far beyond what was proposed by the Royal Commission. The Commission had decided

61 ibid [36].

62 ibid.

63 See E Cape, 'Rebalancing the Criminal Justice Process: Ethical Challenges for Criminal Defence Lawyers' (2006) 9 *Legal Ethics* 56, 75–77; F Garland and J McEwan, 'Embracing the Overriding Objective: Difficulties and Dilemmas in the New Criminal Climate' (2012) 16 *E&P* 233, 247–248. However, the Law Society advises that the duty to conduct the case in accordance with the overriding objective of the CrimPR, which includes respecting the rights of the defendant, means that a court cannot ask solicitors to reveal what a defendant has told them if it is protected by legal professional privilege, unless the defendant consents. See the Law Society's practice note, *Criminal Procedure Rules 2015: Solicitors' Duties*, available at <www.lawsociety.org.uk/support-services/advice/practice-notes/the-criminal-procedure-rules-2015-solicitors-duties/> accessed 1 April 2016.

64 While adverse comment and inferences can follow non-compliance, it is generally not permissible to sanction a failure to mention a witness by refusal to allow that witness to be called. This also brings into question the enforceability of s 6A(2). See *R (on the application of Tinnion) v Reading Crown Court* [2009] EWHC 2930 (Admin), (2010) 174 JP 36; *R v Ullah* [2011] EWCA Crim 3275.

not to recommend the disclosure of the names and addresses of defence witnesses, partly on the basis that:

> such a requirement might lead to a breach of the principle that the defence should not be required to help the prosecution prove its case because the prosecution might itself call any witnesses disclosed by the defence whom the defence in the event decided not to call.[65]

Concerns have also been expressed about the implications of police interviewing proposed defence witnesses.

In the light of the extra time and resources that would be required, it is unlikely that police will routinely interview defence witnesses. Nonetheless, the police could put pressure on defence witnesses and 'use the interview to browbeat, cajole or wheedle the witness to change his evidence or, failing that, not to testify for the defence'.[66] Zander contends that giving the police the power to influence witnesses is itself an invitation to poison the well by 'undue influence', as they naturally want to get the evidence that will convict the defendant.[67] In response to concerns about police conduct, section 21A of the CPIA 1996 provides for a Code of Practice regulating police interviews of defence witnesses. The Code of Practice requires the police to notify the defence before the interview and, if the witness consents, to give an opportunity for the defendant's solicitor to be present at any such interview.[68] It also states that the witness must consent to the interview and is entitled to be accompanied by a solicitor.[69]

There are a number of shortcomings with the Code of Practice.[70] For instance, where the witness gives consent for the defendant's solicitor to attend, her role is limited to that of observer.[71] The defendant's solicitor is not entitled to intervene if the police questioning becomes inappropriate, thus preventing her from serving a useful purpose during the interview. The witness must also consent before the defendant can receive a copy of the record of interview.[72] Where consent is not forthcoming, it may be open to the prosecution to ambush the defence. For example, the prosecution may put an adverse matter from the interview to the

65 Royal Commission on Criminal Justice, *Report* (Cm 2263, 1993) 99.

66 M Zander, 'Consultation on Proposals for Advance Disclosure of Defence Witness Lists and Unused Defence Expert Witness Reports' (2002) 2. Available at <www.lse.ac.uk/collections/law/staff%20publications%20full%20text/zander/adv.discl..pdf> accessed 1 April 2016.

67 ibid.

68 Code of Practice for Arranging and Conducting Interviews of Witnesses Notified by the Accused, paras 4.1 and 6.

69 ibid para 3.1. However, para 3.1 makes it clear that the Code does not create any duty to provide funding for attendance of a solicitor.

70 See P Hungerford-Welch, 'Prosecution Interviews of Defence Witnesses' [2010] *Crim LR* 690.

71 Code of Practice for Arranging and Conducting Interviews of Witnesses Notified by the Accused, para 8.2.

72 ibid paras 3.2 and 11.2.

witness during cross-examination, including matters relating to her consistency and credibility.[73] Such matters would not need to be disclosed as part of the prosecution's CPIA 1996 obligations if they assist the prosecution case or undermine the defence case, rather than undermine the prosecution or assist the defence.[74] The possibility that section 6C exposes the defence to ambush is ironic, given that the CPIA 1996 was enacted, in part, as a response to concerns about ambush defences. While the prosecution ambush may not go directly to an issue in the case in the same way as an ambush by the defence can, the distinction between a fact in issue and the credibility of a witness can be difficult to draw, and of little significance.[75] There is, thus, a contradiction in this approach.

Where witnesses decline to be interviewed by the police, the prosecution may wish to cross-examine them on their refusal, in an attempt to undermine the credibility of their evidence. This places the defendant in danger of being prejudiced by a refusal to cooperate over which he may have little or no control.[76] The defence case may, therefore, be damaged, and the defendant put at a detriment, by the witness's unwillingness to be subject to scrutiny or to confirm the defence's case prior to trial. This would appear to extend the expectation of active participation beyond the defendant and his representatives, to anyone who is affiliated with the defence.

Section 6D (which is not yet in force) requires disclosure of the names and addresses of experts consulted by the defence, but not used. This provision is presumably intended to prevent the defence from 'shopping around' for experts to support its case. Shopping around occurs very rarely in practice.[77] Where it does occur, it may be necessary because, for example, the case concerns a developing field, or a medical opinion is needed in connection with a mental condition for which diagnosis is not an exact science. The number of experts consulted may have no impact on the validity of their views. It is, nonetheless, possible for the prosecution to benefit from disclosure under section 6D. From the jury's point of view, the adverse view of an expert originally consulted by the defence might carry more weight than that of other prosecution experts because it would seem to be evidence coming from the defence stable.[78] Moreover, the defendant may

73 P Hungerford-Welch, 'Prosecution Interviews of Defence Witnesses' [2010] *Crim LR* 690, 696.

74 CPIA 1996, s 7A. See also, *R v H* [2004] UKHL 3, [2004] 2 AC 134 [35], where Lord Bingham states that: 'If material does not weaken the prosecution case or strengthen that of the defendant, there is no requirement to disclose it. . . . Neutral material or material damaging the defendant need not be disclosed and should not be brought to the attention of the court.'

75 See S Seabrooke, 'The Vanishing Trick – Blurring the Line Between Credit and Issue' [1999] *Crim LR* 387.

76 P Hungerford-Welch, 'Prosecution Interviews of Defence Witnesses' [2010] *Crim LR* 690, 699.

77 M Zander, 'Consultation on Proposals for Advance Disclosure of Defence Witness Lists and Unused Defence Expert Witness Reports' (2002) 12. Available at <www.lse.ac.uk/collections/law/staff%20publications%20full%20text/zander/adv.discl..pdf> accessed 1 April 2016.

78 ibid 14.

be prejudiced by disclosing the fact that numerous experts were approached. The jury might over speculate to the detriment of the defendant. However, any instructions which the expert received from the defence are privileged. In most cases, the prosecution will not be able to gain anything useful from knowledge of unused experts. For this reason, this duty of notification has been described as 'largely a waste of time'.[79] Both sections 6C and 6D give the impression that they are designed more for their symbolic resonance than for their practical utility.[80] The provisions raise difficulties of enforceability and address no obvious problem. Yet, they emphasise the desire to secure the participation of the defendant, as well as the defence as a party, throughout the criminal process.

In comparison to the defendant's previous position of generally not being required to disclose any information before the trial, the CPIA 1996 has placed what are arguably vast and detailed participatory obligations upon him. However, compliance with the disclosure obligations is not always forthcoming. In an examination of the original CPIA 1996, Plotnikoff and Woolfson found that 41 per cent of defence statements contained only a denial of guilt, and a further 13 per cent fell short of the requirements set out for them.[81] Following the CJA 2003 amendments, there remain concerns about compliance.

It is the content of defence statements which seems to have caused the most concern for the courts.[82] In *Bryant,* for example, it was stated that the defence statement in issue was 'woefully inadequate'.[83] It consisted of a general denial of the counts in the indictment accompanied by the sentence, 'The defendant takes issue with any witness purporting to give evidence contrary to his denials.' The Court of Appeal took the view that 'That sort of observation is not worth the paper it is written on. It is not the purpose of a defence case statement.'[84] Concern about defence cooperation with the disclosure regime was also expressed in a review of disclosure, undertaken by Lord Justice Gross for the Judiciary of England and Wales in 2011 (the Gross Report). The Report declared that 'a defence refusal to engage in the disclosure process, coupled with persistent sniping at its suggested inadequacies, is unacceptable – and reflects a culture with which the system should not rest content'.[85] This statement is indicative of a view that the courts should not tolerate disclosure failures and should be willing to penalise non-compliance.

79 I Dennis, *The Law of Evidence,* 5th edn (London, Sweet & Maxwell, 2013) 364.

80 M Redmayne, 'Criminal Justice Act 2003: (1) Disclosure and Its Discontents' [2004] *Crim LR* 441, 448.

81 J Plotnikoff and R Woolfson, '*A Fair Balance?' Evaluation of the Operation of Disclosure Law* (RDS Occasional Paper No. 76) (London, Home Office, 2001) 55.

82 On the varying judicial attitudes towards defence statements, see P Darbyshire, 'Judicial Case Management in Ten Crown Courts' [2014] *Crim LR* 30, 40–41.

83 *R v Bryant* [2005] EWCA Crim 2079 [12] (Judge LJ).

84 ibid.

85 Lord Justice Gross, *Review of Disclosure in Criminal Proceedings* (London, Judiciary of England and Wales, 2011) 75.

7.3.2 Penalising disclosure failures

Section 11 Faults in disclosure by accused:

(5) Where this section applies —

(a) the court or any other party may make such comment as appears appropriate;

(b) the court or jury may draw such inferences as appear proper in deciding whether the accused is guilty of the offence concerned.

Defence disclosure is enforced through section 11 of the CPIA 1996, under which failure to disclose a defence statement, late disclosure or departure from the statement can result in adverse comment and adverse inferences being drawn against the defendant. Such inferences may be drawn in deciding whether the defendant is guilty. A failure to participate can, therefore, be used as evidence of guilt and contribute to a finding of guilt. By way of safeguards, section 11(8) states that where the accused puts forward a defence which is different to that in his defence statement, the court should have regard to the extent of the differences between the defences, and to whether there is any justification for a change in defence. By virtue of section 11(9), the court should also have regard to any justification for a failure to give notice of a defence witness, and, pursuant to section 11(10), the accused cannot be convicted solely on an inference drawn under section 11(5).[86]

Withholding information on the basis of legal advice will not in itself preclude adverse comment or inferences. In *Essa,* a claim that legal advice explained the absence of a defence statement did not prevent the prosecution from making comments and cross-examining the defendant about the disclosure failure.[87] Had there been evidence of the solicitor's advice, the Court of Appeal felt that it should have been dealt with in the same way as advice to remain silent.[88] This approach to the relevance of legal advice may force the defendant to second guess the advice of his lawyer and risk the value of legal advice becoming eroded, as it has in relation to silence.[89] However, legal advice is less likely to be an issue in relation to disclosure. The Court of Appeal made it clear that, where the legislation requires disclosure of a defence statement, it is not open to lawyers to advise their clients not to give a defence statement.[90]

Despite the fact that defence statements often lack the required detail, judges have seemed reluctant to sanction defendants with adverse inferences. This is evidenced by the lack of case law dealing directly with the conditions under which

86 It is likely that, following Strasbourg's approach to inferences from silence, disclosure failures should not be a main decisive factor. See *Murray v UK* (1996) 22 EHRR 29 [47].

87 *R v Essa* [2009] EWCA Crim 43.

88 ibid [21].

89 See the discussion on legal advice to remain silent in ch 6.3.1.

90 *R v Essa* [2009] EWCA Crim 43 [18].

an adverse inference can be drawn from non-disclosure, when compared to that concerning adverse inferences drawn from silence under the CJPOA 1994.[91] The courts appear to be more concerned with the inadequacy of defence statements from a managerial point of view, and it makes little sense to invite inferences of guilt on the basis that non-disclosure interferes with efficiency. However, a recent recommendation that the sanctions within section 11 be 'used to their full effect',[92] may increase the prevalence of adverse comment and inferences.

The link between non-disclosure and guilt is even more tenuous than the link between silence and guilt, discussed in the previous chapter. The CJPOA 1994 relies on a supposed link between silence and guilt, under which silence in the face of police questioning or in court is in itself suspicious. Adverse inferences from non-disclosure, on the other hand, depend on the creation of disclosure duties.[93] The defendant's failure to disclose the details of his defence before trial is only suspicious because the law places an obligation on him to do so. Ashworth and Redmayne note that, for this reason, the inference that the defence is fabricated (or that the defendant is guilty) is surely a weak one.[94] This is particularly true where the non-disclosure relates to a point of law, where disclosure is late or where the problem is an insufficiently detailed defence statement but the defence raised is along the same lines as that disclosed. It is difficult to see how the lack of detail can point to guilt. This is not to say that non-disclosure of evidence presented at trial is never the result of fabrication or guilt, but that the link is not a straightforward or obvious one. Some judges may, therefore, feel that it is inappropriate to invite the jury to make a direct link between non-disclosure and guilt.

Aside from the insufficient link between the breach and the punishment, judges may have felt reluctant to give an adverse inference direction under the original CPIA 1996 because fault in defence disclosure was likely to lie with the defence representative rather than the defendant.[95] As a response, the CJA 2003 amendments imposed a tougher regime on defendants. The amendments removed the requirement for leave to be given by the court before 'such comment as appears appropriate' is made by the prosecutor or co-defendant.[96] In addition,

91 The body of case law concerning the applicability of s 11 has grown in recent years. For four recent cases, see *R v Gregory* [2011] EWCA Crim 3276; *R v Haynes* [2011] EWCA Crim 3281; *R v Haigh* [2013] EWCA Crim 2359; *R v Adeyinka* [2014] EWCA Crim 504. For two significant older cases, see *R v Tibbs* [2000] 2 Cr App R 309 (CA); *R v Terry* [2003] EWCA Crim 1800.

92 Lord Justice Gross and Lord Justice Treacy, *Further Review of Disclosure in Criminal Proceedings: Sanctions for Disclosure Failure* (London, Judiciary of England and Wales, 2012) 8.

93 M Redmayne, 'Criminal Justice Act 2003: (1) Disclosure and Its Discontents' [2004] *Crim LR* 441, 447.

94 A Ashworth and M Redmayne, *The Criminal Process*, 4th edn (Oxford, Oxford University Press, 2010) 263.

95 M Redmayne, 'Criminal Justice Act 2003: (1) Disclosure and Its Discontents' [2004] *Crim LR* 441, 446.

96 Leave is still required where the failure is in not having disclosed a point of law that was relied on or the names and addresses of witnesses called. See CPIA 1996, ss 11(6) and 11(7).

section 6E provides that, unless the contrary is proved, defence statements will be deemed to have been given with the authority of the accused. The effect of section 6E is that, even if the defendant has not signed the statement, it will be regarded as his statement made by his authorised agent. It is, therefore, admissible as part of the prosecution case. If, for example, the defence statement contains admissions or inconsistencies with the defendant's testimony at trial, he may be cross-examined on it.[97]

Where there is a dispute as to whether the defence statement has been given with the authority of the defendant, the defendant bears the responsibility and burden of showing that it is not 'his' statement. The burden will not be discharged by the fact that he has not signed the statement and denies having seen it.[98] In *Haynes*, it was suggested that the defendant should have called his solicitors or the person from whom initial instructions had been taken to disprove that the statement was his.[99] If the defendant cannot convince the court that it is not his statement, the prosecution may be able to use it against him and it may become difficult to escape adverse inferences being drawn. Thus, while section 6E is unlikely to change the fact that it is defence lawyers who generally take responsibility for disclosure, it has made it easier to penalise the defendant for disclosure failures. Section 6E has also increased the pressure on the defendant to participate in the criminal process as an individual, by either cooperating in the disclosure exercise prior to the trial or by actively proving that the statement is not his at the trial.[100]

The 2011 Gross Report endorsed a participatory role for the defendant. It suggested that, provided the prosecution take a grip of its disclosure obligations from the outset, 'There is also much to be said for the proposal that in appropriate cases the Court should press for involvement from the defendant personally – not merely from his legal representatives.'[101] In the Report, Lord Justice Gross also recommended scant tolerance of late or uninformative defence statements.[102] He contended that, provided the prosecution's tackle is in order, there can generally 'be no excuse for a defence failure to engage and at an early stage in the proceedings'.[103]

The extent to which the defendant can be penalised for disclosure failures, beyond adverse comment and adverse inference, has raised issues in the courts. In *Rochford*,[104] a judge at a plea and case management hearing attempted to extend the penalties by imposing a 28 day sentence of imprisonment for contempt of

97 *R v Haynes* [2011] EWCA Crim 3281.
98 ibid.
99 ibid [4].
100 A Owusu-Bempah, 'Defence Participation through Pre-Trial Disclosure: Issues and Implications' (2013) 17 *E & P* 183, 187–188.
101 Lord Justice Gross, *Review of Disclosure in Criminal Proceedings* (London, Judiciary of England and Wales, 2011) 75.
102 ibid.
103 ibid 76.
104 [2010] EWCA Crim 1928, [2011] 1 WLR 534.

court against a defendant who had submitted an uninformative defence statement. However, the Court of Appeal recognised that the sanctions for non-cooperation are confined to those in section 11 and it is not until the case has gone before a jury that the court can determine whether an uninformative statement breaches section 6A. The Court held that 'It is not open to the court to add an additional extra statutory sanction of punishment for contempt of court.'[105]

In *R (on the application of Tinnion) v Reading Crown Court*,[106] the Divisional Court clarified that the sanction against someone who fails to give notice of an alibi defence and intention to call witnesses for that defence is adverse comment and adverse inferences, not inadmissibility of the evidence. The trial judge may have been confused as the pre-1996 penalty for failure to disclose a defence of alibi was exclusion of the evidence. This decision was upheld in *Ullah*,[107] where the trial judge made an error in principle by not allowing the evidence of a surprise alibi witness who had appeared in court after the close of the defence case. Likewise, in *T*,[108] the Court of Appeal found that the trial judge had erred in refusing to allow the defence to adduce relevant evidence of a complainant's sexual history on the basis that no advance notice had been given.

Although the Gross Report anticipated that, subject to the interests of justice, late disclosure of material may be capable of resulting in the exclusion of such material from trial,[109] a Further Review of Disclosure in Criminal Proceedings showed no enthusiasm for a general exclusionary rule when there has been a disclosure failure.[110] The review was conducted by Lord Justice Gross and Lord Justice Treacy in order to consider whether the current sanctions are adequate to secure compliance with disclosure duties, and whether there are options to strengthen those sanctions. It did not recommend the creation of any additional sanctions for disclosure failures. A general power to exclude otherwise admissible and relevant evidence was thought to be contrary to the principles of a fair trial and carry the risk of miscarriages of justice.[111] However, the review did recognise that exceptions could be made. The incremental development of the common law was considered to be an appropriate mechanism for dealing with relatively unusual problems which arise.[112] It, thus, appears open to the courts to exclude previously undisclosed evidence at common law, though this should occur 'very rarely'.[113] The case law so far suggests that it is usually not appropriate,

105 ibid [18] (Hughes LJ).
106 [2009] EWHC 2930 (Admin), (2010) 174 JP 36.
107 [2011] EWCA Crim 3275.
108 [2012] EWCA Crim 2358, [2013] Crim LR 596.
109 Lord Justice Gross, *Review of Disclosure in Criminal Proceedings* (London, Judiciary of England and Wales, 2011) 9.
110 Lord Justice Gross and Lord Justice Treacy, *Further Review of Disclosure in Criminal Proceedings: Sanctions for Disclosure Failure* (London, Judiciary of England and Wales, 2012).
111 ibid 3.
112 ibid 7.
113 ibid 6.

and against principle, to exclude relevant evidence where there has been a breach of the requirements of the CPIA 1996. However, previously undisclosed evidence has been excluded where there has been a breach of the CrimPR.[114]

Defence representatives can be penalised for failures to comply with the requirements of the CPIA 1996 through wasted costs orders, requiring them to meet the costs incurred as a result of the failure. In *Re Joseph Hill & Company Solicitors*, the Court of Appeal quashed a wasted costs order against a firm of solicitors who had failed to provide details of potential alibi witnesses. The decision was reached, in part, because there had been a widely held view among criminal practitioners that such details should not be disclosed until the witnesses had provided signed witness statements. Thus, the solicitors' conduct could not be characterised as improper or unreasonable.[115] However, the Court made it clear that any practice of not disclosing details of alibi witnesses until they had signed proofs of evidence was wrong and a breach of the requirements of section 6A(2)(a) of the 1996 Act. Having properly explained the requirements of section 6A, the Court took the view that 'no one can reasonably make this mistake again'.[116]

An assessment of the current law and practice suggests that defence statements often lack the required detail, and that, in comparison to a defendant's silence, the courts have been relatively reluctant to penalise this type of participatory failure. However, the CPIA 1996 has not failed to have an impact on the role of the defendant. Like the CJPOA 1994, the CPIA 1996 has created an expectation of defendant participation. While adverse inferences may be permissive rather than mandatory, it is the availability of a penalty which creates the expectation of participation. The relationship between the CPIA 1996 and the CrimPR has served to reinforce this expectation.

7.4 Disclosure and case management

The Royal Commission on Criminal Justice had supported defence disclosure for largely pragmatic reasons. Among other efficiency benefits, it was thought that defence disclosure would reduce the number of ambush defences.[117] The courts had also become increasingly concerned with the use of ambush defences, in terms of both positive defences being presented for the first time at trial, as well as the defence raising previously undisclosed points of law and prosecution errors. The courts advocated a managerialist approach to criminal procedure which requires the early and active participation of the defence. In *Gleeson*, a case in which the defence had waited until the end of the prosecution case to raise a point of law in support of a submission of no case to answer, the Court of Appeal stated that:

114 See *R v Musone* [2007] EWCA Crim 1237, [2007] 1 WLR 2467; *R v Ensor* [2009] EWCA Crim 2519, [2010] 1 Cr App R 18. See also the discussion on case management in ch 3.2.1.
115 *Re Joseph Hill & Company Solicitors* [2013] EWCA Crim 775, [2014] 1 WLR 786 [40].
116 ibid (Openshaw J).
117 Royal Commission on Criminal Justice, *Report* (Cm 2263, 1993) 97.

> [A] prosecution [should] not be frustrated by errors of the prosecutor, unless such errors have irremediably rendered a fair trial for the defendant impossible. For defence advocates to seek to take advantage of such errors by deliberately delaying identification of an issue of fact or law in the case until the last possible moment is, in our view, no longer acceptable, given the legislative and procedural changes to our criminal justice process in recent years.[118]

This line of thinking was reinforced by the introduction of the CrimPR in 2005. As explained in Chapter 3, under the CrimPR, the court must further the overriding objective of dealing with cases justly by actively managing the case. Dealing with cases justly includes dealing with cases efficiently and expeditiously as well as, *inter alia*, acquitting the innocent and convicting the guilty.[119] Each participant in the case must prepare and conduct the case in accordance with the overriding objective.[120]

Prior to the CPIA 1996 and the rise of managerialism, there were fewer constraints on the defence's ability to pursue what was in the defendant's best interest, for example, by relying on a point of law in support of a submission of no case to answer at the close of the prosecution case. The CrimPR now indicate that the defence's primary concern should not just be to win its own case, but also to ensure that the guilty are convicted and that the case is dealt with efficiently. This is inconsistent with a traditional adversarial role. As noted by McEwan, defence disclosure 'confronts lawyers with some challenging questions of professional ethics in terms of the competing interests of court and client, conflicting loyalties unknown in traditional adversarial settings'.[121] Cases such as *Re Joseph Hill & Company Solicitors*, discussed above, demonstrate how defence lawyers can now be expected to act in the interests of the administration of justice rather than the interests of their clients.[122]

There is a link between the defence disclosure obligations under the CPIA 1996 and the case management provisions found in part 3 of the CrimPR. It is worth noting that while the CPIA 1996 imposes disclosure obligations directly on 'the accused', the CrimPR impose participatory duties on both the defendant and his

118 *R v Gleeson* [2003] EWCA Crim 3357, [2004] 1 Cr App R 29 [35] (Auld LJ).

119 CrimPR, r 1.1(2).

120 ibid r 1.2(1)(a).

121 J McEwan, 'From Adversarialism to Managerialism: Criminal Justice in Transition' (2011) 31 *Legal Studies* 519, 532. See also F Garland and J McEwan, 'Embracing the Overriding Objective: Difficulties and Dilemmas in the New Criminal Climate' (2012) 16 *E & P* 233; M McConville and L Marsh, 'Adversarialism Goes West: Case Management in Criminal Courts' (2015) 19 *E & P* 172.

122 See also *R v SVS Solicitors* [2012] EWCA Crim 319, [2012] 3 Costs LR 502; *Re West* [2014] EWCA Crim 1480, [2015] 1 WLR 109. On *Re West*, see generally M McConville and L Marsh, 'Adversarialism Goes West: Case Management in Criminal Courts' (2015) 19 *E & P* 172.

representatives.[123] Case management includes early identification of the issues,[124] and rule 3.3 requires the parties to actively assist the court in fulfilling its case management duties. Since 2015, the CrimPR specify that 'active assistance' includes communication between the parties so as to find out whether the defendant is likely to plead guilty or not guilty; what is agreed and what is likely to be disputed; what information, or other material, is required by one party of another, and why; and what is to be done, by whom and when.[125] The 2015 amendments to rule 3.3 are intended to give effect to the recommendation of Sir Brian Leveson P that the CrimPR need to 'make clear that the parties are under a duty to engage at the first available opportunity'.[126] In addition, rule 3.11(a) provides that in order to manage a trial or appeal 'the court must establish, with the active assistance of the parties, what are the disputed issues'. Rule 3.11 allows the court to place participatory requirements on the parties, including requirements to identify points of law the parties intend to raise and information about witnesses and the order of their evidence. Although most disclosure obligations under the CPIA 1996 are mandatory only in the Crown Court, these case management provisions are equally applicable in the magistrates' court. The defence can, therefore, be required to reveal details of its case prior to summary trials.

The courts have tended to take their case management role seriously and, following *Gleeson*, have made much of the changing nature of the criminal process, particularly with regard to defence tactics designed to ambush the prosecution, including failure to correct prosecution mistakes. This is supported by the 'grassing up' clause in rule 1.2(1)(c), which requires the participants to inform the court and all parties of any significant failure to comply with the CrimPR or case management directions (whether or not that participant is responsible for that failure). As explained in Chapter 4, from an adversarial standpoint, in which the trial takes the form of a competition between two equal sides, a failure to mention or rectify a mistake made by the prosecution is not ordinarily objectionable. Nor is it objectionable from the perspective of calling the state to account for the allegations made against the defendant. It is explained in the following section that defence disclosure is designed to assist the prosecution, but that is not the job of the defendant. However, a move away from this perspective is evidenced in the *Chorley Justices* case:

> If a defendant refuses to identify what the issues are, one thing is clear: he can derive no advantage from that or seek . . . to attempt an ambush at trial. The

123 Part 1 of the CrimPR refers to the 'participants' and pt 3 refers to the 'parties'. See E Cape, 'Rebalancing the Criminal Justice Process: Ethical Challenges for Criminal Defence Lawyers' (2006) 9 *Legal Ethics* 56, 75.

124 CrimPR, r 3.2(2)(a).

125 ibid r 3.3(2).

126 Sir Brian Leveson, *Review of Efficiency in Criminal Proceedings* (London, Judiciary of England and Wales, 2015) 11.

> days of ambushing and taking last-minute technical points are gone. They are not consistent with the overriding objective of deciding cases justly, acquitting the innocent and convicting the guilty.[127]

The above statement has been influential in later decisions.[128] In *Penner*, for example, the Court of Appeal reaffirmed the position by stating that 'It is no longer possible to have cases . . . where points occur to someone and then an attempt is made to ambush the prosecution by a submission of no case to answer.'[129] In *Malcolm*, it was explained that 'It is the duty of the defence to make its defence and issues that it raises clear to both the prosecution and the court at an early stage.'[130] The case of *Firth* confirmed that the CrimPR reflect a new approach to the administration of criminal justice in which both sides, rather than the prosecution alone, are required to disclose the nature of their case well before trial.[131] In *Santos*, it was held that a technical point should not avail the applicant for judicial review of a refusal to state a case following conviction, since he had failed to raise the matter at his trial before the magistrates' court.[132] More recently, in *Farooqi*, Lord Judge reiterated that 'the trial process is not a game' and that 'ambush defence or arguments are prohibited'.[133] The courts have been willing to penalise failures to comply with the CrimPR by, for example, excluding evidence or imposing costs orders.[134] However, there is a preference for less formal sanctions, particularly 'compliance court appearances' and judicial chastisement of non-compliance in court.[135]

The majority of the cases noted above are not directly concerned with the CPIA 1996, but they do demonstrate the general change in attitude which has occurred as a result of the disclosure regime. The ever-increasing rigour of defence disclosure requirements is also revealing of a transfer of control over the conduct

127 *R (on the application of DPP) v Chorley Magistrates' Court* [2006] EWHC 1795 (Admin) [26] (Thomas LJ).

128 See, for example, *Writtle v DPP* [2009] EWHC 236 (Admin), (2009) 173 JP 224; *Brett v DPP* [2009] EWHC 440 (Admin), [2009] 1 WLR 2530.

129 *R v Penner* [2010] EWCA Crim 1155, [2010] Crim LR 936 [19] (Thomas LJ).

130 *Malcolm v DPP* [2007] EWHC 363 (Admin), [2007] 1 WLR 1230 [31] (Stanley Burnton J).

131 *R (on the application of Firth) v Epping Magistrates' Court* [2011] EWHC 388 (Admin), [2011] 1 WLR 1818 [5].

132 *R (on the application of Santos) v Stratford Magistrates' Court* [2012] EWHC 752 (Admin) [17].

133 *R v Farooqi* [2013] EWCA Crim 1649, [2014] 1 Cr App R 8 [114].

134 See, for example, *R v Musone* [2007] EWCA Crim 1237, [2007] 1 WLR 2467; *R v Ensor* [2009] EWCA Crim 2519, [2010] 1 Cr App R 18; *R v SVS Solicitors* [2012] EWCA Crim 319, [2012] 3 Costs LR 502.

135 See F Garland and J McEwan, 'Embracing the Overriding Objective: Difficulties and Dilemmas in the New Criminal Climate' (2012) 16 *E&P* 233; P Darbyshire, 'Judicial Case Management in Ten Crown Courts' [2014] *Crim LR* 30; Sir Brian Leveson, *Review of Efficiency in Criminal Proceedings* (London, Judiciary of England and Wales, 2015) 55; Criminal Practice Directions 2015 [2015] EWCA Crim 1567 paras 3A.26–3A.28.

of the case, from the parties to the court.[136] The judiciary's case management role has been described as 'of the first importance' for the proper operation of the present disclosure regime.[137] The Gross Report advocates robust case management of disclosure matters by the judiciary, and states that there is undoubted room for improvement in judicial performance in this area.[138] The 2015 Review of Efficiency in Criminal Proceedings also advocates robust case management, stating that 'all parties must be required to comply with the Criminal Procedure Rules and to work to identify the issues so as to ensure that court time is deployed to maximum effectiveness and efficiency'.[139] The Review of Efficiency has been followed up by a Better Case Management initiative, the aims of which are: robust case management; reduced number of hearings; maximum participation and engagement from every participant within the system; and efficient compliance with the CrimPR, Practice and Court Directions.[140]

As a result of the CPIA 1996, the CrimPR and the judicial approach to case management, the defendant as an individual and the defence as a party are now expected to participate constructively in the criminal process. They must disclose the nature of their case in terms of both facts they rely on and facts they take issue with, and points of law they rely on as well as points of law they take issue with. In addition, they may be penalised for altering the details of their case or surprising the prosecution with a defence at trial, and are no longer at liberty to take advantage of prosecution errors. As a result, the disclosure regime has had a significant effect on the voluntary nature of defendant participation. This has occurred primarily in pursuit of efficient fact-finding and, as contended below, at the expense of the values which legitimise the criminal process.

7.5 Reconsidering defence disclosure

The objections to the defence disclosure regime which are put forward in this section are similar to those presented in the previous chapter, in relation to drawing inferences from silence. In particular, both the CJPOA 1994 and the CPIA 1996 raise issues of compatibility with fair trial rights. It could be argued that the position of the defendant is different, and better, at the time of disclosure than it is at the time of police interview, as he will have had better access to legal advice and broad disclosure of the prosecution's case (assuming there has been compliance with the prosecution's disclosure obligations). Consequently, one

136 J McEwan, 'From Adversarialism to Managerialism: Criminal Justice in Transition' (2011) 31 *Legal Studies* 519, 530.

137 Lord Justice Gross, *Review of Disclosure in Criminal Proceedings* (London, Judiciary of England and Wales, 2011) 44.

138 ibid 76.

139 Sir Brian Leveson, *Review of Efficiency in Criminal Proceedings* (London, Judiciary of England and Wales, 2015) 12.

140 Courts and Tribunals Judiciary, *Better Case Management*, available at <www.judiciary.gov.uk/publications/better-case-management> accessed 1 April 2016.

could argue that the defence disclosure regime is less objectionable than the reforms to the right to silence. However, the level of disclosure required under the 1996 Act goes beyond that which can reasonably be expected at police interview. Accordingly, the disclosure regime has greater potential to assist the prosecution in building and presenting its case. Moreover, the position of the defendant at the time of providing a defence statement is arguably worse than it is when a final decision must be reached as to whether he will give evidence in court, at which point he will have heard the prosecution's case in its entirety.

This section examines the implications of the disclosure regime for the enforceability of fair trial rights, a 'no-assistance' approach to the defendant's role in the criminal process and the nature of criminal procedure. The fair trial rights which may be hampered by requirements on the defence to disclose the details of its case, prior to trial, include the privilege against self-incrimination, the presumption of innocence and the prosecution's burden of proof. This is primarily a consequence of the assistance which obligatory disclosure can provide to the prosecution.

Like the silence provisions in the CJPOA 1994, the disclosure regime is at odds with the normative proposition that the state should account for the accusations of criminal wrongdoing that it brings against its citizens, without the co-opted assistance of the accused. This proposition has been grounded in the autonomy and dignity which should be afforded to citizens in a liberal democracy, and the need to regulate state power in order to prevent abuses of such power. If we are to be treated with dignity, we must be treated as subjects of state power, and not as objects for the extraction of information.[141] If our autonomy is to be respected, we must be afforded the freedom to choose whether to actively participate in criminal proceedings. While the normative proposition does not advocate absolute freedom, it was explained in Chapter 1 that it is particularly important to protect freedom during the criminal process, where there is a structural imbalance between the state and the accused, and where much is at stake for the accused.

The theory of calling the state to account provides a basis for interpreting fair trial rights broadly. In practice, however, the courts have been willing to restrict the potentially broad applicability of certain fair trial rights.[142] The compatibility of the defence disclosure requirements with Article 6 of the ECHR has yet to be considered by the European Court of Human Rights.[143] Given the Court's

141 See C McCrudden, 'Human Dignity and Judicial Interpretation of Human Rights' (2008) 19 *European Journal of International Law* 655; LR Barroso, 'Here, There, and Everywhere: Human Dignity in Contemporary Law and in the Transnational Discourse' (2012) 35 *Boston College International and Comparative Law Review* 331.

142 See, for example, *Salabiaku v France* (1988) 13 EHRR 379; *Murray v UK* (1996) 22 EHRR 29; *Saunders v UK* (1997) 23 EHRR 313. See also the discussion on the scope of the privilege against self-incrimination and the right to silence in chs 5 and 6.

143 The Court of Appeal has taken the view that ss 6A and 11(5) of the CPIA 1996 are compatible with fair trial rights. See *R v Essa* [2009] EWCA Crim 43; *R v Rochford* [2010] EWCA Crim 1928, [2011] 1 WLR 534.

approach to rights, such as the right to silence, it is likely that the disclosure regime would be upheld as compliant with Article 6. The broad approach to fair trial rights taken in this section may thus go beyond that afforded to them under the ECHR.

7.5.1 Defence disclosure and the right to a fair trial

To assume that it is legitimate to require the defendant to provide the prosecution with information that may assist in securing a conviction sits uneasily with the privilege against self-incrimination.[144] As defined in Chapter 5, the privilege means that a suspect cannot be required to provide the authorities with information that might be used against him in criminal proceedings. Disclosure may lead to self-incrimination by establishing the *actus reus* through a defence, such as self-defence. This situation arose in *Firth*,[145] which concerned a charge of assault occasioning actual bodily harm. During a committal hearing, the prosecution were allowed to rely on a case progression form prepared by the defence when the allegation was one of common assault. The form stated that 'Only contact was made in self-defence.' This was held to amount to evidence of acceptance that the defendant was involved in a physical encounter with the complainant. Since the defence submitted at the hearing that there was no case to answer, as there was no identification evidence, the earlier disclosure assisted the prosecution in strengthening, if not establishing, its case. However, this decision has been complicated by the later case of *Newell*[146] in which it was held that, although a statement in a Plea and Case Management Hearing Form was admissible at trial against the defendant, the judge should have used his discretion under section 78 of PACE 1984 to exclude it.

The charge in *Newell* was possession of cocaine with intent to supply. On the form, the defence had written 'no possession', whereas in a later defence statement, and at trial, the defence admitted possession, but denied intent to supply. The prosecution had used the earlier form to show the inconsistency and rely on it as evidence of guilt. As a consequence of this case, judges should use their discretion to exclude evidence against the defendant in case management forms. However, this is on the condition that the defence followed the 'letter and spirit of the Criminal Procedure Rules'.[147] This means that directly incriminating evidence from such forms can be rightly admitted where the defence fails to comply with case management directions, or attempts to ambush the prosecution, or perhaps even fails to provide a defence statement, as required by the CPIA 1996. In

144 See A Owusu-Bempah, 'Defence Participation through Pre-Trial Disclosure: Issues and Implications' (2013) 17 *E&P* 183, 193–196.

145 [2011] EWHC 388 (Admin), [2011] 1 WLR 1818.

146 [2012] EWCA Crim 650, [2012] 1 WLR 3142. See generally R Munday, 'Case Management, Disclosure and the Rules of Evidence, or (With Apologies to Ogden Nash) "What's *Newell*, Pussycat?" ' (2012) 176 *Criminal Law and Justice Weekly* 377.

147 *R v Newell* [2012] EWCA Crim 650, [2012] 1 WLR 3142 [36].

Newell, the defendant had been subject to an adverse inference direction due to late disclosure of his defence statement. The defence statement made the case clear and the inconsistent Plea and Case Management Hearing Form caused no disadvantage to the Crown. These factors contributed to the court's finding that the evidence in the form should have been excluded. However, because this case concerned the use of case management forms rather than defence statements, it remains open for incriminating or inconsistent information contained in defence statements to be used against the defendant as part of the prosecution case; the defendant may face cross-examination on the content of the statement and become the subject of adverse comment and inferences.

The Royal Commission rejected the objection that defence disclosure infringes the privilege against self-incrimination on the basis that disclosure of the substance of the defence case at an earlier stage will no more incriminate the defendant nor help prove the case against him than it does when it is given in evidence at the hearing.[148] The Commission believed that the matter was simply one of timing.[149] The Court of Appeal took a similar view in *Rochford*.[150] However, even where disclosure does not directly incriminate the defendant, it may lead the police or prosecution to uncover incriminating information. In this way, the defendant will have assisted the prosecution in incriminating him. For example, details of defence witnesses disclosed under sections 6A(2) or 6C will provide material for investigation, and may lead to defence witnesses changing their evidence or incriminating the defendant. When coupled with pressures to participate stemming from the CJPOA 1994, there is a significant danger that defendants will be coerced into providing incriminating information to the prosecution.

To claim that the defendant is not being compelled to say anything incriminating has been described as 'naïve'.[151] Richardson notes that '[c]ompelling a defendant to identify that which is in dispute inevitably involves forcing him to admit that which is not in dispute'.[152] A clear notion of the scope and rationale of the privilege might help to determine how far the defence disclosure obligations interfere with it. As demonstrated in Chapter 5, a precise scope or rationale is difficult to determine. However, since the privilege provides a specific right not to assist in the criminal process, it should be applied such that it is contrary to the privilege to require the defendant to disclose information which can result in incrimination.

Linked to the implications which the disclosure obligations have for the privilege against self-incrimination are concerns for the impact on the presumption of innocence.[153] As previously explained, a broad interpretation of the

148 Royal Commission on Criminal Justice, *Report* (Cm 2263, 1993) 84.

149 ibid 98.

150 [2010] EWCA Crim 1928, [2011] 1 WLR 534.

151 J Richardson, 'A "Just" Outcome: Losing Sight of the Purpose of Criminal Procedure' (2011) *Journal of Commonwealth Criminal Law* 105, 117.

152 ibid.

153 See A Owusu-Bempah, 'Defence Participation through Pre-Trial Disclosure: Issues and Implications' (2013) 17 *E & P* 183, 196–197.

presumption should operate as a direction to treat the accused as if he were innocent throughout the criminal process, until guilt has been established. To treat him as innocent is to treat him as if he had nothing to account for. Rather, the state should account for the accusations of criminal wrongdoing which it has brought against him. The accused should not have to actively contribute to the discharge of the state's obligation to prove guilt, either expressly or in consequence of a procedural requirement. Requiring the defendant to supply even potentially incriminating information, such as the details of his witnesses, is not in the spirit of this broad conception of the presumption of innocence. To associate late, inconsistent or non-disclosure with guilt by way of adverse inferences is also damaging to the principle of the presumption of innocence. Like the CJPOA 1994, the CPIA 1996 improperly links non-cooperation to guilt.

The defence disclosure obligations also compromise a narrow interpretation of the presumption of innocence, which simply reflects the prosecution's burden of proof. Although the prosecution must prove its case at trial beyond a reasonable doubt, like the reforms to the right to silence, the disclosure regime has an impact on the burden of proof, through its potential to assist the prosecution in discharging its burden. Where the disclosure requirements are not complied with, the adverse inferences of guilt which may be drawn could assist the prosecution in meeting its burden and reaching a standard of proof beyond reasonable doubt.[154]

The burden of proof may also be compromised where the disclosure requirements are complied with. Richardson has argued that, because it is for the prosecution to adduce evidence to establish all the elements of the offence charged and show why the defendant is guilty, the imposition of an obligation on the defendant to say why he is not guilty immediately eases the burden on the prosecution.[155] The burden may be eased as a result of the defendant supplying information which the prosecution can use against him, or which the prosecution would otherwise have difficulty proving. For example, the prosecution may seek admissions of fact in relation to elements of the offence that have not been flagged as being in issue, thus sparing themselves the necessity of obtaining evidence on the matters.[156] The defence is also required to point out defects in the prosecution case, ensuring that the case against the defendant can proceed. While in some instances this may advance the aim of accurate fact-finding, this should not be the responsibility of the defendant. Where fair trial rights, including the burden of proof, constrain the aims of the criminal process, they do so in order to legitimise the process and the outcome of trials, as explained in Chapter 2.

Early indication of the proposed defence case can be used to improve the prosecution case even if it is not intended to help establish it. As Edwards notes, 'the defence becomes an object of investigation, and the prosecution case is

154 See the discussion in ch 6.7 on adverse inferences from silence and the burden of proof.

155 J Richardson, 'A "Just" Outcome: Losing Sight of the Purpose of Criminal Procedure' (2011) *Journal of Commonwealth Criminal Law* 105, 117.

156 ibid.

reinforced as a result'.[157] Arguably, the assistance which the disclosure regime can provide to the prosecution, even if inadvertent, undermines the presumption of innocence and the burden of proof.

7.5.2 A 'no-assistance' approach

Although the Royal Commission believed it to be simply a matter of timing, there are important differences between imposing penalty-backed obligations on the defendant to disclose the details of his case prior to trial and requiring the defence to disclose the nature and basis of its case, and discharge evidential burdens, in court.[158] An evidential burden requires the defence to adduce sufficient evidence in order to raise an issue. If the defence wish to raise an issue, but fail to satisfy the evidential burden, the prosecution still bears the legal burden of proof in relation to the charge, and there are no provisions for adverse inferences stemming from the defence's failure. The obligation to discharge an evidential burden is not without consequence, as the defendant may need to participate in order to discharge it. However, it may also be discharged through other means, such as the testimony of witnesses, or by pointing to some evidence already adduced by the prosecution. Unlike the pre-trial disclosure regime, the imposition of an evidential burden places no formal penalty-backed requirements on the defendant to actively participate. Furthermore, requirements to disclose the details of one's defence at trial will not assist the prosecution in the same way as pre-trial disclosure. It does not afford the prosecution with the time or opportunity to gather new evidence, strengthen or significantly alter its case, based on what is discovered through the obligatory participation of the defendant. Hence, it does not have the same implications for the privilege against self-incrimination, the presumption of innocence or the burden of proof.

In Zander's view, with the 'reasonable exceptions' of disclosure of alibi and expert evidence, 'it is wrong to require the defendant to be helpful by giving advance notice of his defence and to penalise him by adverse comment if he fails to do so'.[159] This critique of defence disclosure reflects a 'no-assistance' approach to the defendant's role in the criminal process; the defendant should not be required to actively participate in a way that may assist the prosecution in establishing its case. Any active participation on the part of the defendant should be voluntary. A strict 'no-assistance' approach, based on a broad interpretation of the presumption of innocence and the burden of proof, would ensure that the state can account for the accusations of criminal wrongdoing that it makes against the accused. It would eliminate the requirement for the defendant to disclose the details of his defence prior to trial, including alibi and expert evidence. If the state cannot make a case without the defence's help, it should not bring a case to trial.

157 A Edwards, 'Do the Defence Matter?' (2010) 14 *E & P* 119, 127.

158 A Owusu-Bempah, 'Defence Participation through Pre-Trial Disclosure: Issues and Implications' (2013) 17 *E & P* 183, 197.

159 Royal Commission on Criminal Justice, *Report* (Cm 2263, 1993) 221.

Likewise, if the prosecution cannot anticipate a defence, its case deserves to fail. Although this claim may appear brazen, it is not necessarily unreasonable. Prior to the CPIA 1996, in the vast majority of cases, the prosecution were able to anticipate the defence and were seldom successfully ambushed.[160]

It has been argued that the absolutist 'no-assistance' position goes too far by permitting defence tactics specifically designed to throw the prosecution off balance.[161] Redmayne has contended that ambush defences cannot be justified in that manner, and that the system has no reason to accommodate tactics designed to gain illegitimate acquittals.[162] He contends that the absolutist 'no-assistance' position can be modified to make it more attractive, by distinguishing two different ways in which the defence can assist the prosecution. While knowing something about the defence that will be presented may help the prosecution to anticipate attacks on its case at trial, disclosure of the defence case will not necessarily help the prosecution establish a *prima facie* case. However, in some cases, disclosure can help the prosecution to make a *prima facie* case.[163] For example, disclosure of a defence, such as self-defence or duress, may help the prosecution establish the *actus reus* of an offence, and the disclosure of an alibi may assist the prosecution by providing the police with a time frame of the defendant's whereabouts and movements. To ensure that disclosure does not assist the prosecution in making a *prima facie* case, Redmayne suggests that, under the modified 'no-assistance' approach, the prosecution could be prevented from using the fruits of disclosure as part of its case in chief.[164] However, this would be difficult to apply in practice, and there would be no way to guarantee that the defence disclosure had not provided assistance to the prosecution in establishing its case. For example, incriminating information might have been obtained during an interview of a defence witness, or the disclosure of an alibi might have prompted the prosecution to reconsider the time at which the offence was committed.

In practice, the courts have not made a clear distinction between using information disclosed by the defence to anticipate attacks on the prosecution's case and using it to establish a *prima facie* case against the defendant. As a result of *Firth* and *Newell*, at least where it can be said that the defence has not followed the letter and spirit of the CrimPR, the fruits of disclosure can be used as evidence to establish a *prima facie* case. Moreover, such cases as *Essa* and *Haynes* show that the prosecution are able to cross-examine the defendant on disclosure failures

160 See the discussion in ch 7.1 on the introduction of the CPIA 1996, and the discussion on reform to the right to silence in ch 6.2. Although there was a duty to disclose alibi and expert evidence prior to the CPIA 1996, this was rarely enforced: Royal Commission on Criminal Justice, *Report* (Cm 2263, 1993) 97.

161 M Redmayne, 'Criminal Justice Act 2003: (1) Disclosure and Its Discontents' [2004] *Crim LR* 441, 450.

162 ibid 451.

163 ibid.

164 ibid.

pursuant to the CPIA 1996, even where the defendant denies responsibility for the failure.

In his dissent from the Royal Commission's proposals, Zander stated that defence disclosure is:

> designed to be helpful to the prosecution and, more generally, to the system. But it is not the job of the defendant to be helpful either to the prosecution or to the system. His task, if he chooses to put the prosecution to proof, is simply to defend himself.[165]

Normatively, the right of the defendant not to actively participate in proceedings against himself should be strong enough to justify an absolute rule against obligatory pre-trial defence disclosure. Where particularly significant problems arise for the prosecution, and the interests of justice are at stake, short adjournments could be used to allow time for the prosecution to address new or unanticipated evidence or arguments raised by the defence. Although this would upset the current emphasis on efficiency, it should be recalled that delays and adjournments are commonplace within the existing disclosure regime.[166] If any concessions are to be made to a 'no-assistance' approach, it is important that procedural rights designed to ensure fairness and legitimise the criminal process are not compromised.

7.5.3 The nature of criminal procedure

Owing to the long-standing general principle which placed no obligation upon the defendant to disclose his case before trial, it is understandable that a defence non-disclosure norm might be perceived as being an intrinsic part of the adversarial system.[167] However, during the height of adversarialism in the nineteenth and twentieth centuries, although prosecution disclosure became important, defence non-disclosure was not in itself essential. Nonetheless, in the light of the wider impact of requiring defence participation, imposing obligations on the defence to provide the prosecution with the details of its case interferes with norms which are associated with adversarialism.[168] These norms tend to allow the defendant to

165 Royal Commission on Criminal Justice, *Report* (Cm 2263, 1993) 221.

166 See HM Crown Prosecution Service Inspectorate, *Disclosure: A Thematic Review of the Duties of Disclosure of Unused Material Undertaken by the CPS* (London, HMCPSI, 2008); Lord Justice Gross and Lord Justice Treacy, *Further Review of Disclosure in Criminal Proceedings: Sanctions for Disclosure Failure* (London, Judiciary of England and Wales, 2012); Lord Justice Gross, His Honour Judge Kinch and H Riddle, *Magistrates' Court Disclosure Review* (London, Judiciary of England and Wales, 2014).

167 M Redmayne, 'Criminal Justice Act 2003: (1) Disclosure and Its Discontents' [2004] *Crim LR* 441, 449.

168 A Owusu-Bempah, 'Defence Participation through Pre-Trial Disclosure: Issues and Implications' (2013) 17 *E & P* 183, 200.

take a passive role and enable him to choose whether or not to participate. They allow the prosecution to be put to proof and the prosecution's case to be tested. Emphasising the defendant's new participatory role through the assumption that defence statements have been given with his authority,[169] and through suggestions that the court should press for his involvement personally,[170] also has an impact on adversarialism, by focusing on the defendant as an individual and detracting from the defence's role as a party.[171] Consequently, although defence non-disclosure may not be an essential aspect of adversarialism, in terms of the increased participatory requirements on the defendant and the defence, the current regime has undoubtedly contributed to a shift in the nature of criminal procedure, away from an adversarial system.

The dual focus of the disclosure regime on efficient fact-finding might seem indicative of a shift towards inquisitorialism[172] or managerialism.[173] However, what is most prevalent is the impact that defence disclosure has on the voluntary nature of participation within the criminal process. The CPIA 1996, together with the CrimPR, has created expectations of constructive participation, with the defendant facing indirect compulsion to provide information. Leng notes that:

> [T]o those familiar with the traditional model of adversarial criminal justice in which prosecution is something which happens to a non-volunteer, who is fully entitled to devote his energies to defending himself, the theme of the defendant as a participant with responsibilities in connection with the efficient running of the system is disturbing.[174]

The defence disclosure regime is not only disturbing to those familiar with the traditional adversarial model of procedure. It is also disturbing from the perspective of the normative theory of calling the state to account, as the defendant is now expected to provide an account of why he is not guilty, before the trial has even begun. This is intensified by the provisions of the CJPOA 1994 which create an expectation that defendants will respond to official questioning, or

169 CPIA 1996, s 6E.

170 Lord Justice Gross, *Review of Disclosure in Criminal Proceedings* (London, Judiciary of England and Wales, 2011) 75.

171 Recognition of the defence as a party was an important aspect of adversarial development which allowed the defendant to take a more passive role. See ch 4.2.

172 This is unlikely given that prosecution non-disclosure presents a greater threat to truth-finding than defence non-disclosure, and modern 'inquisitorial' type jurisdictions, such as France, neither require defence disclosure, nor do they attach penalties for failure to disclose evidence. See J Hodgson, 'The Future of Adversarial Criminal Justice in 21st Century Britain' (2010) 35 *North Carolina Journal of International Law and Commercial Regulation* 319, 330.

173 See J McEwan, 'From Adversarialism to Managerialism: Criminal Justice in Transition' (2011) 31 *Legal Studies* 519.

174 R Leng, 'Losing Sight of the Defendant: The Government's Proposals on Pre-Trial Disclosure' [1995] *Crim LR* 704, 711.

else risk their silence being used against them. The defendant's freedom to choose whether or not to respond to the accusations against him, to provide information or to assist the state in establishing guilt has been severely undermined by the availability of penalties for non-cooperation. The defence disclosure regime has, thus, contributed to the emergence of a system in which participation is an obligation.

8 Participation and the future of criminal procedure

The participatory requirements imposed on the defendant demonstrates that the fact-finding aim has been prioritised at the expense of fairness and respect for the rights of the defendant.[1] The participatory requirements can be observed in the limitations to the privilege against self-incrimination, in the curtailment of the right to silence and in the defendant's duty to disclose the details of his case prior to trial. If the defendant fails to meet these participatory requirements, he may be penalised by way of criminal sanction or through adverse inferences, linking his failure directly to guilt.

There are further instances within the criminal process in which individuals can be required to participate and penalised for a failure to do so. These include the harsher sentence which follows a refusal to plead guilty, and sanctions for failure to comply with case management directions. Many other instances will concern passive participation, particularly during the initial stages of the process, such as where a refusal to submit to a police stop and search results in arrest. Requirements of passive participation, and their wider implications, fall outside of the scope of this book, which has been concerned with the active participation of the defendant.[2] There is, however, one further example of a requirement to actively participate which warrants consideration. This participatory requirement arises in consequence of a reverse burden of proof. The nature of this participatory requirement differs from the other requirements that have been explored, as does the penalty for non-cooperation. For these reasons, reverse burdens of proof are not examined to the same extent as the privilege against self-incrimination, the right to silence or pre-trial disclosure. However, brief consideration of reverse burdens within the context of this book provides a more comprehensive picture of the participatory role of the defendant.

8.1 Reverse burdens of proof

In previous chapters, it has been argued that the presumption of innocence should be interpreted and applied widely, as a direction to officials to treat the accused as

1 On the aims and values of the criminal process, see ch 2.

2 As explained in ch 1, active participation will ordinarily involve mental effort or voluntary physical movement on the part of the defendant, resulting in the production of information.

if he were innocent at all stages of the criminal process, until guilt is proved. At its narrowest, however, the presumption of innocence is simply a reflection of the prosecution's burden of proof at trial. The prosecution ordinarily bears the legal burden of proving, or disproving, all of the facts in issue in the case, to the standard of proof beyond reasonable doubt. The presumption of innocence, in its narrow sense, is widely accepted as a fundamental principle and constitutes a 'golden thread' of the English criminal law.[3]

There are, however, instances in which the legal burden of proof is reversed, and the defence must disprove an element of the offence or prove a defence, with the standard of proof being a balance of probabilities.[4] With the exception of the common law defence of insanity, all reverse burdens of proof are either expressed or implied in statutes.[5] As a result of Parliament's unfettered power to enact reverse burdens, as far back as 1996, no fewer than 40 per cent of offences triable in the Crown Court appeared to impose a legal burden on the defence.[6] Reverse burdens are not a recent invention.[7] However, one might have expected little tolerance of them following the enactment of the Human Rights Act 1998, which provides that, so far as it is possible to do so, legislation must be read and given effect in a way which is compatible with the Convention rights,[8] including the presumption of innocence.

Reverse burdens of proof are objectionable on the grounds that they *prima facie* violate even a very narrow conception of the presumption of innocence; the defendant is taken to be guilty unless the defence can prove or disprove a particular issue. Yet, the courts have been willing to uphold reverse burdens of proof where they are considered to be a proportionate response to a legitimate aim.[9] There is,

3 *Woolmington v DPP* [1935] AC 462 (HL) 481.

4 Much has been written on the presumption of innocence and burdens of proof. See generally P Roberts, 'Taking the Burden of Proof Seriously' [1995] *Crim LR* 783; A Ashworth and M Blake, 'The Presumption of Innocence in English Criminal Law' [1996] *Crim LR* 306; P Roberts, 'The Presumption of Innocence Brought Home? *Kebilene* Deconstructed' (2002) 118 *Law Quarterly Review* 41; V Tadros and S Tierney, 'The Presumption of Innocence and the Human Rights Act' (2004) 67 *MLR* 402; I Dennis, 'Reverse Onuses and the Presumption of Innocence: In Search of Principle' [2005] *Crim LR* 901; A Ashworth, 'Four Threats to the Presumption of Innocence' (2006) 10 *E & P* 241; D Hamer, 'The Presumption of Innocence and Reverse Burdens: A Balancing Act' (2007) 66 *Cambridge Law Journal* 142; A Stumer, *The Presumption of Innocence: Evidential and Human Rights Perspectives* (Oxford, Hart Publishing, 2010); F Picinali, 'Innocence and Burdens of Proof in English Criminal Law' (2014) 13 *Law, Probability & Risk* 243.

5 *Woolmington v DPP* [1935] AC 462 (HL) 481.

6 A Ashworth and M Blake, 'The Presumption of Innocence in English Criminal Law' [1996] *Crim LR* 306.

7 Reverse burdens were common prior to the decision in *Woolmington v DPP* [1935] AC 462 (HL). See A Stumer, *The Presumption of Innocence: Evidential and Human Rights Perspectives* (Oxford, Hart Publishing, 2010) 5–8.

8 Human Rights Act 1998, ss 3 and 6.

9 See, for example, *R v Johnstone* [2003] UKHL 28, [2003] 1 WLR 1736; *Sheldrake v DPP* [2004] UKHL 43, [2005] 1 AC 264.

thus, not an absolute right to be presumed innocent,[10] and Article 6(2) of the European Convention on Human Rights has been balanced against the public interest in crime control, despite Article 6 not being explicitly qualified by balancing considerations. In determining the proportionality of particular reverse burdens of proof, the courts have taken a number of factors into account on a case by case basis. These factors include the nature and seriousness of the offence charged, the ease of discharging the burden and whether the defendant has peculiar knowledge of the issue.[11] The overall effect of the judicial approach to reverse burdens has been to create a great deal of uncertainty and inconsistency in this area of law. Where the reverse burden cannot be justified on proportionality grounds, it can be read down to an evidential burden,[12] requiring the defence to adduce sufficient evidence to raise the issue, but not requiring the defendant to assume a risk of conviction, as the prosecution will carry the legal burden of disproving the issue.

The imposition of a legal burden of proof on the defence creates a participatory requirement. The defence, as a party, must actively participate in the trial proceedings in order to discharge the burden, by raising arguments and adducing evidence. The defendant's participation may also be required. For example, if a reverse burden requires the defence to prove knowledge or belief as to the existence or non-existence of certain facts,[13] the defendant will likely need to give direct evidence as to his thought process at the time of the alleged offence. In fact, it may be difficult for the defence to prove or disprove any issue which goes to the defendant's state of mind without the testimony of the defendant.[14] Yet, reverse burdens differ from the other examples of participatory requirements explored in this book, as, on the face of it, the requirement is to discharge a burden of proof and not to participate. However, in consequence of the requirement to discharge the burden, participation will often be essential. Reverse burdens of proof can, therefore, be conceived of as placing a participatory requirement on the defendant in so far as the defendant will need to participate in order to discharge the burden.

Where the defence fail to discharge the burden, the defendant will be convicted. The defendant's participation may thus be necessary in order to avoid a substantial and detrimental consequence. The conviction which follows a failure to discharge the burden can be conceived of as a penalty for the failure to participate. Again, this penalty differs from the others explored in this book. On the face of it, the conviction is a consequence of failing to discharge the burden of proof, and not

10 *Salabiaku v France* (1988) 13 EHRR 379.

11 See I Dennis, 'Reverse Onuses and the Presumption of Innocence: In Search of Principle' [2005] *Crim LR* 901; A Ashworth, 'Four Threats to the Presumption of Innocence' (2006) 10 *E&P* 241.

12 *R v Lambert* [2001] UKHL 37, [2002] 2 AC 545.

13 See, for example, *R v Johnstone* [2003] UKHL 28, [2003] 1 WLR 1736; *Sheldrake v DPP* [2004] UKHL 43, [2005] 1 AC 264.

14 Except in situations where, for example, there is sufficient medical evidence to support the defendant's claim of insanity or diminished responsibility.

failing to participate. Moreover, the defence may fail to discharge the burden notwithstanding the active participation of the defendant. However, since the defendant can be convicted as a direct consequence of his failure to participate, reverse burdens constitute a further example of the way in which defendants can face compulsion to actively participate in the criminal process.

Reverse burdens of proof allocate the risk of misdecision to the defence. In so doing, they increase the prospect of wrongful conviction. They also have implications for a no-assistance approach to the criminal process and the relationship between citizen and state. The imposition of a reverse burden is of assistance to the prosecution; the primary purpose of requiring the defence to prove an issue is to make the prosecution's task easier, and to save the prosecuting authorities time and money. The presumption of innocence gives effect to a claim to fair treatment by the state.[15] It is an important mechanism to ensure that the state can account for its accusations against its citizens, before subjecting them to condemnation and punishment. Where the burden is on the defence to prove innocence, it is the accused, and not the state, that is being called to account. This completely undermines the proposition that the state should treat all citizens as law-abiding until it proves otherwise.

Aside from raising significant matters of principle, reverse burdens of proof are arguably unnecessary in the light of the evidential burden. As explained in the previous chapter, if the defence wish to raise an issue or rely on a particular defence, they must adduce sufficient evidence in support of it.[16] The mechanism of an evidential burden has been described as 'a convenient and efficient method of narrowing the matters in issue in a criminal trial'.[17] There is no universally accepted formula to describe how much evidence is needed to satisfy the burden, and much will depend on the nature of the issue to which the burden relates.[18] It may become necessary for the defendant to testify in order to discharge it,[19] but the evidential burden does not require defendant participation in the same way as a legal burden. The evidential burden could be discharged by, for example, the testimony of other witnesses or through evidence adduced by the prosecution. If the defence cannot adduce sufficient evidence to support an issue, the consequence is that the fact-finder need not consider that issue, but the prosecution will remain obligated to prove the offence. Consequently, the burden of adducing evidence is not a burden of proof.[20]

15 I Dennis, 'The Human Rights Act and the Law of Evidence Ten Years On' (2011) 33 *Sydney Law Review* 333, 354.

16 See generally R Glover, 'Codifying the Law on Evidential Burdens' (2008) 72 *Journal of Criminal Law* 305.

17 A Stumer, *The Presumption of Innocence: Evidential and Human Rights Perspectives* (Oxford, Hart Publishing, 2010) 16.

18 ibid 17.

19 In *R v Lambert* [2001] UKHL 37, [2002] 2 AC 545 [90]–[91], Lord Hope suggested that discharging the evidential burden would require evidence of a degree little short of that necessary to discharge the legal burden.

20 *Jayasena v R* [1970] AC 618 (PC) 624.

The presumption of innocence is a fundamental right, enshrined in international human rights documents. Many other fair trial rights exist in consequence of the presumption of innocence, and as a means of reinforcing the presumption.[21] In addition to the implications for the defendant's participatory role, the judicial willingness to uphold reverse burdens of proof sends a clear message about the prioritisation of efficient fact-finding above fairness concerns.

8.2 The nature of criminal procedure in the light of defendant participation

This book has demonstrated that, within the current system in England and Wales, defence rights have been marginalised, interpreted narrowly, subjected to exceptions and balanced away against the 'public interest' in convictions. These rights, including the presumption of innocence, privilege against self-incrimination and right to silence, provide the freedom to choose whether to actively participate in the criminal process. They developed, or at least became workable, with the rise of adversarialism, when defence lawyers made it possible to organise criminal trials around the presumption of innocence and defend a silent accused.[22] The marginalisation of defence rights and the increase in participatory requirements indicate that, despite retaining some of the form of adversarialism, England no longer has an adversarial system. The problem is not so much that English criminal procedure has moved on from adversarialism. Adversarialism has shortcomings of its own,[23] and it is natural for systems to change over time. Rather, the problem is that we have also moved away from fairness norms which work as part of an adversarial system.[24]

The shift away from adversarialism within England and Wales has been accompanied by a shift away from inquisitorialism in a number of European jurisdictions.[25] Due to the constantly developing and diverse nature of individual legal systems, the adversarial and inquisitorial divide does not provide a satisfactory means of characterising modern Western criminal justice systems. It is, in fact, difficult to adequately categorise systems into any pre-defined procedural model,

21 See, for example, the discussion on the justifications for the privilege against self-incrimination in ch 5.1.1.

22 See JH Langbein, *The Origins of the Adversary Criminal Trial* (Oxford, Oxford University Press, 2003).

23 See, for example, the wealth and combat effect discussed in JH Langbein, *The Origins of the Adversary Criminal Trial* (Oxford, Oxford University Press, 2003).

24 A number of commentators who have noted recent ad hoc developments to criminal procedure have also expressed concern about the consequences for procedural guarantees. See, for example, J Hodgson, 'The Future of Adversarial Criminal Justice in 21st Century Britain' (2010) 35 *North Carolina Journal of International Law and Commercial Regulation* 319; J McEwan, 'From Adversarialism to Managerialism: Criminal Justice in Transition' (2011) 31 *Legal Studies* 519.

25 See ch 3.1.

based on a particular form or structure. This poses a challenge in terms of identifying the current state of English criminal procedure.

A central proposition advanced in this book is that the nature of criminal procedure is affected by the role of the defendant in the criminal process. A means of characterising criminal procedure, based on the role of the defendant, was identified in Chapter 3; the system may be characterised by either the obligatory or voluntary nature of defendant participation. It will be recalled that a system which imposes requirements on the defendant to actively participate, whether through direct or indirect compulsion, can be characterised by the obligatory nature of participation. Such a system may provide for defence rights, but the pursuit of accurate verdicts takes priority. A system of obligatory participation is also likely to be concerned with the efficient running of the criminal process, seeking to save time and money through robust management of criminal cases. On the other hand, a system which seeks to give maximum effect to fair trial rights and individual autonomy can be characterised by the voluntary nature of participation. Although concerned with reaching accurate outcomes, it does not subject the defendant to laws which seek to penalise non-participation.

In practice, it may not be easy to determine whether a system provides for voluntary or obligatory participation. It is unlikely that any system would compel participation at all stages of the criminal process. Likewise, systems which appear to respect individual autonomy are likely to exert some pressure on accused persons to actively participate. The pressure may simply take the form of a warning that when incriminating evidence stands unchallenged by the defendant, the prospect of conviction may increase.[26] Thus, whenever there is evidence against the defendant, there will be some degree of inherent pressure to participate. Broadly, however, the dividing line between voluntary and obligatory participation is the existence of compulsion to participate. There is compulsion to participate where the defendant lacks freedom to exercise his rights not to participate, and where adverse legal consequences, or penalties, are attached to non-participation.

It is worth reiterating that this means of characterising criminal procedure is not intended to replace or supplement the pre-defined procedural models which are often relied on to compare different legal systems. It is not presented as a normative construct on which to model criminal procedure, as it requires no particular form or structure for the criminal justice system. Rather, the purpose is to highlight the significant impact which the participatory role of the defendant can have on the nature of criminal procedure. It provides a way of identifying the current state of English criminal procedure, which does not conform to the pre-defined models, particularly adversarialism or inquisitorialism.

26 Even if adverse inferences from silence are not permitted, the lack of exculpatory explanation of the case against the defendant could impact the fact-finder's decision. See J Jackson and S Summers, *The Internationalisation of Criminal Evidence: Beyond the Common Law and Civil Law Traditions* (Cambridge, Cambridge University Press, 2012) 265.

In the light of the increase in penalty-backed legislative requirements to participate, and the narrow interpretation afforded to many fair trial rights by the courts, if the nature of English criminal procedure is to be characterised, it can be done so on the basis of obligatory participation. The rules of the criminal process now reflect a *prima facie* obligation to participate, and the courts have been reluctant to interfere with this. The current system of obligatory participation has not been developed by design; rather it is the result of reforms aimed at obtaining the perceived benefits of the defendant's participation, with little, if any, regard for their wider consequences. The adoption of a system of obligatory participation has, thus, gone largely unchecked by any serious consideration for due process concerns. It is reminiscent of the pre-adversarial altercation trial in which the defendant's participation was essential. Although what we see now is different in form, both rely on a lack of procedural protection for the defendant in order to secure his participation in pursuance of the process aims.

8.3 The future of criminal procedure

The current emphasis on defendant participation, and the imposition of penalties to secure it, calls into question the legitimacy of the criminal process. We must consider whether we can accept as legitimate a verdict which has been obtained in defiance of the defendant's rights not to actively participate, or whether we can rest content with a system which treats individuals as objects for the extraction of evidence, rather than as dignified and autonomous individuals. If we cannot accept these things, reform to the current system should be considered.

One means of rectifying the situation is to adopt the normative position which has been advanced in this book. That is, the state should account for the accusations of criminal wrongdoing which it brings against the accused and its request for his condemnation and punishment. This normative theory of the criminal process has been founded on a broad interpretation of the presumption of innocence, the right to a fair trial and a conception of the relationship between citizen and state in a liberal democracy in which autonomy must be protected. The state should not use its potentially oppressive powers to enforce the criminal law against its citizens without first proving and justifying its allegations against them. This should be done without resource from the accused. Adopting this position would give effect to a system of voluntary participation.

However, at present, it is the accused who is expected to account for the accusations against him. The accused is expected to plead guilty to the offence charged, or else face a harsher sentence. The accused is expected to respond to allegations of his involvement in criminal activity both to the police and in court, or else his silence may be used against him as evidence of guilt. The accused is expected to provide a written account of the accusations against him, and explain why he is not guilty, or else he may face inferences of guilt. Where a legal burden is imposed on the defence, the accused is expected to prove his innocence, or else be convicted. The accused can also be required, on pain of criminal sanction, to provide information which can lead to prosecution or be used against him in criminal proceedings. Where the accused succumbs to compulsion to participate, his participation can assist the state. Answers to questions, material evidence, such as documents, and information contained in defence statements can all provide material for investigation or be presented against the defendant in court.

The normative theory, on the other hand, advocates a 'no-assistance' approach to the defendant's role in the criminal process. Instead of directing the jury that they may draw adverse inferences from a defendant's silence, the normative approach requires the judge to direct the jury that innocent reasons for silence exist and that silence should not be used as evidence of guilt. It can accommodate a broad interpretation of the privilege against self-incrimination which does not distinguish between evidence dependent or independent of the will of the accused. It can also prevent the defendant from having to disclose the details of his defence prior to trial. Moreover, the no-assistance approach does not accept the imposition of reverse burdens of proof; it requires the prosecution to prove all aspects of the offence and disprove any defence at trial. In order to put this theory into practice, reverse burdens of proof should be read down to evidential burdens.[27] The privilege against self-incrimination should be interpreted and applied broadly, as proposed in Chapter 5. The silence provisions of the Criminal Justice and Public Order Act 1994 should be repealed, along with the provisions of the Criminal Procedure and Investigations Act 1996 (CPIA 1996) which require defence disclosure. In addition, the Criminal Procedure Rules (CrimPR) should be revised, such that the defendant as an individual, and the defence as a party, should not be tasked with convicting the guilty, and certainly not in the same context as acquitting the innocent or ensuring fairness. It is also important that the duties of defence representatives to the court do not unduly prevent them from acting in the best interests of the defendant.

The existence and enforceability of rights not to participate does not in itself discourage participation, as the very nature of the criminal process is inherently coercive, and many may feel that participation is in their best interest. Moreover, affording a wide scope to the privilege against self-incrimination and the right to silence is unlikely to have major practical consequences, as a minority of suspects rely on these rights, and silence is not a major obstacle to convicting the guilty.[28] We can thus take rights seriously without substantially constraining the aim of accurate fact-finding.[29] Reform to the CPIA 1996 and the CrimPR is also unlikely to constrain the aim of accurate fact-finding or substantially reduce efficiency. There are significant issues of compliance with the CPIA 1996 and the CrimPR,[30]

27 This is consistent with the recommendations of the Criminal Law Revision Committee, *Eleventh Report, Evidence (General)* (Cmnd 4991, 1972).

28 See Royal Commission on Criminal Justice, *Report* (Cm 2263, 1993) 53–54.

29 A L-T Choo, *The Privilege Against Self-Incrimination and Criminal Justice* (Oxford, Hart Publishing, 2013) 119.

30 See, for example, HM Crown Prosecution Service Inspectorate, *Disclosure: A Thematic Review of the Duties of Disclosure of Unused Material Undertaken by the CPS* (London,

and ambush defences have never been a significant problem.[31] There are a limited number of issues which can be raised in each case, and the prosecution has traditionally been well equipped to predict the line of defence at trial. In addition, the evidential burden can act as a mechanism for filtering out weak defences.

Active participation of the defendant can be valuable to the pursuit of the aims of the criminal process. The participation of the defendant may be helpful not only to the prosecution in establishing and presenting its case, but also to the defence. Information provided by the defendant could lead to the prosecution dropping the case, or it could expose weaknesses in the prosecution case at trial, particularly if the defendant is free to communicate with his legal representatives. Moreover, a failure to participate, particularly at trial, could increase the risk of conviction, as the absence of any explanation from the defendant of the evidence against him may harm the defence. In order to reap the benefits of participation, without obligations or penalties for non-compliance, participation could be encouraged through non-coercive means. At the investigative stage, participation could be facilitated through improved protections for the accused. Jackson and Summers suggest that increased safeguards for the defence at this stage should include improved access to legal advice, disclosure of the evidence against the accused and a guarantee of an authenticated recording of any interview, *before* police questioning takes place.[32] Such safeguards could reduce improper physical and psychological pressure, thus reducing the risk of abuse of power or of the defendant being tricked or misconstrued. In consequence, some of the defence's concerns about participating at this stage might be alleviated, and informed and effective participation could be facilitated. It is, however, important that additional safeguards are not seen to be replacing the rights not to participate.

To the extent that participation is currently discouraged at trial, this is likely to stem from the structure, professionalisation and formality of the criminal process, rather than as a direct consequence of fair trial rights. It was explained in Chapter 4 that, at trial, there are a number of barriers to meaningful communication between the defendant and the court, particularly for vulnerable defendants. Participation could be encouraged through less formal, and more relatable, criminal justice processes, focused on creating a less intimidating and isolating environment for the defendant. Simple changes, such as adapting the language

HMCPSI, 2008); Lord Justice Gross and Lord Justice Treacy, *Further Review of Disclosure in Criminal Proceedings: Sanctions for Disclosure Failure* (London, Judiciary of England and Wales, 2012); Lord Justice Gross, His Honour Judge Kinch and H Riddle, *Magistrates' Court Disclosure Review* (London, Judiciary of England and Wales, 2014); HM Crown Prosecution Service Inspectorate, *CPS London Inspection Report* (London, HMCPSI, 2014).

31 See R Leng, *The Right to Silence in Police Interrogation: A Study of Some of the Issues Underlying the Debate*, Royal Commission on Criminal Justice Research Study No. 10 (London, HMSO, 1993); M Zander and P Henderson, *The Crown Court Study*, Royal Commission on Criminal Justice Research Study No. 19 (London, HMSO, 1993).

32 J Jackson and S Summers, *The Internationalisation of Criminal Evidence: Beyond the Common Law and Civil Law Traditions* (Cambridge, Cambridge University Press, 2012) 275–277.

used in court and ordinarily allowing defendants to sit with their legal representative, could go some way to improving the situation. Greater availability and use of special measures for vulnerable defendants may also be of some assistance in encouraging and facilitating participation. With these measures in place, the defendant may feel more willing and able to participate, where it is in his best interest to do so. Moreover, both the defendant and the public may be more willing to accept the outcome of criminal cases if the defendant is afforded an adequate opportunity to meaningfully participate, thus increasing the legitimacy of the criminal process.[33] The efforts of the government and the judiciary would be best spent facilitating effective voluntary participation, rather than creating or enforcing penalties for participatory failures. Respect for individual dignity and autonomy requires that we do not oblige defendants to actively participate in proceedings against themselves, but at the same time, that we provide an opportunity to participate meaningfully, and that we take due account of what the defendant has to say.

If the normative theory advanced in this book were to be put into practice, with the defendant facing no formal consequences for choosing not to actively participate in the criminal process, it is likely that some would see it as a step backwards. Yet, the old common law positions on the right to silence and defence disclosure are preferable, and most post-*Funke*[34] cases concerning the privilege against self-incrimination would be better off reversed. Following this path would lead to greater respect and concern for a wide interpretation of the presumption of innocence, the right to a fair trial and a conception of the relationship between citizen and state in which state power is controlled, and liberty and autonomy are protected. However, it may be that, rather than go backwards, the system can only evolve. If this is the case, then the theory still has a place in the evolving system. It can provide a normative yardstick by which to measure developments in criminal procedure and the law of evidence. It can be used to prevent the pursuit of efficient fact-finding from leading to further participatory requirements.

Unfortunately, the prioritisation of time and cost saving measures, along with the political appeal of being tough on crime, has created a real threat of further participatory requirements. For example, the increasingly limited scope of the privilege against self-incrimination could become even more restricted, with the availability of criminal sanctions against those who refuse to incriminate themselves (or others) being extended. Taken to the extreme, this could completely jeopardise the right to silence in the police station and at trial. It could lead to greater risk of defendants being coerced into offering unreliable evidence; of their being convicted on the basis of their true, but unconvincing, testimony; or being convicted for offences of failing to answer questions. While this would obviously raise Article 6 issues, it could perhaps be achieved on proportionality and public interest grounds. The existing intrusions on defence rights are not always glaringly

33 ibid 24–25.
34 (1993) 16 EHRR 297.

obvious, and sometimes depend on broad interpretations of rights, beyond that which the courts have been willing to give them. Until we encounter the kind of obvious injustice to innocent defendants which leads to the strengthening of due process rights,[35] requirements of defendant participation may continue to develop.

8.4 Conclusion

The political determination to be tough on crime and increase conviction rates has persisted over the past 20 years, and the demand for efficiency in fact-finding is ever-increasing.[36] While it is hoped that the yardstick provided by the normative theory presented in this book can constrain future developments of participatory requirements, there has undoubtedly been a 'cultural change' in criminal procedure.[37] In particular, England can no longer be described as having a system akin to adversarialism. Once we recognise the significant effect which the participatory obligations have had on the nature of criminal procedure, we must decide whether to abandon them or change how we define and understand our system. The latter includes recognition that the pursuit of efficient fact-finding has been given priority over respect for autonomy and the rights of the defence, and that the English system of criminal procedure can now be characterised by the obligatory nature of defendant participation.

35 Such as the miscarriages of justice which contributed to the development of the adversarial system, particularly the Treason Trials Act of 1696 and, more recently, to the enactment of the Police and Criminal Evidence Act 1984.

36 See, for example, Sir Brian Leveson, *Review of Efficiency in Criminal Proceedings* (London, Judiciary of England and Wales, 2015).

37 The language of 'culture change' is evident in discussions on the perceived need to increase compliance and cooperation within the criminal process. See, for example, Sir Brian Leveson, *Review of Efficiency in Criminal Proceedings* (London, Judiciary of England and Wales, 2015).

Bibliography

Ashworth A, 'Crime, Community and Creeping Consequentialism' [1996] *Crim LR* 220

—— 'Responsibilities, Rights and Restorative Justice' (2002) 42 *British Journal of Criminology* 578

—— 'Four Threats to the Presumption of Innocence' (2006) 10 *E & P* 241

—— 'Case Comment: Human Rights: Article 6(1) – Privilege Against Self-Incrimination – Offence Under the Road Traffic Act 1988 s.172 of Failing to Furnish Information' [2007] *Crim LR* 897

—— 'Self-Incrimination in European Human Rights Law – A Pregnant Pragmatism?' (2008) 30 *Cardozo Law Review* 751

—— 'The Exclusion of Evidence Obtained by Violating a Fundamental Right: Pragmatism Before Principle in the Strasbourg Jurisprudence' in P Roberts and J Hunter (eds), *Criminal Evidence and Human Rights: Reimagining Common Law Procedural Traditions* (Oxford, Hart Publishing, 2012)

—— *Sentencing and Criminal Justice*, 6th edn (Cambridge, Cambridge University Press, 2015)

—— and Blake M, 'The Presumption of Innocence in English Criminal Law' [1996] *Crim LR* 306

—— and Redmayne M, *The Criminal Process*, 4th edn (Oxford, Oxford University Press, 2010)

Auld LJ, *Review of the Criminal Courts of England and Wales* (London, The Stationery Office, 2001)

Bar Standards Board, *Bar Barometer: Trends in the Profile at the Bar* (The General Council of the Bar of England and Wales, June 2014)

—— *Handbook,* 2nd edn (April 2015): <www.barstandardsboard.org.uk/media/1731225/bsb_handbook_sept_2015.pdf> (accessed 1 April 2016)

Barkow RE, 'Separation of Powers and the Criminal Law' (2006) 58 *Stanford Law Review* 989

Barroso LR, 'Here, There, and Everywhere: Human Dignity in Contemporary Law and in the Transnational Discourse' (2012) 35 *Boston College International and Comparative Law Review* 331

Beattie JM, *Crime and the Courts in England 1660–1800* (Oxford, Clarendon Press, 1986)

—— 'Scales of Justice: Defense Counsel and the English Criminal Trial in the Eighteenth and Nineteenth Centuries' (1991) 9 *Law and History Review* 221

Beccaria C, *On Crimes and Punishments and Other Writings* (R Bellamy ed, R Davies tr, Cambridge, Cambridge University Press, 1995)

Bentham J, *Rationale of Judicial Evidence, Specially Applied to English Practice* (London, Hunt & Clarke, 1827)

Berlin I, 'Two Concepts of Liberty' in I Berlin, *Four Essays on Liberty* (Oxford, Oxford University Press, 1969)

Birch D, 'Suffering in Silence: A Cost-Benefit Analysis of Section 34 of the Criminal Justice and Public Order Act 1994' [1999] *Crim LR* 769

Blake M and Ashworth A, 'Ethics and the Criminal Defence Lawyer' (2004) 7 *Legal Ethics* 167

Bridges L, 'The Ethics of Representation on Guilty Pleas' (2006) 9 *Legal Ethics* 80

Bucke T, Street R and Brown D, *The Right to Silence: The Impact of the Criminal Justice and Public Order Act 1994* (Home Office Research Study No. 199) (London, Home Office, 2000)

Cape E, 'Sidelining Defence Lawyers: Police Station Advice After Condron' (1997) 1 *E & P* 386

——'Rebalancing the Criminal Justice Process: Ethical Challenges for Criminal Defence Lawyers' (2006) 9 *Legal Ethics* 56

—— Hodgson J, Prakken T and Spronken T (eds), *Suspects in Europe: Procedural Rights at the Investigative Stage of the Criminal Process* (Antwerp, Intersentia, 2007)

Choo A L-T, '"Give Us What You Have" – Information, Compulsion and the Privilege Against Self-Incrimination as a Human Right' in P Roberts and J Hunter (eds), *Criminal Evidence and Human Rights: Reimagining Common Law Procedural Traditions* (Oxford, Hart Publishing, 2012)

—— *The Privilege Against Self-Incrimination and Criminal Justice* (Oxford, Hart Publishing, 2013)

Cooper S, 'Legal Advice and Pre-Trial Silence – Unreasonable Developments' (2006) 10 *E & P* 60

Cottu C, *On the Administration of Criminal Justice in England; and the Spirit of the English Government* (anon tr, London, Richard Stevens, 1822)

Criminal Cases Review Commission, *Annual Report and Accounts 2013/14* (London, HMSO, 2014)

Criminal Justice Joint Inspection, *Meeting the Needs of Victims in the Criminal Justice System* (CJJI, 2015)

Criminal Law Revision Committee, *Eleventh Report, Evidence (General)* (Cmnd 4991, 1972)

Crown Prosecution Service, *The Prosecutors' Pledge*: <www.cps.gov.uk/publications/prosecution/prosecutor_pledge.html> (accessed 1 April 2016)

Crown Prosecution Service, *Victims' Right to Review Scheme*: <www.cps.gov.uk/victims_witnesses/victims_right_to_review> (accessed 1 April 2016)

Damaska M, 'Evidentiary Boundaries to Conviction and Two Models of Criminal Procedure: A Comparative Study' (1973) 121 *University of Pennsylvania Law Review* 506

—— 'Structures of Authority and Comparative Criminal Procedure' (1975) 84 *Yale Law Journal* 480

—— *The Faces of Justice and State Authority: A Comparative Approach to the Legal Process* (New Haven, Yale University Press, 1986)

—— 'The Uncertain Fates of Evidentiary Transplants: Anglo-American and Continental Experiments' (1997) 45 *American Journal of Comparative Law* 839

Darbyshire P, 'The Mischief of Plea Bargaining and Sentencing Rewards' [2000] *Crim LR* 895

—— 'Judicial Case Management in Ten Crown Courts' [2014] *Crim LR* 30

Dennis I, 'The Criminal Justice and Public Order Act 1994: The Evidence Provisions' [1995] *Crim LR* 4

—— 'Instrumental Protection, Human Right or Functional Necessity? Reassessing the Privilege Against Self-Incrimination' (1995) 54 *Cambridge Law Journal* 342

—— 'Silence in the Police Station: The Marginalisation of Section 34' [2002] *Crim LR* 25

—— 'Reverse Onuses and the Presumption of Innocence: In Search of Principle' [2005] *Crim LR* 901

—— 'The Right to Confront Witnesses: Meanings, Myths and Human Rights' [2010] *Crim LR* 225

—— 'The Human Rights Act and the Law of Evidence Ten Years On' (2011) 33 *Sydney Law Review* 333

—— *The Law of Evidence*, 5th edn (London, Sweet & Maxwell, 2013)

—— 'Quashing Acquittals: Applying the "New and Compelling Evidence" Exception to Double Jeopardy' [2014] *Crim LR* 247

Denyer RL, 'Non-Compliance with Case Management Orders and Directions' [2008] *Crim LR* 784

—— 'The Defence Statement' [2009] *Crim LR* 340

—— *Case Management in Criminal Trials*, 2nd edn (Oxford, Hart Publishing, 2012)

Doak J, *Victims' Rights, Human Rights and Criminal Justice* (Oxford, Hart Publishing, 2008)

Dolinko D, 'Is There a Rationale for the Privilege Against Self-Incrimination?' (1986) 33 *UCLA Law Review* 1063

Dorange A and Field S, 'Reforming Defence Rights in French Police Custody: A Coming Together in Europe?' (2012) 16 *E & P* 153

Duff A, *Trials and Punishments* (Cambridge, Cambridge University Press, 1986)

—— 'Who is Responsible, for What, to Whom?' (2005) 2 *Ohio State Journal of Criminal Law* 441

—— Farmer L, Marshall S and Tadros V (eds), *The Trial on Trial 1: Truth and Due Process* (Oxford, Hart Publishing, 2004)

—— Farmer L, Marshall S and Tadros V (eds), *The Trial on Trial 2: Judgment and Calling to Account* (Oxford, Hart Publishing, 2006)

—— Farmer L, Marshall S and Tadros V (eds), *The Trial on Trial 3: Towards a Normative Theory of the Criminal Trial* (Oxford, Hart Publishing, 2007)

Easton S, 'Legal Advice, Common Sense and the Right to Silence' (1998) 2 *E & P* 109

—— *Silence and Confessions: The Suspect as the Source of Evidence* (Basingstoke, Palgrave Macmillan, 2014)

Edwards A, 'Do the Defence Matter?' (2010) 14 *E & P* 119

Edwards I, 'An Ambiguous Participant: The Crime Victim and Criminal Justice Decision Making' (2004) 44 *British Journal of Criminology* 967

Garland F and McEwan J, 'Embracing the Overriding Objective: Difficulties and Dilemmas in the New Criminal Climate' (2012) 16 *E & P* 233

Gerstein RS, 'Privacy and Self-Incrimination' (1970) 80 *Ethics* 87

Glover R, 'Codifying the Law on Evidential Burdens' (2008) 72 *Journal of Criminal Law* 305

Goldstein A, 'Reflections on Two Models: Inquisitorial Themes in American Procedure' (1974) 26 *Stanford Law Review* 1009

Goss R, *Criminal Fair Trial Rights: Article 6 of the European Convention on Human Rights* (Oxford, Hart Publishing, 2014)

Greenawalt K, 'Silence as a Moral and Constitutional Right' (1981) 23 *William & Mary Law Review* 15

Greer S, 'The Right to Silence: A Review of the Current Debate' (1990) 53 *MLR* 709

—— 'The Right to Silence, Defence Disclosure, and Confession Evidence' (1994) 21 *Journal of Law and Society* 102

Gross LJ, *Review of Disclosure in Criminal Proceedings* (London, Judiciary of England and Wales, 2011)

—— and Treacy LJ, *Further Review of Disclosure in Criminal Proceedings: Sanctions for Disclosure Failure* (London, Judiciary of England and Wales, 2012)

—— Kinch HHJ and Riddle H, *Magistrates' Court Disclosure Review* (London, Judiciary of England and Wales, 2014)

Gudjonsson GH, *The Psychology of Interrogations and Confessions: A Handbook* (Chichester, Wiley, 2003)

Hall M, 'The Relationship Between Victim and Prosecutors: Defending Victims Rights?' [2010] *Crim LR* 31

Hamer D, 'The Presumption of Innocence and Reverse Burdens: A Balancing Act' (2007) 66 *Cambridge Law Journal* 142

Harding C, Fennell P, Jorg N and Swart B (eds), *Criminal Justice in Europe: A Comparative Study* (Oxford, Clarendon Press, 1995)

Hay D, 'Property, Authority and the Criminal Law' in D Hay, P Linebaugh, JG Rule, EP Thompson and C Winslow (eds), *Albion's Fatal Tree: Crime and Society in Eighteenth Century England* (New York, Pantheon Books, 1975)

Helmholz RH, 'The Privilege and the *Ius Commune:* The Middle Ages to the Seventeenth Century' in RH Helmholz, CM Gray, JH Langbein, E Moglen, HE Smith and AW Alschuler, *The Privilege Against Self-Incrimination: Its Origins and Development* (Chicago, University of Chicago Press, 1997)

Higher Education Statistics Agency, *Students in Higher Education Institutes 2011/12* (Higher Education Statistics Agency, 2013)

HM Crown Prosecution Service Inspectorate, *Thematic Review of the Disclosure of Unused Material* (London, HMCPSI, 2000)

—— *Disclosure: A Thematic Review of the Duties of Disclosure of Unused Material Undertaken by the CPS* (London, HMCPSI, 2008)

—— *CPS London Inspection Report* (London, HMCPSI, 2014)

Ho HL, *A Philosophy of Evidence Law* (Oxford, Oxford University Press, 2008)

—— 'Book Review: Duff, Farmer, Marshall and Tadros, The Trial on Trial (vol. 3): Towards a Normative Theory of the Criminal Trial' (2008) 6 *International Commentary on Evidence* Article 3

—— 'Liberalism and the Criminal Trial' [2010] *Singapore Journal of Legal Studies* 87

—— 'The Presumption of Innocence as a Human Right' in P Roberts and J Hunter (eds), *Criminal Evidence and Human Rights: Reimagining Common Law Procedural Traditions* (Oxford, Hart Publishing, 2012)

—— 'The Privilege Against Self-Incrimination and Right of Access to a Lawyer: A Comparative Assessment' (2013) 25 *Singapore Academy of Law Journal* 826

Hodgson J, 'Human Rights and French Criminal Justice: Opening the Door to Pre-Trial Defence Rights' in S Halliday and P Schmidt (eds), *Human Rights Brought Home: Socio-legal Perspectives on Human Rights in the National Context* (Oxford, Hart Publishing, 2004)

—— *French Criminal Justice* (Oxford, Hart Publishing, 2005)

—— 'Conceptions of the Trial in Inquisitorial and Adversarial Procedure' in A Duff, L Farmer, S Marshall and V Tadros (eds), *The Trial on Trial 2: Judgment and Calling to Account* (Oxford, Hart Publishing, 2006)

—— 'The Future of Adversarial Criminal Justice in 21st Century Britain' (2010) 35 *North Carolina Journal of International Law and Commercial Regulation* 319

Home Office, *Disclosure: A Consultation Document* (Cm 2864, 1995)

—— *Justice for All* (Cm 5563, 2002)

Home Office Working Group on the Right of Silence, *Report* (London, HMSO, 1989)

Hood R, *Race and Sentencing* (Oxford, Oxford University Press, 1992)

House of Commons Justice Committee, *Criminal Courts Charge Second Report of Session 2015–16* HC586 (London, The Stationery Office, 2015)

Hoyano L, 'Striking a Balance Between the Rights of Defendants and Vulnerable Witnesses: Will Special Measures Directions Contravene Guarantees of a Fair Trial?' [2001] *Crim LR* 948

—— 'Coroners and Justice Act 2009: Special Measures Directions Take Two: Entrenching Unequal Access to Justice?' [2010] *Crim LR* 345

—— 'What is Balanced in the Scales of Justice? In Search of the Essence of the Right to a Fair Trial' [2014] *Crim LR* 4

Hungerford-Welch P, 'Prosecution Interviews of Defence Witnesses' [2010] *Crim LR* 690

Hurd D, 'Police Foundation Lecture' (London, The Police Foundation, 1987)

Jackson J, 'Recent Developments in Criminal Evidence' (1989) 40 *Northern Ireland Legal Quarterly* 105

—— 'Interpreting the Silence Provisions: The Northern Ireland Cases' [1995] *Crim LR* 587

—— 'Silence Legislation in Northern Ireland: The Impact After Ten Years' (2001) 6 *Journal of Civil Liberties* 134

—— 'Managing Uncertainty and Finality: The Function of the Criminal Trial in Legal Inquiry' in A Duff, L Farmer, S Marshall and V Tadros (eds), *The Trial on Trial 1: Truth and Due Process* (Oxford, Hart Publishing, 2004)

—— 'The Effects of Human Rights on Criminal Evidentiary Processes: Towards Convergence, Divergence or Realignment?' (2005) 68 *MLR* 737

—— 'Re-Conceptualizing the Right to Silence as an Effective Fair Trial Standard' (2009) 58 *International and Comparative Law Quarterly* 835

—— and Kovalev N, 'Lay Adjudication and Human Rights in Europe' (2006) 13 *Columbia Journal of European Law* 83

—— and Summers S, *The Internationalisation of Criminal Evidence: Beyond the Common Law and Civil Law Traditions* (Cambridge, Cambridge University Press, 2012)

Jaconelli J, 'Rights Theories and Public Trial' (1997) 14 *Journal of Applied Philosophy* 169

—— *Open Justice: A Critique of the Public Trial* (Oxford, Oxford University Press, 2002)

Jorg N, Field S and Brants C, 'Are Inquisitorial and Adversarial Systems Converging?' in C Harding, P Fennell, N Jorg and B Swart (eds), *Criminal Justice in Europe: A Comparative Study* (Oxford, Clarendon Press, 1995)

Judicial Studies Board, *Crown Court Bench Book: Directing the Jury* (Judicial Studies Board, 2010)

Lord Judge, 'Constitutional Change: Unfinished Business' (University College London, 4 December 2013)

Kant I, *Political Writings* (HS Reiss ed, HB Nisbet tr, Cambridge, Cambridge University Press, 1991)

—— *Groundwork of the Metaphysics of Morals* (New York, Cambridge University Press, 1996)

Landsman S, *The Adversary System: A Description and Defense* (Washington DC, American Institute for Public Policy Research, 1984)

Langbein JH, *Torture and the Law of Proof: Europe and England in the Ancien Régime* (Chicago, University of Chicago Press, 1977)

—— 'The Historic Origins of the Privilege Against Self-Incrimination at Common Law' (1994) 92 *Michigan Law Review* 1047

—— *The Origins of the Adversary Criminal Trial* (Oxford, Oxford University Press, 2003)

Langer M, 'The Rise of Managerial Judging in International Criminal Law' (2005) 53 *American Journal of Comparative Law* 835

Lawrence D, Neyroud P and Starmer K, *Recommendations on a Victims' Law: Report for the Labour Party by the Victims' Taskforce* (The Labour Party, February 2015)

Laws LJ, 'Do Human Rights Make Bad Citizens?' (Northumbria University Inaugural Lecture, November 2012)

—— 'The Common Law Constitution' *The Hamlyn Lectures* (Cambridge University Press, July 2014)

Law Society, *Practice Note: Criminal Procedure Rules 2015: Solicitors' Duties* (29 February 2016): <www.lawsociety.org.uk/support-services/advice/practice-notes/the-criminal-procedure-rules-2015-solicitors-duties> (accessed 1 April 2016)

Legrand P, 'European Legal Systems Are Not Converging' (1996) 45 *International and Comparative Law Quarterly* 52

Leng R, *The Right to Silence in Police Interrogation: A Study of Some of the Issues Underlying the Debate*, Royal Commission on Criminal Justice Research Study No. 10 (London, HMSO, 1993)

—— 'Losing Sight of the Defendant: The Government's Proposals on Pre-Trial Disclosure' [1995] *Crim LR* 704

—— 'The Right to Silence Reformed: A Re-appraisal of the Royal Commission's Influence' (2001) 6 *Journal of Civil Liberties* 107

—— 'Silence Pre-trial, Reasonable Expectations and the Normative Distortion of Fact Finding' (2001) 5 *E & P* 240

Leveson Sir Brian, *Review of Efficiency in Criminal Proceedings* (London, Judiciary of England and Wales, 2015)

Levy LW, *Origins of the Fifth Amendment: The Right Against Self-Incrimination* (New York, Oxford University Press, 1968)

Lewis A, 'Bentham's View of the Right to Silence' (1990) 43 *Current Legal Problems* 135

Lippke RL, *The Ethics of Plea Bargaining* (Oxford, Oxford University Press, 2011)

—— 'Justifying the Proof Structure of Criminal Trials' (2013) 17 *E & P* 323

Lord Judge, 'Constitutional Change: Unfinished Business' (University College London, 4 December 2013)

MacCulloch A, 'The Privilege Against Self-Incrimination in Competition Investigations: Theoretical Foundations and Practical Implications' (2006) 26 *Legal Studies* 211

Mark R, 'Minority Verdict' (The 1973 Dimbleby Lecture) (London, BBC, 1973)

Markesinis BS (ed), *The Gradual Convergence: Foreign Ideas, Foreign Influences, and English Law on the Eve of the 21st Century* (Oxford, Clarendon Press, 1994)

Markovits I, 'Playing the Opposites Game: On Mirjan Damaska's The Faces of Justice and State Authority' (1989) 41 *Stanford Law Review* 1313

Marks A, 'Evidence of Drug Traces: Relevance, Reliability and the Right to Silence' [2013] *Crim LR* 810

McConville M and Marsh L, 'Adversarialism Goes West: Case Management in Criminal Courts' (2015) 19 *E & P* 172

McCrudden C, 'Human Dignity and Judicial Interpretation of Human Rights' (2008) 19 *European Journal of International Law* 655

McEwan J, 'Ritual, Fairness and Truth: The Adversarial and Inquisitorial Models of Criminal Justice' in A Duff, L Farmer, S Marshall and V Tadros (eds), *The Trial on Trial 1: Truth and Due Process* (Oxford, Hart Publishing, 2004)

—— 'From Adversarialism to Managerialism: Criminal Justice in Transition' (2011) 31 *Legal Studies* 519

—— 'Vulnerable Defendants and the Fairness of Trials' [2013] *Crim LR* 100

McInerney P, 'The Privilege Against Self-Incrimination from Early Origins to Judges' Rules: Challenging the "Orthodox View"' (2014) 18 *E & P* 101

Meyerson D, 'Why Courts Should Not Balance Rights Against the Public Interest' (2007) 31 *Melbourne University Law Review* 873

Miller J, 'A Rights-Based Argument Against the Dock' [2011] *Crim LR* 216

Ministry of Justice, *Swift and Sure Justice: The Government's Plans for Reform of the Criminal Justice System* (Cm 8388, 2012)

—— *Code of Practice for Victims of Crime* (London, The Stationery Office, 2015)

—— *Criminal Court Statistics: April–June 2015 (Main Tables)* (Ministry of Justice, September 2015)

—— *Statistics on Race and the Criminal Justice System 2014* (Ministry of Justice, November 2015)

—— 'Government Response to Review of Efficiency in Criminal Proceedings' (11 March 2015): <www.gov.uk/government/uploads/system/uploads/attachment_data/file/411854/response-to-leveson-review.pdf> (accessed 1 April 2016)

Morgan R, 'The Process is the Rule and the Punishment is the Process' (1996) 59 *MLR* 306

Munday R, 'Case Management, Disclosure and the Rules of Evidence, or (With Apologies to Ogden Nash) "What's *Newell*, Pussycat?"' (2012) 176 *Criminal Law and Justice Weekly* 377

Lord Neuberger, 'The Role of Judges in Human Rights Jurisprudence: A Comparison of the Australian and UK Experience' (Conference at the Supreme Court of Victoria, Melbourne, 8 August 2014)

Nijboer JF, 'Common Law Tradition in Evidence Scholarship Observed from a Continental Perspective' (1993) 41 *American Journal of Comparative Law* 299

Owusu-Bempah A, 'Judging the Desirability of a Defendant's Evidence: An Unfortunate Approach to s.35(1)(b) of the Criminal Justice and Public Order Act 1994' [2011] *Crim LR* 690

—— 'Defence Participation through Pre-Trial Disclosure: Issues and Implications' (2013) 17 *E & P* 183

—— 'Silence in Suspicious Circumstances' [2014] *Crim LR* 126

—— 'Vulnerable Defendants and the Right to Silence: *O'Donnell* v *United Kingdom* [2015] ECHR 16667/10' (2015) 79 *Journal of Criminal Law* 322

Packer H, *The Limits of the Criminal Sanction* (Stanford, Stanford University Press, 1968)

Panzavolta M, 'Reforms and Counter Reforms in the Italian Struggle for an Accusatorial Criminal Law System' (2005) 30 *North Carolina Journal of International Law and Commercial Regulation* 577

Pattenden R, 'Silence: Lord Taylor's Legacy' (1998) 2 *E & P* 141

Phillips C and Brown D, *Entry into the Criminal Justice System: A Survey of Police Arrests and Their Outcomes* (Home Office Research Study No. 185) (London, Home Office, 1998)

Picinali F, 'Innocence and Burdens of Proof in English Criminal Law' (2014) 13 *Law, Probability & Risk* 243

Pizzi WT, 'The American Adversary System' (1998) 100 *University of West Virginia Law Review* 847

—— and Montagna M, 'The Battle to Establish an Adversarial Trial System in Italy' (2004) 25 *Michigan Journal of International Law* 429

Plotnikoff J and Woolfson R, *'A Fair Balance?' Evaluation of the Operation of Disclosure Law* (RDS Occasional Paper No. 76) (London, Home Office, 2001)

Quirk H, 'The Significance of Culture in Criminal Procedure Reform: Why the Revised Disclosure Scheme Cannot Work' (2006) 10 *E & P* 42

—— 'Twenty Years On, the Right of Silence and Legal Advice: The Spiralling Costs of an Unfair Exchange' (2013) 64 *Northern Ireland Legal Quarterly* 465

Radzinowicz L, *A History of English Criminal Law and its Administration from 1750, Volume 4: Grappling for Control* (London, Stevens and Sons, 1968)

Rawls J, *A Theory of Justice,* rev edn (Massachusetts, The Belknap Press of Harvard University Press, 1999)

Redmayne M, 'Process Gains and Process Values: The Criminal Procedure and Investigations Act 1996' (1997) 60 *MLR* 79

—— 'Criminal Justice Act 2003: (1) Disclosure and Its Discontents' [2004] *Crim LR* 441

—— 'Rethinking the Privilege Against Self-Incrimination' (2007) 27 *Oxford Journal of Legal Studies* 209

—— 'English Warnings' (2008) 30 *Cardozo Law Review* 1047

Richardson J, 'A "Just" Outcome: Losing Sight of the Purpose of Criminal Procedure' (2011) *Journal of Commonwealth Criminal Law* 105

Riddle H and Jones S, 'Trial in Absence in a Magistrates' Court' [2013] *Crim LR* 750

Roberts A, 'Case Comment: *R v Dixon*: Evidence – Failure to Give Evidence – Adverse Inference' [2014] *Crim LR* 141

Roberts P, 'Taking the Burden of Proof Seriously' [1995] *Crim LR* 783

—— 'The Presumption of Innocence Brought Home? *Kebilene* Deconstructed' (2002) 118 *Law Quarterly Review* 41

—— 'Loss of Innocence in Common Law Presumptions' (2014) 8 *Criminal Law and Philosophy* 317

Royal Commission on Criminal Justice, *Report* (Cm 2263, 1993)

Royal Commission on Criminal Procedure, *Report* (Cmnd 8092, 1981)

Schulhofer SJ, 'Some Kind Words for the Privilege Against Self-Incrimination' (1991) 26 *Valparaiso University Law Review* 311

Seabrooke S, 'The Vanishing Trick – Blurring the Line Between Credit and Issue' [1999] *Crim LR* 387

Seidmann DJ and Stein A, 'The Right To Silence Helps the Innocent: A Game-Theoretic Analysis of the Fifth Amendment Privilege' (2001) 114 *Harvard Law Review* 430

Sentencing Guidelines Council, *Reduction in Sentence for a Guilty Plea: Revised Guideline* (Sentencing Guidelines Secretariat, 2007)

Sharpe SD, 'The Human Rights Act 1998: Part 3: Article 6 and the Disclosure of Evidence in Criminal Trials' [1999] *Crim LR* 273

Skinns L, 'The Right to Legal Advice in the Police Station: Past, Present and Future' [2011] *Crim LR* 19

Sklansky D, 'Anti-Inquisitorialism' (2009) 122 *Harvard Law Review* 1634

Smith HE, 'The Modern Privilege: Its Nineteenth Century Origins' in RH Helmholz, CM Gray, JH Langbein, E Moglen, HE Smith and AW Alschuler, *The Privilege Against Self-Incrimination: Its Origins and Development* (Chicago, University of Chicago Press, 1997)

Starmer K, 'Finality in Criminal Justice: When Should the CPS Reopen a Case?' [2012] *Crim LR* 526

—— 'Human Rights and Victims: The Untold Story of the Human Rights Act' [2014] *European Human Rights Law Review* 215

—— 'Human Rights, Victims and the Prosecution of Crime in the 21st Century' [2014] *Crim LR* 777

Stewart H, 'The Right to be Presumed Innocent' (2014) 8 *Criminal Law and Philosophy* 407

Stumer A, *The Presumption of Innocence: Evidential and Human Rights Perspectives* (Oxford, Hart Publishing, 2010)

Summers S, *Fair Trials: The European Criminal Procedural Tradition and the European Court of Human Rights* (Oxford, Hart Publishing, 2007)

Lord Sumption, 'The Limits of the Law' (27th Sultan Azlan Shah Lecture, Kuala Lumpur, 20 November 2013)

Sward E, 'Values, Ideology, and the Evolution of the Adversary System' (1989) 64 *Indiana Law Journal* 301

Tadros V, 'Rethinking the Presumption of Innocence' (2007) 1 *Criminal Law and Philosophy* 193

—— 'The Ideal of the Presumption of Innocence' (2014) 8 *Criminal Law and Philosophy* 449

—— and Tierney S, 'The Presumption of Innocence and the Human Rights Act' (2004) 67 *MLR* 402

Tan A, 'Adverse Inferences and the Right to Silence: Re-examining the Singapore Experience' [1997] *Crim LR* 471

Taylor C, 'The Evolution of the Defence Statement' (2010) 74 *Journal of Criminal Law* 214

—— 'The Disclosure Sanctions Review: Another Missed Opportunity?' (2013) 17 *E & P* 272
Taylor N and Ormerod D, 'Mind the Gaps: Safety, Fairness and Moral Legitimacy' [2004] *Crim LR* 266
Theophilopoulos C, 'The Privilege Against Self-Incrimination and the Distinction Between Testimonial and Non-Testimonial Evidence' (2010) 127 *South African Law Journal* 107
Trechsel S, *Human Rights in Criminal Proceedings* (Oxford, Oxford University Press, 2005)
van Koppen P and Penrod S (eds), *Adversarial Versus Inquisitorial Justice: Psychological Perspectives on Criminal Justice Systems* (New York, Kluwer Academic/Plenum Publishers, 2003)
Vogler R, *A World View of Criminal Justice* (Aldershot, Ashgate Publishing, 2005)
Ward T and Gardner P, 'The Privilege Against Self-Incrimination: In Search of Legal Certainty' [2003] *European Human Rights Law Review* 388
Williams G, 'Law and Fact' [1976] *Crim LR* 472
Wolfe-Robinson M and Bowcott O, 'Lord Irvine: Human Rights Law Developed on False Premise' *The Guardian* (London, 14 December 2011): <www.theguardian.com/law/2011/dec/14/lord-irvine-human-rights-law> (accessed 1 April 2016)
Zander M, 'Consultation on Proposals for Advance Disclosure of Defence Witness Lists and Unused Defence Expert Witness Reports' (2002): <www.lse.ac.uk/collections/law/staff%20publications%20full%20text/zander/adv.discl.pdf> (accessed 1 April 2016)
—— and Henderson P, *The Crown Court Study*, Royal Commission on Criminal Justice Research Study No. 19 (London, HMSO, 1993)

Index